Neutrality and International Sanctions

Neutrality and International Sanctions

Sweden, Switzerland and Collective Security

By
John F. L. Ross

PRAEGER

New York
Westport, Connecticut
London

Library of Congress Cataloging-in-Publication Data

Ross, John F. L.
    Neutrality and international sanctions: Sweden, Switzerland, and collective security
    / John F. L. Ross
      p.   cm.
    Bibliography: p.
    ISBN 0-275-93349-0 (alk. paper)
    1. Sweden—Neutrality. 2. Switzerland—Neutrality. 3. United Nations—Sweden.
    4. United Nations—Switzerland. 5. United Nations—Sanctions. I. Title.
    JX4031.R68   1989
    341.6'4—dc20   89-32270

Library of Congress Catalog Card Number: 89-32270
ISBN: 0-275-93349-0

First published in 1989

Praeger Publishers, One Madison Avenue, New York, NY 10010
A division of Greenwood Press, Inc.

Printed in the United States of America

The paper used in this book complies with the Permanent
Paper Standard issued by the National Information Standards
Organization (Z39.48—1984).

10 9 8 7 6 5 4 3 2 1

To Rebecca

Contents

Tables

Preface

The problem of reconciling a policy of neutrality with participation in collective security systems has been a continually significant issue for neutral states during this century. The establishment of the League of Nations and its successor organization the United Nations, both for the purpose of maintaining international peace and security, has posed a challenge and a dilemma for neutrals; indeed, in pure theory, neutrality and collective security are inconsistent—even antithetical—conceptions. A status of neutrality implies abstention from conflict and assumes free choice, whereas collective security operations require the common participation of most or all states in concerted enforcement measures (sanctions), if called for by a recognized international authority.

Despite this clear theoretical dilemma, both neutrality policies and sanctions systems have managed to coexist since World War I. There has been in fact a striking historical parallel between the League and UN systems: both appeared to eliminate the traditional régime of neutrality by undermining its basic premises, yet in subsequent practice, they have allowed for a reassertion of neutrality. Thus in terms of practical policy, the neutrals have had to establish a viable modus vivendi with international organizations. As a result, this work proceeds from the assumption that the history of modern neutrality can be read largely in terms of how far neutral states have been able to adapt their policies to enable their cooperation with, and participation in, sanctions operations. Attitudes toward sanctions thus represent an important litmus test for determining the relative success or failure of neutrality in the modern international system.

Despite the seemingly straightforward nature of the neutrality-sanctions problem, the existing body of literature on the subject is conspicuous for its lack of any systematic, much less comprehensive, study of this relationship.

Most writings on problems of neutrality have taken either one of two forms. One approach, influenced by the Cold War and thus particularly prevalent in the postwar period, examines neutrality within the context of East-West relations, that is relative to international security issues in the narrow sense. The second approach, deriving from international law, tends to focus on the legal and theoretical side of neutrality. While not surprising in itself, given that neutrality traditionally has been considered a term of law rather than one of politics, this type of analysis nonetheless often lacks a valid empirical basis. Thus while both approaches are useful and necessary, neither addresses squarely the issue of compatibility between policies of neutrality and collective security obligations.

My aim, rather, is to examine the neutrality-security issue within the broader context of international sanctions operations, with special reference to two neutral states, Sweden and Switzerland. In pursuit of this aim, two primary and interconnected questions will be posed. First, what is the extent to which neutral states can participate in sanctions operations without relinquishing or compromising their neutrality? Second, to what extent have Sweden and Switzerland been able to adapt their policies in order to overcome this dilemma? These two issues in turn give rise to other important questions: How and why have Swedish and Swiss policies toward sanctions differed? What factors have accounted for their variation? Are those factors case-specific, or are they generally operative? What do their respective responses tell us about neutrality policy in general? In other words, to what extent can we generalize about neutrality from a comparative study of two states whose policies reflect, to a degree, common aims? I propose to examine these issues by means of a direct comparative analysis of Sweden's and Switzerland's responses to two of the most significant cases of collective international sanctions yet imposed: the League of Nation's operation against Italy in 1935–36, and the UN's operation against Rhodesia (now Zimbabwe) in 1965–79.

The usefulness of examining the neutrality-sanctions issue has been enhanced by the recent visibility and increasingly prominent role of neutral states in the international system. To take but one example, the contributions of the neutral states in the ongoing Conference on Security and Cooperation in Europe (CSCE), both prior to and following the 1975 Helsinki Accords, have been pivotal in enhancing the renewed climate of détente in Europe by the late 1980s. Similarly, the UN's return to favor and its successful efforts to reduce international conflicts—highlighted by the Namibian agreement and by the 1988 Nobel Peace Prize, which was awarded to the United Nations peacekeeping forces—have been as sudden as they have been striking. In light of these developments, the time would appear to be ripe for an analysis of neutrality within international organizations.

The study is divided into four main parts. Part I introduces the major themes: Chapter 1 examines the conceptual bases of neutrality and collective security systems, and discusses general aspects of the neutrality-sanctions problem. Chapter 2 sets out the comparative framework for analyzing Swedish and Swiss policy relative to the sanctions issue. Part II examines the neutrals' responses to the League's sanctions operation against Italy. After a brief survey of the crisis itself and its aspects relating to neutrality in general (chapter 3), Sweden's and Switzerland's policies in the crisis are considered separately (chapters 4 and 5). Part III focuses on neutrality relative to the United Nations system and the UN operation against Ian Smith's Rhodesia. Chapter 6 outlines the dispute itself and the sanctions called for, and relates the issues to neutrality. Chapters 7 and 8 analyze Swedish and Swiss policies, vis-à-vis the UN's operation. Chapter 9 summarizes the four case studies, and proposes a set of explanatory factors relating to how source states, neutral and other, might respond to similar sanctions operations. It concludes with a discussion of the extent to which the neutrality-sanctions problem has been resolved insofar as the neutral states themselves are concerned.

The breadth of the study precludes detailed examination of several important related issues. It will not discuss neutral policies during the two world wars, as the issue here is one of peacetime coercion relative to sanctions as a means of averting war itself. Second, the complex and unresolved legal debate since 1918 over whether the traditional laws of neutrality remain in force will be discussed only in relation to how it has affected the two countries' policies; this study focuses mainly on neutrality as policy rather than as law. Third, the neutrals' attitudes toward sanctions prior to the two operations will be discussed only to the extent that they relate to, and help explain, their responses to the crises themselves. This precludes, for example, detailed examination of the Korean, Suez, and Congo crises, all of which elicited significant UN involvement with active neutral participation. Finally, the study does not attempt to elbow its way into an already crowded field of excellent works which analyze the overall effectiveness of sanctions as an instrument of policy; thus rather than examining the effect of sanctions on the target state(s), it will examine their actual and potential effect on the (neutral) source states themselves—those actually imposing them.

This book was conceived and written while I was in residence at the London School of Economics. Hence my debts to the LSE are considerable. Financial support from the School in the form of the Montague Burton award and two grants from the Central Research Fund of the University of London, as well as outside awards from the Gilbert Murray Trust Fund and the Committee of Vice Chancellors and Principals in Britain, helped me both to get started and later to complete the necessary field research. On the personal level, help of a very individual nature was provided by J. T. S. Madeley, friend and colleague; N. A. Sims, who was most generous with making suggestions, and who provided a stimulating forum, his research seminar on international organization, within which to discuss related issues; and P. G. Taylor, whose encouragement was instrumental in the publication of this work. Thanks are also due to Roderick Ogley, formerly of Sussex University, for his remarkably detailed suggestions, particularly in improving a misguided earlier version of chapter 9.

Help was also provided by the staffs of the Eidgenossische Parlaments- und Zentralbibliothek in Bern, Switzerland, particularly Annemarie Amacher; the United Nations Library in Geneva; the Swedish Institute for International Affairs and Kungliga Biblioteket, both in Stockholm; and the British Museum and the British Library for Political and Economic Studies in London. I also greatly benefited from conversations and encouragement from, among many others, Prof. Jürg Steiner; Docent Krister Wahlbäck; Dr. Katarina Brodin; and Prof. Nils Andrén. I am particularly grateful to my editor at Praeger, Mary Glenn, for all her help and timely advice.

I should also thank my family—both in the United States and abroad—for their unstinting support. My most enduring gratitude extends to my wife Rebecca, who knows the contribution she has made. The book is dedicated to her.

Abbreviations

AJIL	*American Journal of International Law*
AK	Andra Kammaren (prior to 1971)
AKU	Aktstycken utgivna av Kungl. Utrikesdepartementet
BRP	*Bihang till Riksdagens Protokoll*
BS	*Bulletin sténographique officielle de l'Assemblée fédérale suisse*
BYBIL	*British Year Book of International Law*
C&C	*Cooperation and Conflict*
CE	Conseil des Etats
CF	Conseil fédéral
CN	Conseil national
CSCE	Conference on Security and Cooperation in Europe
DSFP	*Documents on Swedish Foreign Policy*
DIA	*Documents on International Affairs*
DN	*Dagens Nyheter*
EEC	European Economic Community
EFTA	European Free Trade Association
FF	*Feuille fédérale*
FK	Första Kammaren (prior to 1971)
FN	Förenta Nationerna
FT	*Financial Times*
GAOR	*United Nations General Assembly, Official Records*
GATT	General Agreement on Tariffs and Trade
GNP	Gross National Product
ICJ	International Court of Justice
ICRC	International Committee of the Red Cross
IDA	International Development Association
IEA	International Energy Agency

ILA	International Law Association
ILC	International Law Commission
IMF	International Monetary Fund
KU	Konstitutions Utskottet
LDC	Less Developed Country
NATO	North Atlantic Treaty Organization
NF	Nationernas Förbund
NR	Nordiska Rådet
NZZ	*Neue Zürcher Zeitung*
OAU	Organization for African Unity
OECD	Organization for Economic Cooperation and Development
OEEC	Organization for European Economic Cooperation
OJ	*League of Nations Official Journal*
RCF	*Rapport du Conseil fédéral a l'Assemblée fédérale sur la gestion en 19...*
RO	*Recueille Officielle des Lois et Ordonnances de la Confédération Suisse*
RP	*Riksdagens Protokoll*
SAP	Sveriges Socialdemokratiska Arbetarpartiet
SCOR	*United Nations Security Council, Official Records*
SEK	Swedish kronor
SFS	*Svensk Författningssamling*
SIA	*Survey of International Affairs*
SIDA	Swedish International Development Authority
SKM	*Sveriges Kommersiella Meddelanden*
SOS	*Sveriges Officiella Statistik*
SOU	*Statens Offentliga Utredningar*
SPC	United Nations General Assembly, Special Political Committee
SS	Special Supplement
SwFr	Swiss Francs
TG	*Tribune de Genève*
UD	Utrikesdepartementet
UNCTAD	United Nations Conference on Trade and Development
UU	Utrikesutskottet
VPK	Vänsterpartiet kommunisterna
YUN	*Yearbook of the United Nations*

Part I

Introduction

1

The Neutrality–Collective Security Problem

THE CONCEPTUAL BASES OF NEUTRALITY

The term *neutrality* is derived from the medieval Latin adjective *neutralis*, meaning "neither of the two." It implies a position in a conflict which is identifiable with neither of the antagonists; the legal status of the neutral is essentially determined by the existence of the dispute itself, yet the neutral must be distinguished from both parties to it. This attitude of separateness, of abstention from conflict, has tended to impart negative connotations to the modern term *neutrality*. However, the extrapolation of this purely legal concept onto the moral and political plane has led to numerous misrepresentations of the term in modern political thought.[1]

Historical Development

In various forms neutrality has been an option for political associations for far longer than the modern concept of sovereignty has existed. There was little or no notion of neutrality in antiquity, nor even a law of nations, though noninvolvement in war has been a possible policy option for third states since the beginning of armed conflict. In his classic historical volume, Thucydides mentioned a form of neutrality taken by Greek city-states during the Peloponnesian Wars (431–404 B.C.). Still earlier, the biblical account of Isaiah mentioned the neutrality of the Hebrew state in wars between the Egyptians and Assyrians.

However, the rise of the European nation-state system required the development of a standardized procedure for governing interstate relations, particularly a system to regulate conflicts which inevitably disrupted normal trade patterns. This need gave rise to a rudimentary system of international law, which in turn included a set of rules governing the general conduct of war and of neutrality; the laws of war and of neutrality have long maintained a close, symbiotic association (Cohn 1939, 12). The first neutrality laws pertained to maritime rather than land warfare, given the importance of European sea trade even in the Middle Ages (Jessup 1935–36, 1: 22–23). Already by the fifteenth century the *Consolato del Mare* (1494) had given rudimentary expression to rules governing maritime conflict. This work set out the first restrictions on neutral trade: it specified that neutral goods seized aboard enemy ships had to be restored, but that all enemy goods aboard neutral ships could be freely confiscated by the belligerent; the important principle "free ships, free goods" was not established until the nineteenth century. However, even this general rule was very loosely interpreted, for there were few clear guidelines concerning the treatment of neutral vessels trading with belligerents. No general principle on the seizure of war contraband existed, nor restrictions on the right of belligerents to search neutral vessels for enemy goods, even on the high seas. This lack of clarity led to considerable dispute during the various maritime wars of the eighteenth century, particularly the Franco-British dispute which led to the so-called "Rule of the War" of 1756.

The first use of the specific term *neutrality* was made in Neumayr de Ramsla's 1620 work *Von der Neutralität und Assistenz in Kriegzeiten*. Thus the term was known, if not in general circulation, at the time of Hugo Grotius, whose work is often considered the precursor of modern international law. Grotius, however, dealt only superficially with neutrality per se; only one chapter of his seminal three-volume *De Jure Belli ac Pacis* (The Law of War and Peace) even discusses the term. Grotius established two cardinal principles for conduct by a neutral state, which he called *in bello medii*: (1) the neutral must not aid an "unjust cause" in a war, nor hinder a "just" one; and (2) when there is doubt as to which party's cause is the more just, the neutral must treat both parties equally. Thus he provided the first formal codification of the medieval "just war" (*jus ad bellum*) theory, and the Grotian conception became established authority as early as 1653, when cited by a French prize court. Even so, it lacked two of the key aspects of modern neutrality. First, there was no requirement that neutral territory be considered inviolable, nor that the neutral treat the belligerents impartially in every dispute. Second, the presumption of a linkage between neutrality and a just cause immediately raised the problem of determining who was to make such a judgment; it was apparent, given the lack of an overall international authority (following the breakup of European Christendom and the resulting decline in the temporal power of the papacy) that only the neutral state itself could make such a determination. Neutrality thus remained subject to interpretation by parties to each individual dispute as it arose, based on ad hoc rather than predetermined criteria.

The modern notion of impartiality as an integral feature of neutrality law developed through the works of several eighteenth century positivist writers, although inconsistency remained a hallmark of the concept. Among these writers was Samuel Pufendorf, whose theory derived from the same "just war" concept; however, he also held that it was dangerous to allow neutral states themselves to determine independently which cause in a war was the more just. A somewhat clearer interpretation was provided by Cornelius von Bynkershoek in his *Quaestiones Juris Publici* (1737). He argued that neutrals were *non hostis*, meaning "of neither party" to a conflict, and in that capacity must serve both sides impartially. He also defined *war* in a much more modern sense, as "a contest between independent persons," each of which was asserting its sovereign rights by use of force; this formulation strongly implied that all parties to a dispute had, in a sense, a just cause, and that therefore it was misleading to suppose that one had to choose either side (Borchard 1941, 621). Like Pufendorf, he argued that the neutral alone could not determine the justice of a cause; however, his formulation suffered from inconsistency since he also stated that a neutral could refuse the passage of troops to any belligerent waging war for an unjust cause.

Yet another formulation was proposed by Emerich de Vattel who in *Le Droit des gens* held that "Neutral nations, during a war, are those who take no one's part, remaining friends common to both parties, and not favoring the armies of one of them to the prejudice of the other" (de Vattel 1916, 3: 102). However, de Vattel confused the legal and moral dimensions of neutrality even while formally separating them; he required "exact impartiality" from neutrals in all wars, yet also asserted that a neutral must not help any state waging an "evidently unjust war."

These earlier theories of land warfare, as with the maritime rules, resembled the modern concept of neutrality in neither form nor conduct. For example, a neutral state could still grant limited assistance to one belligerent in the form of cash payments, mercenary troops (either individually or in group consignments), or the right of passage, particularly if such aid was stipulated in a previous treaty concluded between the belligerent and the neutral; neutral states could thus be "bought" by one of the belligerents, to "keep them neutral" (Cohn 1939, 13). Such treaties could also obligate the neutral to abstain from aiding another state in case of war. Likewise, the belligerent was free to levy troops on neutral territory, and to grant "letters of marque" to its merchantmen. The observance of neutrality in the seventeenth and eighteenth centuries depended upon the wording of individual agreements tailored to specific situations, rather than upon universally accepted rules of conduct. This particularist arrangement often led to serious disagreement between states concerning the point at which the duties of neutrality had been breached; this problem was compounded by the frequency of wars and shifting political coalitions during the eighteenth century.

The concept of neutrality was first set out with clarity and consistency in Galiani's 1782 work *De' doveri de' principi neutrali*. He asserted that potential neutral states must consider the moral implications of participating in warfare, particularly for their own citizens. This formulation made an important distinction between individual and state morality; he argued that, while individuals were bound morally to aid human victims of strife and conflict, states could not be held to a similar obligation to interfere in wars for the purpose of helping another nation victimized by aggression. This view was based on a realistic appraisal of the economic and moral decay which often follows a state's entry into a war; the neutral state's first responsibility is to protect the welfare of its own citizens, and helping other states was secondary. This was an argument for neutral abstention from all conflict, even if moral propriety clearly rested with one party. These considerations provided the basis for the passivity and disinterestedness which came to characterize neutrality in the nineteenth century.

These still unrefined neutral guidelines found concrete expression in a number of early attempts by groups of neutral states to protect their shipping from attack, if necessary through the joint use of force. The first such agreement tied the Dutch States General and the city of Lübeck in 1613 (officially recognized the following year by the Swedish Crown); later, in 1670, an Anglo-Danish convention bound each to refrain from supplying the other's enemies with munitions, soldiers, or arms, and to prevent their subjects from doing so. On this basis, Denmark and Sweden concluded two ambitious bilateral agreements in 1691 and 1693, both providing for mutual assistance in wartime through the use of armed convoys; the latter agreement even stipulated a common obligation to mediate between the belligerents (Jessup 1932, 789–90).

The most significant attempts at collective enforcement of neutrality were the "Leagues of Armed Neutrality" of 1780 and 1800, formed in retaliation for British interference in neutral shipping during the American War of Independence. The first League was initiated by Catherine the Great of Russia, and was based upon five principles: (1) free trade rights for all neutral vessels; (2) freedom from seizure of all enemy goods aboard neutral vessels, except contraband of war; (3) general acceptance of a 1766 Anglo-Russian agreement on rules for contraband; (4) general recognition of a blockaded port only if vessels were "sufficiently near"; and (5) compensation for neutrals if their detained vessels were found by a prize court to be not at fault (Scott 1918, 313–14). The League's main aims were to limit wars by localizing them, and to protect the commerce of all nations, including neutrals (Cohn 1939, 25). The agreement was limited initially to Denmark, Sweden, and Russia in an effort to neutralize the Baltic waterways, although subsequently the Netherlands, Portugal, Prussia, Austria, and the Kingdom of the Two Sicilies also joined. However, the unstable alliance pattern of the era contributed to the demise of the League, specifically Russia's agreement with Britain which led to Russia's own blockade of French ports to all neutral shipping.

The second League, again initiated by Russia (Czar Paul I), was established in 1800 due to Britain's refusal to grant immunity to neutral vessels under convoy from its general practice of "visit and search." The agreement obligated Russia, Denmark, Sweden, and Prussia to defend the principle that a neutral convoy was immune from visit and search, provided its commanding officer declared that no war contraband was being carried; it also asserted that neutrals were entitled to formal notification by belligerents of an effective blockade. Although British opposition (and Czar Paul's death in 1801) contributed to the League's collapse, the subsequent Maritime Convention between the ascendant Czar Alexander I and the British Crown was more consequential. Through it the British accepted that neutral vessels could navigate freely between belligerent ports, and that blockades had to be effective in order to be recognized; in return, Russia accepted that enemy goods aboard neutral ships could be seized, and that the British fleet could refuse to recognize the immunity of neutral vessels under convoy from visit and search procedure (Oppenheim 1952, 631, n. 2). Although Russia annulled this specific agreement in 1807, the principles underlying it, especially freedom of neutral shipping and the need for physically effective blockades, were important steps toward the eventual codification of maritime neutrality rules in the nineteenth century. Even so, the Leagues of Armed Neutrality were essentially mutual defense pacts, which involved a commitment to use force in defense of another (neutral) country; hence they were neither passive nor impartial.

The widespread violation of neutral rights during the Napoleonic Wars led directly to further refinement and circumscription of the legal guidelines for neutral activity. The relatively stable nineteenth-century balance of power system, sustained by the great powers through the Congress system and later the Concert of Europe, set the political framework for two separate developments. One was a collective undertaking by the powers to place certain states and territories under international guarantee through treaty, in order to ensure that they did not become future theaters of war (Wicker 1911, 3). This procedure, called "neutralization," represented an extension of certain neutral principles from wartime to peacetime policy (Black et al. 1968, 108); the main aim was to "localize" future European conflicts, by setting out strict requirements for both the neutral state and its guarantors. The first states whose permanently neutral status was ensured in this manner were Cracow and Switzerland, through the 1815 treaties, although several earlier attempts had been made (for example, concerning Malta, through the 1803 Peace of Amiens). Later both Belgium (1839) and Luxembourg (1867) were also neutralized, following international recognition of their independence. Other such areas have included the Ionian islands of Corfu and Paxi (1864), the Congo Basin (1885), Albania (1913, though never officially recognized in law), and still later Austria (1955) and Laos (1962). A similar régime, "internationalization," applies to international waterways (the Suez, Panama, and Kiel canals, and the Elbe, Rhine, and Danube rivers); the status of "demilitarization" describes the legal régimes governing the Norwegian island of Spitsbergen, and the Åland Islands under the Finnish flag. Still other agreements have rendered inviolable the facilities of national Red Cross societies (through the Geneva Red Cross Conventions of 1864, 1906, 1929, and 1949 and reiterated in the two Additional Protocols of 1977).

The second advance in the nineteenth century was the extensive codification of the rules of neutral conduct in wartime. Although some continued to hold to the earlier moralist overtones (Mazzini, for example, called neutrality in a war of principles "political atheism" [W.P. Grieve 1948, 105]), neutrality emerged as an essentially legal concept, limited and well-defined in scope. One major development was the 1856 Declaration of Paris concerning neutrality in maritime law, brought about by serious violations of neutrality during the Crimean War. The Paris Declaration established rules for contraband, privateering (which was abolished), and blockade (which had to be proven physically effective to be recognized by the neutral). Most importantly, the Declaration established the principle "free ships, free goods," by which neutral shipping was immune from random visit and search; under this rule, neutral goods aboard enemy ships, with the exception of contraband of war, could not be legally seized (Bowles 1900, chapter 7). This represented the first general recognition of the right of neutrals to conduct unhindered free trade even in wartime, and provided the basis for many neutral rights which characterize the modern laws of neutrality. Later, the Treaty of Washington of 1871, concluded in the wake of the American Civil War, set stricter guidelines for neutrals to use "due diligence" in enforcing the laws of neutrality through stricter domestic legislation (which was modified in the 1907 Hague Neutrality Conventions to read "the means at its disposal"). The Washington rules prevented belligerents from using neutral territory or ports for warlike purposes such as outfitting vessels, recruiting troops, or basing military operations. New and stricter rules for neutral conduct in land warfare were also set out in the 1874 Brussels Conference (Cohn 1939, 34).

The Hague Rules of Neutrality

The Hague Peace Conferences of 1899 and 1907 (somewhat misnamed, since they did not conclude a war) codified these hitherto disparate guidelines for conduct in war and neutrality in their most extensive form to date. Both Conferences made important strides toward establishing a system for the peaceful resolution of international disputes, although the specific guidelines for neutral conduct were concentrated in the Fifth and Thirteenth Conventions of 1907, governing, respectively, the rights and duties of neutrals in land and maritime warfare. Neutral duties include abstention from participating in the conflict: Art. 6 of Convention XIII prohibits the supply of war matériel to belligerents, as well as the transport of troops and provisions; however, Art. 7 allows the neutral to export general goods which might be used for military purposes. Another basic requirement is the equal treatment of the belligerents in a conflict; Art. 9 of both Conventions states that "Every measure of restriction or prohibition taken by a neutral power . . . must be impartially applied by it to both belligerents." From these general rules flow more specific requirements for the neutral: for example, it must prevent the use of its territory as a base for belligerent operations or the recruitment of troops; the stationing of foreign troops or convoys (of either munitions or supplies) on or across its territory (Art. 2, Convention V); the outfitting of belligerent ships in its ports and the establishment of prize courts. Both Conventions (Art. 5 of Convention V; Art. 25 of Convention XIII) also require the neutral to repel all attacks against its territory, thereby stipulating a posture of armed neutrality. Erik Castrén (1954, 15–16) suggests three categories of neutral duties: (1) the duty of prevention (protection of its territory from violation); (2) the duty of abstention (no supply of war matériel, loans, or other aid to the belligerent), and (3) the duty of impartiality (equal treatment of each belligerent).

Aside from these duties, the Hague Conventions give the neutral considerable leeway to conduct its own affairs freely, even during hostilities; in fact, the Conventions are weighted in favor of neutrals' rights. The basic right comes through Art. 1 of Convention V, which states that "the territory of neutral powers is inviolable." The rights of neutrals are essentially the reverse of belligerent duties; belligerents are prevented from moving troops, armed convoys, arms, munitions, or other supplies across neutral territory, and from perpetrating acts of hostility within neutral territorial waters (Art. 2, Convention XIII). Probably the most open-ended neutral right is the freedom to conduct trade freely with both belligerents, unless prohibited by an effective blockade; this protects the neutral from random visit and search, and also upholds the doctrine of "free ships, free goods," whereby neutral goods aboard enemy ships (except contraband of war) and enemy goods aboard neutral ships (with the same exception) cannot be confiscated. Moreover, the neutral is free to restrict its own trade, although such restrictions "must be uniformly applied" against both belligerents equally (Art. 9, Convention V). This proviso has given rise to a number of problems of interpretation such as whether, in a war, the neutral must alter its prewar pattern of trade (Wengler 1964). Furthermore, Art. 5 of Convention V frees the neutral state from the duty of preventing its nationals from engaging in unneutral activity, such as blockade running, dealing in contraband, or even enlisting in belligerent forces; it is up to the belligerents to punish such actions (Oppenheim 1952, 656–57, n. 5). On the other hand, the neutral state must be able to control the activities of its citizens insofar as their actions could otherwise transform the neutral's territory into a base for war operations. Neutrals are also given the right to offer their good offices and mediation in conflicts. Finally, Art. 10 of Convention V gives neutrals the right to repel all attacks against their territory without it being regarded as an act of war, which fully legitimizes the use of force in neutral self-defense.

The rules governing neutrality in maritime warfare were supplemented by the Declaration of London of 1909, issued at the conclusion of the London Naval Conference. These guidelines clarified many of the terms of maritime conflict such as unneutral service, destruction of neutral prizes, blockade, enemy character, convoy, transfer of flag, resistance to search, and compensation. The most significant result was a more precise definition of "contraband," which was subdivided into categories of "absolute" and "conditional." The latter classification was subject to capture only if it could be proven to be destined for use by the government or armed forces of a belligerent power.

This relative lack of restrictions on neutral activity reflected certain nineteenth century presuppositions which underlay the Hague Conventions. First, the Hague rules assume the sovereign right of states to conduct war in defense, or in pursuit, of their national interests, or as theorized by Karl von Clausewitz, a "continuation of political relations through other means." This right reflected the prevailing political theory of Social Darwinism, and was questioned by neither socialists (e.g., Bakunin, Marx) nor conservatives (Bismarck). The prevailing emphasis on positivist rather than Grotian "just war" principles, which accepted the incidence of war as "an evil which could not be controlled" (Wright 1936b, 54), merely reflected this political trend. The Hague Peace Conferences attempted only to regulate certain aspects of the conduct of war, as through Conventions II and III of 1907 concerning, respectively, the Limitation of the Employment of Force for the Recovery of Contract Debts, and the Opening of Hostilities. This principle also reflected the traditionally anarchic system of sovereign nation-states acting as the supreme judge of their own actions, which had developed out of the formal recognition of the breakup of European Christendom through the Treaties of Westphalia (1648) and Utrecht (1713), and theorized by Jean Bodin as the "divine right" of sovereigns to rule over their own territories.

Another basic precondition for the Hague system, and for classical neutrality, was the existence of a stable balance of power system in Europe, which prevailed (apart from the Napoleonic era) from Westphalia until World War I. The establishment of rules of neutrality, and the success of neutral policy, depended directly on the maintenance of such a system; so long as neutral states could play off the powers against each other, their status was protected. The reverse situation was equally true: so long as it was in the interests of the powers to respect a state's neutrality, its success was ensured. Even so, this nineteenth-century framework underpinning the Hague system was being eroded simultaneously by a sharp deterioration in the international political climate, including the establishment of competing alliances, the Triple Alliance and the Triple Entente; the intense imperial competition for overseas colonies; and the trend since the 1870s toward economic protectionism. Thus, paradoxically, the Hague Conventions codified a system of accepted thought which was dated even in its own time (Wright 1933, 58). Even so, they presumably remain a fully valid and functioning source of international law, since they have been neither reformulated nor legally renounced since that time.

Classical neutrality is limited to a legal, contractual relationship between the neutral and the belligerents, commencing at the outbreak of hostilities and remaining in effect only for the duration of the conflict: neutrality ceases to have effect when hostilities end. Once a state of war is established, it is up to the (potential) neutral to declare its status, either through official statement or by its actions; an express declaration of neutrality is not strictly required, but one is often made, even in advance, in the interests of political credibility (Oppenheim 1952, 654). Thus Hans Morgenthau's definition of neutrality, "a legal status that aims at keeping the neutral state out of war" (1938, 560) is inaccurate, although his formulation does broach the important distinction between the law and politics of neutrality. Neutral states are those which pursue a foreign policy in peacetime by which they aim for neutrality in the event of war; their peacetime policies are not, however, governed by the Hague neutrality rules. The decision on whether to remain neutral or not at the outbreak of war is one of policy rather than law (Oppenheim 1952, 653), unless a treaty stipulates otherwise.

Nonetheless, the overall position of any state that maintains a continuous desire to avoid participation in all wars (i.e., the neutral state) is constrained by certain peacetime duties or "ancillary effects" of neutrality. For example, it cannot conclude defensive alliances with other states which would prevent a neutral position should war break out. This has provided the rationale for the neutrals' refusal to join NATO and even (with the sole exception of Ireland) the European Community, due to its widely perceived overt identification with the Atlantic alliance. Occasional attempts have been made to demonstrate the existence of anticipatory legal effects of neutrality even in peacetime, of which the clearest obligation would compel the belligerents to treat the neutral state as a "sphere of no interest" (Wengler 1964); this characterization is, however, usually reserved for those perpetually neutral or neutralized states whose policies are based on international treaties.[2] More generally, it can hardly be disputed that the political attitude of any state in peacetime will affect its position in the event of war; for example, a disarmed neutral will be unable to defend its neutrality and territory from attack. Thus the strict distinction between the law and politics of neutrality is somewhat misleading; there is a necessary and indeed inevitable overlap from one to the other. This situation has given rise to numerous quasi-legal designations such as "qualified" or "differential" neutrality (as related to neutral members of international organizations), and later, to "nonbelligerency," which attempts to limit neutral duties while preserving neutral rights in time of war.[3]

COLLECTIVE SECURITY AND SANCTIONS: SCOPE AND APPLICATION

Definitions and Guidelines

The term *collective security* denotes a system of mutual guarantees formed to provide for the security and other common purposes which unite the constituent members. It has been defined variously as "the idea that the unlawful use of force by one nation will be met by the combined force of all others" (Claude 1964, 244), or in Sir Alfred Zimmern's more all-encompassing description, "the safety of all by all" (1936b, 3). An operative collective security system is generally based on two interlinking requirements: first, that states resolve their international disputes peacefully, through such procedures as judicial settlement, arbitration, mediation, or conciliation; and second, that any state that flouts this procedure is subject to collective punishment by the other members, in some form of sanctions. At its most theoretical level, collective security presupposes a vague, almost ethereal, "ideology of solidarity" (Undén 1963, 38), or what E. H. Carr (1939) criticized as the false presumption of a "harmony of interests," by which a higher "common good," recognized by all civilized states, would replace selfish national concerns. In this respect, collective security represents a partial throwback to the medieval *jus ad bellum* principle.

Collective security must also be distinguished from collective defense, which is aimed at checking aggression from a predetermined source (whether one state or an alliance). Collective security, however, is based upon the principle of "anonymity" (Undén 1963, 42–43); it aims to stop or prevent the use of force or aggression itself from any source, with no prior designation of friends or enemies. Indeed, in President Woodrow Wilson's formulation, the League of Nations was designed to sweep away the deficiencies of the pre-1914 system of competing politico-military alliances, by superimposing an organized peacekeeping system over the old balance of power arrangement. Later, the League's degeneration into groups of antagonistic states provided an impetus for the establishment of the United Nations as a global peacekeeping system.

Collective security is only realizable by means of an institutionalized international organization, which provides the basis for coordinating discussion about whether, when, and what types of sanctions should be imposed (Doxey 1987, 6). International organizations legitimize the use of sanctions as a means of providing for collective security, through the constitutional authority bestowed upon them by member states. Sanctions themselves are the specific instruments available to the organizations to defend the values of their members. The term *sanctions* is not merely interchangeable with coercive measures or reprisals, which are often applied unilaterally by a state to punish another—although a number of recent analyses of sanctions as an element of statecraft fail to make this distinction clearly (e.g., Baldwin 1985; Hufbauer and Schott 1985, 4–9). True sanctions connote a more noble aim, the defense of international values rather than the mere protection or advancement of narrow national interests. States can nonetheless have many aims in applying international sanctions, not all of which are inherently virtuous (such as pacifying a domestic audience), although two primary aims should be noted: (1) punishment of a wrongdoing actually or allegedly committed; and (2) prevention or deterrence, by which the mere threat of an international embargo may suffice in deterring a state from a certain undesirable course of action (Friedman 1970, 24).

Sanctions have been regarded traditionally as legal instruments—as a means to punish lawbreakers by giving "teeth" to the international legal system, akin to legal procedure within domestic society (Guggenheim 1945, 40). Even so, this narrow, legalistic interpretation is inadequate in the realm of international politics, where despite continuous efforts in this direction, no overarching legal authority higher than the nation-state yet exists (Doxey 1987, 2–3). As such, international organizations are independent actors in the international system in only a very limited sense. Indeed one of the continually vexing problems in the study of international organization is the difficulty in determining universally applicable norms and values, much less rules of foreign policy behavior, in a world of such great cultural, political, and economic diversity. Decisions over whether to impose sanctions against supposed rule-breakers are very often contentious; but an equally difficult problem lies in determining what rules actually exist, apart from certain general (though important) existing principles such as protection of human rights and prohibitions against the use of force.

Thus this work will accept Margaret Doxey's broader definition of international sanctions as "penalties threatened or imposed as a declared consequence of the target's failure to observe international standards or international obligations" (1987, 4). Use of the term *standards* allows for more flexible interpretation of political norms and values (though these can attain quasi-legal status through usage and custom [Higgins 1963]), and is thus more relevant to the practice of foreign policy by states. Of course, within the context of the League of Nations and UN systems, the legal meaning of sanctions is largely preserved, since sanctions are to be applied in response to actions interpreted as breaches of the constitutional documents of the organizations, namely the Covenant and the Charter respectively (although some lawyers have argued against even referring to UN enforcement as "sanctions," since they are not automatic measures applied against lawbreakers).[4]

The potential range of sanctions is considerable, as Doxey (1987, 10–12) demonstrates in a useful fourfold typology. Types of sanctions include: (1) diplomatic and political, including protests, the postponement or cancellation of official visits, and the severance of consular or diplomatic relations; (2) cultural and communications, including interruptions of transportation links; (3) economic, both financial (credit)- and commercial (trade)-related, including the partial or complete interruption of export or import trade, withdrawal of most-favored-nation trading status and bans on access to banking or credit facilities; and (4) measures pertaining to status in international organizations (membership questions, including suspension or expulsion). This typology, however, neglects to include physical sanctions, such as a blockade of the ports of the defaulting state or the deployment of troops under an international flag;

indeed Undén considers that the establishment of an international peace force would represent the "crown" of a true collective security system (1963, 46–47). Even so, organizations based on the principle of upholding the peace can scarcely resort to such forcible measures consistently and still remain credible; and in practice, the military sanctions option has been essentially a nonstarter.

Sanctions under the League Covenant and UN Charter

The League Covenant established a partial set of restrictions on states' right to resort to force, which if disregarded would elicit a collective response in the form of punitive sanctions. These procedures for pacific settlement, set out in Arts. 12–15, included specific requirements that states submit their disputes to arbitration, judicial procedure or inquiry by the League Council. States were then required to delay any warlike action until a three-month cooling off period had elapsed following the award by the arbitrators or the Council's report (Art. 15[7]). These procedures could not, however, be used to redress even legitimate territorial grievances, since the League, through Art. 10, had cemented the political status quo established through the peace treaties following World War I.

According to the Covenant (Art. 11), any war or threat of war was to be regarded as a matter of concern to the whole League. If a state resorted to war in disregard of the procedures outlined in Arts. 12–15, member states were required, under Art. 16, to "undertake immediately to subject it to the severance of all trade and financial relations, the prohibition of all intercourse between their nationals and the nationals of the Covenant breaking state." These economic measures were supplemented by provisions for League military sanctions against designated aggressors (Art. 16[2]), and by provisions for mutual support for member states suffering undue losses (Art. 16[3]); however, all military obligations to the League (except the right of passage) remained optional for member states. These procedures did not distinguish between great and small powers; theoretically, all states were equally subject to the sanctions procedure. Furthermore, Art. 17 provided for the possibility of sanctions against uncooperative nonmember states; and the important but rarely discussed Art. 19 empowered the League Council to give prior consideration to situations which might endanger the peace.

The enforcement system under the UN Charter is based on the similar requirement that states resolve their disputes in peaceful fashion. However, the Charter does not stipulate any set procedure for conflict resolution, but rather allows the disputing parties to choose their own means (Arts. 2[3] and 33[1]). The system is also based on a more all-inclusive ban on the threat or use of force (under Art. 2[4]), although warlike measures are allowable in case of collective or individual self-defense, under Art. 51. The main distinction between the two documents lies in the predominant role of the Security Council in the UN, which according to Art. 24 has "primary responsibility for the maintenance of international peace and security," and can take steps for all states, "on their behalf." Its discretionary powers include the right to investigate any dispute or situation which might give rise to a dispute (Art. 34), and the exclusive right to deal forcibly with any situation which it regards as disturbing the peace (Chapter VII). Member states are bound through certain "positive obligations" (Arts. 2[5]; 25; 49) to fulfill Security Council decisions in good faith. Under this system the General Assembly plays a secondary role; for example, the Assembly can never take binding decisions on a security-related issue (Art. 11[2]), and it is precluded from even discussing such issues unless the Security Council is deadlocked (Art. 12[1]). The Assembly's role was expanded through the Uniting for Peace Resolution (GA Res. 377 [v]) of 1950, although its powers remain advisory only.

The sanctions system (called "enforcement actions" in Charter terminology) is set out in Chapter VII. Art. 39 states that the Security Council shall determine the "existence of any threat to the peace, breach of the peace, or act of aggression." Once its initial determination has been made, the Council has four options: (1) to make recommendations for action under Art. 39; (2) to call for provisional measures under Art. 40; (3) to call on member states to apply nonmilitary sanctions, under Art. 41; or (4) to call on members to apply military sanctions, under Art. 42. Article 41 outlines measures including the "complete or partial interruption of economic relations and of rail, sea, air, postal, telegraphic, radio or other means of communication, and the severance of diplomatic relations." Art. 42 envisions "demonstrations, blockade, and other operations by air, sea, or land forces of Members of the United Nations," although such obligations remained contingent upon the conclusion of special agreements between member governments and the Security Council (Art. 43), to be worked out in conjunction with a military staff committee (Arts. 45–47). Under the terms of such agreements, military sanctions would be compulsory, unlike under the Covenant, when, apart from the right of passage, they remained optional. (In subsequent practice, of course, the military provisions of the Charter have remained a dead letter due to the onset of the Cold War.) The UN's independent authority is also wider than the League's in nonmilitary sanctions, which are mandatory in any case in which the Security Council has made a determination as to the guilty party. The UN's purview is also greater vis-à-vis nonmember states, by which it shall ensure that nonmembers act in accordance with the Charter in order to maintain international peace and security (Art. 2[6]). However, the extent of these nonmember obligations to the UN has been the focus of significant legal controversy.[5]

NEUTRAL STATES AND SANCTIONS

Although participation in a military sanctions operation would appear to be clearly inconsistent with a viable neutral policy, economic and other nonforcible sanctions broach the problematical grey area in which it is difficult to distinguish between allowed and forbidden measures. As mentioned earlier, there is a sharp distinction in pure law between the military aspects of neutrality, which are governed by the Hague rules, and the economic aspects, which are not clearly established. Technically, therefore, participation in an economic embargo could be considered allowable for a neutral state. Even so, given the historical importance of neutrality rules as a means to protect shipping and trade by nonparticipants in armed conflict, this strict separation of the two issues is inadequate. For example, even if the application of economic sanctions against an aggressor is not considered a direct violation of the Hague neutrality rules, it would nonetheless breach the equally important, if more general, neutral principles of abstention from conflict and impartiality of attitude. It has been argued that neutral policy cannot attain complete impartiality in economic warfare, given that all neutral trade helps belligerents in some fashion (Robert 1950, 79–80). Furthermore, several writers (including legal experts in both Sweden and Switzerland) have expressed the view that neutrality in its formal, legal meaning *is* affected by economic sanctions, and hence that neutrality has also an economic role.[6]

Another potential problem for neutrals is that nonviolent sanctions can be a prelude to forcible, even warlike, measures, using a graduated scale of rigor. Indeed the standing threat of escalation to more severe measures is an important component of an operative sanctions system, particularly in light of its deterrent function mentioned earlier. In a recent analysis of the sanctions problem, Stephanie Lenway (1988, 497–526 *passim*) repeatedly emphasizes that sanctions often fail precisely because the states applying them fear that nonviolent sanctions may trigger a war. Even so, sanctions cannot simply be equated with an international "hunger blockade," such as those applied in the Napoleonic Wars and the two world wars.[7] Economic sanctions are much more circumscribed in both aims and usage—although it must be kept in mind that in 1918, 1935, or even 1945, they did not seem nearly so benign as they might today. Indeed the League's sanctions system (in Lord Cecil's view) was conceived largely because of the success of the Allied economic blockade of Germany during World War I; sanctions were regarded as a peacetime application of the same principle, or, as Robin Renwick suggests, a "bloodless substitute for war" (1981, 91). Such considerations are, arguably, even more crucial for neutral states, since the credibility of their policies hinges directly upon their avoidance of war. In fact, this problem of possible escalation proved to be very serious in the Italo-Abyssinian crisis.

Another difficulty for neutrals is the linkage between international security organizations and the wars which preceded them. It is not merely coincidental, as Morgenthau points out, that the most ambitious attempts at establishing an international authority (the Holy Alliance after 1815, the League, and the UN) all emerged after the most destructive wars in history (1960, 427). From their inception, both the League and the UN reflected the intent of the wartime allies to determine the rules of the peace following their victory; and indeed both organizations retained some of the vestiges of a defensive alliance aimed against a resurgent Germany. The neutral state must therefore decide whether to join and participate in such organizations on the basis of promise rather than on performance; and in neither the League nor the UN did the neutrals have direct access to the decision-making process leading to establishment of the organizations.

Neutrality and collective security thus represent conflicting obligations primarily insofar as neutrality is based on the principles of impartiality and abstention from disputes; whereas sanctions, when imposed by international organizations, require partiality and active participation to resolve such disputes. Collective security stems from the realization that in the modern period no state can avoid conflicts simply by remaining indifferent, as in the limited wars of the nineteenth century. This is particularly true for neutral states, whose policies, according to Alfred Verdross, are "justified insofar as [neutrality] has been chosen not only as a means of self-preservation, but also with the conviction that this policy will serve at the same time the higher interests of peace" (1958, 417). A working peace system is therefore also in the neutrals' clear interest, even though the establishment of such a system would, paradoxically, undermine the traditional neutral principles of avoiding political entanglements and conflicts (W. P. Grieve 1948, 115). Thus while their ultimate aims (the preservation of peace) may coincide, the means to achieve those ends—including economic sanctions obligations—create a clear dilemma for neutral states.

Numerous writers and practitioners of politics have indeed accepted the notion that neutrality and sanctions are irreconcilable principles, which according to one are "as immiscible as oil and water" (Woolsey 1936, 259); Hans Morgenthau asserted strongly that "these two principles can neither in theory nor in practice exist together" (1938, 559). The League of Nations Council itself underscored this incompatibility at the very outset of the League era: "The idea of neutrality of Members of the League is not compatible with the other principles that all the members of the League will have to act in common to cause their covenants to be respected" (*OJ*, September 1920, 308). Similarly forceful views were held after World War II,[8] even within the UN.[9] There are in fact two arguments often advanced on the issue. One, mentioned above, refers to the theoretical incompatibility between the two sets of obligations; the other, more far-reaching, asserts that the establishment of collective security systems supercedes the Hague rules and has ruled out the resort to neutrality altogether. Thus according to Nils Ørvik, "neutrality in its original sense is no longer a debatable question. The antiquity and impracticality of traditional, impartial neutrality are today regarded as accepted facts" (Ørvik 1971, 268).

On the other hand, there is a distinctly artificial air about such predictions or even declarations of the decline or end of neutrality, and its replacement by new international obligations. Quite apart from the obvious reality that neutral countries and sanctions systems have continued to exist conjointly since 1918, neither the League Covenant nor the UN Charter so much as mentioned the term neutrality, much less ruled it out explicitly; and both have allowed for neutrality in certain instances. Under the Covenant, for example, both the resort to war and a position of neutrality were allowable if the Council was unable to come to a unanimous recommendation on resolving a dispute, or if an attack occurred more than three months after a decision or award pertaining to the dispute. Individual member states retained the right to determine if and when to apply sanctions, again giving scope for a neutral or quasi-neutral posture. The incomplete, "revolving-door" membership of the League also prevented the establishment of a watertight enforcement system. And under the UN Charter, neutrality appears to be possible in any great power dispute, or indeed in any dispute in which the UN fails to act, due to the stipulation (in Art. 27[3]) that the five permanent Council members must be in agreement before enforcement action can be taken. Thus Inis Claude asserts that the UN Charter represents only an "agreement to agree" on collective security provisions (1962, 173–74).

These confusing signals concerning the compatibility of neutrality with collective security operations indicate that the practical aspects of the neutrality-sanctions problem have received too little attention as yet for decisive conclusions to be drawn. The hypothesis that neutrality is irreconcilable with a sanctions operation has not been subject to sufficient empirical testing. This need for further analysis of the problem indicates the potential usefulness of such a study which moves beyond purely legal and conceptual arguments, and analyzes neutral policies in actual sanctions operations, in order to determine the scope for compatibility between them. The validity of using Sweden and Switzerland as representative neutrals will be set out in the next chapter.

NOTES

1. Perhaps the most notorious example of confusing the legal and moral dimensions was John Foster Dulles's view that "neutralism is, except under very exceptional circumstances . . . an immoral and shortsighted conception"; quoted in Crabb, 1965, pp. 169–73.

2. See Oppenheim, 1952, pp. 655–56; Verdross, 1967, p. 13; Zemanek, 1961, pp. 415–16.

3. See Kelsen, 1957, pp. 110, 159, 162–63; Jessup, 1935-36; Brierly, 1929, p. 209; Wright, 1928, pp. 369–70; Oppenheim, 1952, p. 639; Wright, 1936a, pp. 226–27, Doc. 2; Cohn, 1939; Guggenheim, 1945, pp. 27, 45.

4. Prof. Kelsen, for example, argues that UN measures taken under Chapter VII are "purely political measures . . . which the Security Council may apply at its own discretion to maintain or restore international peace" (1950, p. 733; also pp. 710, 724–25); Halderman, 1968, p. 690.

In Kelsen's view the only true UN "sanctions" include provisions for expulsion from the organization (Art. 6), suspension of Assembly voting rights (Art. 19), and Security Council measures to give effect to an ICJ judgment (under Art. 94[2]).

5. For arguments considering the Charter capable of binding nonmembers, see Lalive, 1947, p. 85; Falk, 1970, pp. 202–3; and Kelsen, 1950, p. 110, even characterized this attempt as "revolutionary."

For opposing views, see Castrén, 1954, p. 433; Bindschedler, 1963, pp. 404–5; and especially W. P. Grieve, 1948, p. 115.

6. Undén, 1939, pp. 29–30; Robert, 1950, pp. 77–79; Gihl, 1936, pp. 24–25; and Gihl, 1938, p. 76, calls such neutral participation in economic sanctions "undeniably a divergence from neutrality."

7. Doxey, 1980, p. 10; Brown-John, 1975, pp. 3–4; Galtung, 1967, pp. 411–12; Muriel Grieve, 1968, p. 433; Lalive, 1947, p. 87; and especially Taylor, 1965, p. 456.

8. For example, in 1944 a nongovernmental committee of jurists headed by Judge Hudson asserted that in the future "no state would be free to frustrate the efforts of the Community of States by relying on the Nineteenth-Century law of neutrality" ("The International Law of the Future," 1944, p. 41). See also Koravin, 1946, p. 754.

9. The UN Conference at San Francisco "tacitly accepted" [sic] the view that a policy of (permanent) neutrality was incompatible with UN membership; see UNCIO, Documents, Vol. 6, Doc. 739, p. 722, and Doc. 944, pp. 459–60; Vol. 7, Doc. 1178, p. 327. It also considered neutrality incompatible with even nonmilitary sanctions (Goodrich et al., 1969, p. 91), which seemed to rule out "qualified" neutrality within the UN. However, the subcommittee appeared to admit of the possibility of "ordinary" neutrality in certain cases of war under the Charter; see Guggenheim, 1945, p. 32; Lalive, 1947, p. 78.

2

Swedish and Swiss Neutrality in Comparative Perspective

THE FEASIBILITY OF COMPARATIVE ANALYSIS

The validity of a comparative study of neutrality is illustrated by the "most similar systems" research design of Przeworski and Teune, who adapted J. S. Mill's rules of concomitant variation to social science methodology. The most similar systems design is based on two requirements: first, that the compared units be as similar as possible along a wide range of factors, thereby reducing the number of explanatory (independent) variables to a reasonable limit. Second, their policy output (the dependent variable) must show divergence which cannot be explained by those common factors, so that their differences in policy will be attributable to a relatively small number of factors (Przeworski and Teune 1970, 32–33).

It is often argued that the Scandinavian states form a useful source for such an inquiry, since their many geographical, cultural, and political similarities cannot in themselves explain the postwar divergence in Scandinavian foreign and security policies (e.g., Petersen 1977, 223–24). A similar case can be made for examining European neutrality within this comparative design, with special reference to Sweden and Switzerland. As a pool of possible case studies, the West European neutrals (Austria, Ireland, Finland, Sweden, and Switzerland) can be distinguished from other states which pursue a policy of disengagement or nonalignment, due to important common features.

Each maintains a strong and stable system of liberal democracy, operates a free trade–oriented industrial economy, and has been shaped by European political culture through centuries of internal consolidation within the Western world; they are also, by all measurements, small states in the international system. In addition, the European neutrals have been associated with the development of Western-based international law, from which the Hague neutrality rules are derived; in this sense they all *aim* for neutrality, in its usual legal sense, in the event of a major war. In all these respects the European neutrals are distinguishable from the Nonaligned or "Group of 77" countries of the developing world, which, although similar in their nonadherence to the East and West blocs, are also characterized by their developing economies, colonial past, and lack of established, indigenous political and administrative structures (Yugoslavia, with features of both systems, presents a special case in itself).

Within this context of European neutrality, Sweden and Switzerland suggest themselves as valid comparable cases. One author asserts that these two countries are "together a class apart" (Lyon 1963, 197), due to their many distinguishing characteristics, four of which will be examined below. On the other hand, their policy output—in this case, their attitudes toward collective security—has shown considerable variation, indicated by Switzerland's nonaccession to the UN Charter in contrast to Sweden's formal UN membership, by which the Swedish but not the Swiss government is bound to comply with Security Council decisions which are mandatory under Art. 25 of the Charter (those pertaining to enforcement). This situation also raises certain methodological problems, such as the lack of an existing data base derived from (Swiss) votes on issues before the UN.

Nonetheless, this problem can be overcome by extending the analytical framework to cover the League as well as the UN periods. Indeed within this broader historical context Switzerland is a more logical choice than would be the other neutral states (Austria, Ireland, Finland) none of which have remained consistently neutral, much less independent, since World War I. In return, Switzerland's anomalous refusal to enter the UN, despite the organization's achievement of virtual universal membership, provokes many interesting and pertinent questions—particularly since this refusal attests to the long-term significance of the neutrality–collective security dilemma discussed in chapter 1. Even so, this approach is not completely exclusionary, and references to other neutrals occasionally will be made in order to place these two states in better perspective.

COMMON FACTORS LINKING SWEDEN AND SWITZERLAND

The Traditional Neutrals

The first distinguishing characteristic of both states has been their longtime success in maintaining neutrality as the basis of their foreign policy, which has given rise to their common designation as the "traditional" (or even "professional") neutrals of Europe. Sustained by the forces of continuity built up over a long period of avoiding wars (including both world wars of this century) and membership in entangling alliances, the neutrality of both states has attained an unmatched degree of international and domestic credibility, which has largely freed their policymakers from charges of opportunism.

Neither state's territory has been violated since the Napoleonic era, although it would be inaccurate to date either state's neutral policy from that time. The development of Swedish neutrality after 1814 (the last point at which Sweden was involved in hostilities, with Denmark) was only slow and incremental; indeed a consistent policy of neutrality did not actually emerge until early in the twentieth century (Håstad 1956, 20). Sweden's neutrality was the fortunate by-product of efforts to reach an adequate modus vivendi with the major Baltic powers during the nineteenth century; Sweden, in fact, managed to avoid involvement in ongoing wars by gravitating toward the predominant power of the era (in turn Russia, Britain, and, after 1870, Germany), which in the latter case was solidified by blood ties between the Swedish Royal Family and the Hohenzollerns. Swedish policy was actually a striking confirmation of Fox's theory of the "anti-balance of power," by which a smaller and weaker state will tend to side with the predominant power in its region in the interests of survival, thus "increasing the imbalance between two power constellations" (Fox 1959, 187). Sweden's relative geopolitical isolation also enabled it to shift its loyalties, by which its "policy of freedom from alliances was the product rather than the cause of Swedish security" (Roberts 1972, 63).

The first unilateral Swedish declaration of neutrality (apart from its earlier participation in the makeshift Leagues of Armed Neutrality of 1780 and 1800) came in 1834 during an Anglo-Russian dispute in the Near East. Although Swedish policy tended to favor British interests (Scott 1977, 319), King Karl XIV told Lord Palmerston that "My policy will be strict neutrality as long as I can preserve it; in no event will I ever embark on hostilities against England, and with Russia only in the last extremity. . . . " (Svänström and Palmstierna 1934, 333). During the Crimean War, Sweden was ultimately a nonparticipant, yet at this high point of its rapprochement with Britain, it came very close to hostilities with Russia.

The advent of Sweden's neutrality as a component of state policy dates from the quasi-utopian "pan-Scandinavian" movement of the mid-nineteenth century, when Swedish Kings Oscar I and Karl XV nearly embroiled Sweden in two wars on the side of Denmark (1848 and 1863) in its ongoing dispute with Prussia. However, in November 1863 Sweden's War Minister Reuterskjöld told the *Riddarhus* that the country lacked the military strength to fulfill the Crown's promise (unless supported by either France or Britain), and that Sweden had therefore to remain neutral, which contributed to Denmark's capitulation to Prussia in 1864. The tendency to remain neutral was strengthened during Prime Minister Manderström's decade-long tenure, when Sweden pursued strict neutrality in the Austro-Prussian and Franco-Prussian wars of 1866 and 1870, and later during the Balkan crises of 1877–78 and 1885–86 (Edberg 1951, 195). The advent of Swedish neutrality thus coincided, and was directly associated, with the decline of royal adventurism in foreign affairs, which was also facilitated by the replacement in 1866 of the antiquated Four-Estate system with a more powerful, bicameral parliament (*Riksdag*).

In later crises, including the break with Norway in 1905 and the Ålands dispute with Finland in 1920–21, circumstances tended to exclude all likelihood of a resort to arms, even though both outcomes are often proclaimed as a triumph of reason over intransigence. The cumulative effect of these various crises was greater than the sum of their parts, for Sweden's fortuitous avoidance of wars gradually strengthened the appeal of neutrality as a long-term strategy (Scott 1977, 326); accordingly, in 1912 Sweden, along with Denmark and Norway, issued its first prior declaration of neutrality, which was then successfully pursued throughout World War I. Its neutrality by that time "came as a natural consequence of long-time isolation from diplomatic entanglement in European affairs" (Abrahamsen 1957, 11).

It is similarly difficult to pinpoint one specific date as the beginning of Switzerland's policy of neutrality, as it too was a direct product of the evolution of the European system. Holt (1978) has noted four different historical phases in this development: (1) prior to 1500, internal neutrality among the Swiss cantons; (2) 1500–1674, occasional neutrality in ongoing wars; (3) 1674–1815, continual, unilaterally declared neutrality; and (4) after 1815, continual, unilaterally declared and internationally recognized neutrality. The first harbinger of Switzerland's determination to remain neutral came in 1481 at the Convention of Stans, when the hermit Nicholas von Flüe averted an impending civil war over the spoils from the victory over the Burgundians by asserting his historic dictum "do not meddle into the disputes of others." This advice was first taken up in 1508, when Switzerland declared neutrality in a dispute between Holy Roman Emperor Maximilian I and Louis XII of France.

Swiss neutrality is customarily dated from 1515, when its great power era in central Europe was brought to a sudden halt by France at the Battle of Marignano in northern Italy. After that time the Swiss summarily withdrew from European power politics, preoccupied by their own internal disputes. Indeed, neutrality was scarcely a conscious choice; it was necessitated by the inability of the quasi-sovereign cantons to cooperate, and described as such by William Martin as "not a principle; it is a negation" (quoted in Wilson 1974, 42).

The specific term *neutrality* was first used for Switzerland in a formal treaty between France and Austria concerning the neutralization of Burgundy and the Franche-Comté in 1522, with Switzerland as the intermediary (Hughes 1975, 149). The Swiss Diet first proclaimed neutrality as the consistent basis of Swiss foreign policy soon after the outbreak of the General (Vermligen) wars between France and the Netherlands of 1672–1713; Swiss historian Edgar Bonjour therefore prefers 1674 as the key point of departure for Switzerland's neutrality. Still later, after suffering repeated territorial violations by the Napoleonic armies after 1798 (and by the Allies after 1813), Switzerland obtained Napoleon's recognition of its neutrality in November 1813 (after his defeat at Leipzig), which set the stage for the formal recognition of its perpetual neutrality in 1815 by the great powers through the Treaties of Vienna and Paris. After that time, neutrality was maintained consistently and within Switzerland's territorial borders, finalized in 1857 (Bonjour 1952, 228); and it was respected by both belligerents during the Austro-Prussian and Franco-Prussian wars of 1866 and 1870, and later during the two world wars.

Due to this strong tradition, neutrality has developed into a national institution with virtually unanimous support in both countries. The sanctity of their neutral tradition has also provided a powerful incentive for a continuation of that policy into the modern era, in spite of the structural changes in the international system which have wholly altered the setting in which their policies are formulated. Adam Roberts agrees with this view: "In Europe those states which have turned the legal status of neutrality into a great national dogma have in fact generally been the more successful neutrals...because their neutrality is widely understood and accepted" (Roberts 1972, 44). This factor has been particularly important due to their avoidance of participation in World War II; in fact, they emerged as the only neutral states directly exposed to the threat of German invasion which escaped from the war years with their neutrality intact. Since that time even tacit Soviet recognition of their neutrality, previously denied, has been forthcoming.[1]

Nonetheless, any state with long-term policy recognition can begin to perceive that policy as worthy of retention in its own right—not only as a means to protect and defend its national interests but as, in itself, an essential interest; such an attitude can in turn blur the "means-ends" relationship of neutrality. Peter Lyon suggests that

> a policy which survives through the years, which generations of statesmen practice and modify, gradually begins to take on the aspect of a dogma and to become independent of the purposes for which it was first devised. To a great extent this is now true of both Swiss and Swedish neutrality policies. Public explanations and justifications of present policies have to be placed in the cherished tradition. (Lyon 1963, 152)

In this respect, the neutral tradition can develop an aura of "permanence" for the neutral state; Roderick Ogley points out that "most akin to the 'neutralized' state is the 'traditional neutral,' of which Switzerland and Sweden are the obvious examples" (1970, 5). Gerald Stourzh maintains that the problem of policy rigidity is most acute in the case of a permanent neutral such as Switzerland, where the constant endeavor to maintain international credibility can lead to an "ideology of neutrality" (Stourzh 1971, 98; Frei 1969, 171–72). Jacques Freymond adds that "its relinquishment would imply a complete break with the past" (1963, 152). Christopher Hughes asserts that "the (Swiss) Assembly declares neutrality rather as other nations declare war" (1954, 44). Similar observations have been made concerning Sweden's neutral policy: Thomas Hart (1976, 44) shows that neutrality is regarded as an "overriding goal" by many Swedish foreign policy élites, which "is so strongly rooted in the minds of many élites that it enjoys a special dignity of its own ... for many, apparently, adherence to nonaligned status has become in itself the extreme goal."

Notwithstanding the clear benefits resulting from such widespread acceptance, the veneration of neutrality can also prevent or hinder necessary alterations in the state's basic policy objectives. The credibility argument can indeed work both ways, since deviations from a longstanding policy may arouse even greater distrust from, for example, the great powers than for a state lacking such an historical basis. The need to maintain policy continuity has been stressed repeatedly by both Swiss and Swedish governments. This need, however, can raise problems for the neutral state when it is faced with major changes in the external system, such as the establishment of sanctions systems, assuming that "the price of effectiveness in foreign policy is eternal vigilance to the changes restlessly at work in world politics" (Northedge 1976, preface). This factor has important bearing on the neutrality-sanctions problem, for a clear dilemma arises between attachment to the old, tried and tested neutral formula and acceptance of new international obligations.

The Armed Neutrals

A second feature common to both countries has been their commitment to a strongly armed neutrality. The military tradition runs deep into the national experience of both states, which are classic examples of "nations in arms" (Roberts 1972, 16); early military success preceded neutrality, yet continued military readiness fostered the development of neutrality as a traditional status. During the Middle Ages, each was the predominant military power in its respective geographical region. Under the Vasa Royal House, Sweden emerged at the end of the sixteenth century as a primary Baltic military power, outstripping Denmark and successfully challenging Russia's traditional control over the area. During the third phase of the Thirty Years War (1630–32), King Gustavus Adolphus led the Protestant forces as far south as the Swiss border, and Sweden enveloped a northern European empire including Finland, Latvia, Lithuania, and Estonia to the east, and many Germanic territories (e.g., Bremen, Verden, Pomerania) to the south.

Another factor enabling Sweden's acquisition of an empire far out of proportion to its overall resources was the important institution of a mostly free, arms-bearing peasantry (*bondi*), the legacy of relatively shallow feudal roots, which was skillfully exploited by successive kings. The death of Karl XII in 1718 quickly terminated Sweden's great power era, although King Gustaf III conducted a more limited military campaign after the reassertion of royal absolutism through the bloodless coup of 1772. Sweden's colonial aspirations came to a decisive end after it won control over Norway from Denmark in 1814 (in recompense for its loss of Finland to Russia in 1809); the Treaty of Kiel of

January 1814 also marked the final physical separation of Sweden from continental Europe. Even so, as noted earlier, Sweden nearly became embroiled in hostilities with both Russia and Prussia in the mid-nineteenth century. Later, the defense issue became the locus of a major political debate with Sweden, leading to an important compromise in 1885 between the advocates of economic protectionism and those wanting a stronger defense, in an unorthodox arrangement linking defense with tax reform (Oakley 1966, 212). Also at this juncture a strong countervailing influence in the form of antimilitarist sentiment grew in Sweden, which lay the groundwork for Sweden's later receptivity to proposals for international disarmament.

The military tradition in Switzerland extends back even further (Caesar reputedly considered the Roman province of Helvetia to contain the empire's best fighters), cited by Arnold Toynbee as an example of the "transmigration of the martial spirit" (1954, 9:493–94). The very genesis of the Swiss Confederation in 1291 came about through bands of mountain peasants attempting to throw off the yoke of corrupt external rule by the Habsburg dynasty (dramatized through Schiller's play *Wilhelm Tell*), a process virtually completed by the end of the fifteenth century (Bonjour 1952, 80). The battles of Sempach (1386) and Näfels (1388) helped consolidate Switzerland's growing military reputation. The Swiss militarist age reached its peak in 1476 with the defeat of the Burgundians under Charles the Bold in the battles of Grandson and Morat, and lasted until 1515 and its precipitous defeat at Marignano, after which the advent of artillery and professional armies rendered obsolete the halberd-bearing bands of peasant foot-soldiers. Even so, Switzerland continued its massive export of professional mercenaries. The *Reislaufen* (parodied in G. B. Shaw's play *Arms and the Man*) included both individual hiring and, more commonly, the practice of cantons concluding "treaties of military capitulation" with foreign powers, providing regiments of soldiers in exchange for payment; this included the élite "Hundred Swiss" regiment in the employ of the Bourbon Monarchy, which was massacred along with Louis XVI in the Tuileries in August 1792. However, due to an increasing conflict with Switzerland's neutrality, military capitulations were banned in the 1848 constitution (Art. 11) and the mercenary service by federal decree in 1859 (Codding 1961, 154). After that time (apart from the ceremonial Swiss Papal Guard) the Swiss military has been used purely for defensive purposes in successfully warding off threats to Switzerland's neutrality, as in compelling the King of Prussia in 1857 to relinquish his antiquated claim to the (Swiss) principality of Neuchâtel.

Since the 1930s a strongly armed neutrality has characterized both countries, arguably contributing to their success in avoiding foreign invasion in World War II (though this point is disputed, particularly in Sweden [e.g., Hägglöf 1960, 163; Carlgren 1977]). Since then, after some debate over joining NATO in the 1950s, both countries operate strikingly similar "total defense" arrangements; neither, however, has elected to procure or develop nuclear weapons due to neutrality considerations. Both states rely heavily on civil, economic, and even psychological defenses as well as military, though this requires spending among the highest levels on defense (3–4 percent of GNP) in the Western world. "Security" policy assumes a much wider meaning for an armed neutral than for an allied state; there is even a direct link between trade and security for the neutrals (Bergquist 1969; Gaudard 1976, 18). For example, in the interests of self-reliance, both states insist on retaining stiff tariff barriers in certain product-areas (agriculture, textiles, pharmaceuticals) deemed vital for military preparedness. Such exceptions to otherwise avowedly free-trade policies have complicated the neutrals' negotiations with both the European Economic Community (EEC) (Bohn 1977, 347) and the General Agreement on Tariffs and Trade (GATT) (Dohlman 1985).

Both states maintain a well-trained but almost entirely conscript army with a small permanent staff (Art. 13 of the 1874 Swiss constitution actually prohibits the establishment of a standing army), which operate on similar doctrines of "deterrence" or "dissuasion," calculated to make the costs of an invasion outweigh the possible gains for a potential enemy. The practice of universal male conscription has yielded the two highest ratios of armed forces to total population in Western Europe: indeed in an emergency, these two states can field the continent's two largest armies.[2] Military self-reliance also requires significant expenditure on weapons research and development (R & D), and on maintaining an indigenous arms manufacturing industry. However, the military and economic necessity of selling arms abroad is strongly counterbalanced by political considerations relating to neutrality, and selling arms abroad can raise moral issues through its apparent inconsistency with a nominally peace-loving neutral attitude; this is particularly true of Sweden, due to long-time Social Democratic rule. It is occasionally claimed, particularly in Switzerland, that arms sales to both belligerents in a war actually enhances the credibility of impartial neutrality and universality (see *Journal de Genève*, 10 January 1983, p. 1). These conflicting considerations and the sensitivity of the issue have resulted in very restrictive arms sale legislation in both countries; even so, numerous violations have occurred.[3]

The maintenance of a wide-ranging armed neutral policy also has direct implications for their attitudes toward collective security, insofar as their purely defensive national security orientation by definition excludes foreign military engagements; this would suggest a strong reluctance to accept any military sanctions obligations. The past and continuing high level of security preparedness clearly demonstrates both states' willingness to defend their territory and neutrality through the force of arms, a duty also stipulated in the Hague Conventions. The neutrals' security policy maintains a dual function: to provide for their own national security needs, and also to contribute to the general security of the international system.

The Humanitarian Neutrals

Swedish and Swiss policy is also linked through a common emphasis on humanitarian aid and international peacekeeping activity. This emphasis has been a direct offshoot of their neutral traditions, having remained at peace and above the fray of European political intrigue for a long period. The neutrals have come to regard activity which contributes to a relaxation of political tensions as a necessary and integral component of neutral policy, even as a specifically neutral duty. Such activity can also serve to counterbalance any negative implications of a policy of armed neutrality and abstention from controversial issues, and thereby enhance their credibility as neutral brokers.

Neutrality is thought to serve the interests of the international system in two ways: first, by the very existence of the neutral state itself (by which, for example, the neutral, in forswearing all participation in wars, thereby creates a "zone of no interest"); and second, by providing an opportunity to serve the international community impartially. Both states have intimated the belief that neutrality policy itself somehow demonstates an inherently peaceful or peace-loving attitude, which has occasionally led to charges of moral righteousness, particularly against Sweden. Yet both states reject all notions of spiritual neutrality and have never disguised their natural ideological affiliation with Western democratic values. Their traditionally liberal policies of political asylum, the availability of good offices and channels of mediation, the granting of foreign aid, and more generally their traditions of democracy, tolerance, and the rule of law all have helped cultivate an ideology of benevolent neutrality.

One particularly important aspect of their policies has been the universality of their relations with other states, which predisposes them to support the cause of universal membership in modern international organizations. Indeed the maintenance of good relations with all states, and the refusal to consider any state as an enemy, are regarded as vital components of neutral policy (Undén 1963, 58–59). As one example, both states played an important role as the Western neutrals on the five-nation Neutral Supervisory Commission to oversee the Korean Armistice after 1953 (J. Freymond 1959). During both world wars and in the Suez crisis of 1956 both states (particularly Switzerland) also fulfilled the vital task of neutral "protecting power," watching over the interests of the various belligerents in countries with which they had broken relations; and this role continues to be utilized even in peacetime (e.g., Switzerland representing U.S. interests in Iran after the 1979 revolution). Furthermore, both states have strongly advocated the development of the international legal order, maintaining what has been called a "legalistic" attitude toward international relations (Eek 1955, 35; Hughes 1975, 151); they much prefer legal to political solutions in international conflict and pursue this aim by championing the establishment of mandatory procedures for peaceful conflict resolution (e.g., mediation, arbitration) as opposed to punitive measures. This emphasis also carries important implications for their attitude toward collective sanctions, which are also measures designed to defend the international order, employed only when peaceful means have failed.

Sweden's internationalist reputation stems largely from its traditional openness to foreign, particularly liberal, influences (Gustafsson 1964, 7), which significantly has been voluntary rather than imposed; apart from a temporary occupation of northern Sweden by Russian troops in 1809, Sweden has never been occupied by a foreign power since its founding as a sovereign state in 1523. One telling historical circumstance was the precipitous changeover of the monarchy in 1809, when the Vasa line was severed with the discredited policies of Gustaf IV Adolf, and replaced by an imported French Marshal, Jean-Baptiste Bernadotte, Prince of Pontecorvo. The significance of the fact that the legendary Vasa dynasty, associated with the very establishment of Swedish national sovereignty and its era as an imperial power, could be successfully replaced by a non-Swedish-speaking French military commander (who just two years previously had stood poised with a large army on a Danish beachhead ready to invade southern Sweden) could hardly be lost upon the Swedes themselves.

Later in the nineteenth century, Swedish internationalist thought was associated variously with the pan-Scandinavian movement; the development of antimilitarist/pacifist philosophy (more closely associated with Sweden's neutrality than were the militarist-minded Conservative élites of the pre-1914 period [Mårold 1974]); and particularly in the free trade movement (influenced by the Manchester Liberalism of Richard Cobden and John Bright). More recently Swedish officials have held that neutrality has a vital peacekeeping effect in the Nordic region (Brodin et al. 1968, 30); and the renowned Swedish welfare state has even been cited as a role model for developing countries. The establishment of peace research institutes at Uppsala, Lund, and Stockholm, as well as the Nobel Foundation, further solidifies this association between humanitarian activity and neutrality. Indeed Norman Angell's "index of national receptivity to world responsibilities" lists Sweden first out of the ninety-one countries studied (with Denmark and Norway second and third), due largely to its postwar expressions of solidarity and international activism (Rosenau 1981, 93).

Similarly, Swiss neutrality is often regarded as inherently virtuous and coincidental with the interests of peace, and not without justification. Through the Treaties of Paris and Vienna in 1815 (and reiterated through the Versailles Treaty of 1919) the powers formally recognized Swiss neutrality as being "in the interests of all Europe," thereby acknowledging the utility of a reliable "island of peace" in the center of a war-torn continent, to be maintained in perpetuity. Thus Switzerland, even in its secondary international role, was given reason to consider its position as special and even unique.

Switzerland's internationalism has also been bolstered by its availability or presence as a neutral meeting ground for disputing parties, which is seen to enhance its reputation for trust and confidentiality. Its "good offices" have been another notable offshoot of permanent neutrality and the universality of its diplomatic relations. The very first international organizations (the International Telegraphic Union in 1865, the Universal Postal Union in 1874) were established in the Swiss capital of Bern; more recently, Geneva (even though it occupies a peculiarly remote position in Swiss society) has gained a reputation as *the* international city, hosting the International Committee of the Red Cross (ICRC), the International Labor Organization (ILO), the League of Nations, and since 1945 the UN's European Office and literally hundreds of specialized agencies, subsidiary UN bodies, and non-governmental organizations (NGOs) holding consultative status with the UN. Swiss territory has also served as the venue for numerous international conferences and treaties (Ouchy in 1912, Lausanne in 1923, Locarno in 1925), and more recently the British-Argentinian talks in Bern in 1982, the Reagan-Gorbachev summit in November 1985, and the perennial East-West nuclear arms talks.

Undoubtedly the most visible and significant Swiss humanitarian contribution has been the work of the all-Swiss ICRC, which, despite being purely a private organization, has certain legal ties with the Swiss state (for example, Switzerland is the official repository of the Geneva Red Cross Conventions and the two Additional Protocols of 1977). More importantly, it has been argued that the Geneva Conventions presuppose the continuance of Swiss permanent neutrality (Kunz 1953, 288). Even so, there is much evidence that the Swiss government has attempted to muddle the distinction between Red Cross operations and official Swiss policy, thereby "hiving off" some of the good reputation of the ICRC to increase the credibility of Swiss neutrality;[4] one writer even asserts that Swiss officials never take an important foreign policy decision without referring directly to the work of the ICRC (Rist 1978, 21).

Due to these factors, it has been claimed that the neutrality of Switzerland shows that it is "eminently at the service of the international community," which constantly has its "windows open on the world" (F. Pictet 1975a, 580–81). These largely passive functions have contributed to Switzerland's strong, but arguably unjustified, reputation for solidarity; and the themes of neutrality and solidarity are "constantly associated in the Swiss political rhetoric" (Rist 1978, 125).

The Wealthy Neutrals

A fourth similarity between Sweden and Switzerland is their position as highly developed, industrialized, strongly free trade-oriented states, "neutrals by tradition, and traders with all comers by necessity" (Stanley and Whitt 1970, 16). Their success in avoiding destruction during World War II has led to unprecedented prosperity and expansion in the postwar period. Another factor is the effective and nearly identical systems of collective bargaining established in both countries in 1937–38, and the relative labor peace they induced, based on loose variations of democratic corporatism (Katzenstein

1985, 136–37). Prior to the first oil shock in 1973, Switzerland and Sweden became distinguished (by OECD statistics) as the two wealthiest countries in the world on a per capita basis; this development merely solidified the widespread perception in both countries of a symbiotic linkage between neutrality and modern economic prosperity.

This linkage is particularly marked in the Swiss case, whose "foreign policy seems to have become largely coterminous with its foreign economic policy" (Katzenstein 1980, 540), best symbolized by the powerful and largely autonomous Swiss Department of Trade. The French philosopher Chateaubriand once castigated the Swiss for growing "rich on the misfortunes of others and founding a bank upon human disasters" (quoted in Ziegler 1978, 129). The significance of wealth has not diminished in subsequent times, although its role vis-à-vis neutrality has been reversed: whereas earlier the avoidance of war facilitated the accumulation of wealth, Switzerland's growing prosperity eventually served to justify and underpin the continuation of a quiescent neutral policy. Neutrality, and its accompanying psychology of confidence (Bohn 1977, 344) has contributed to the widespread perception (however warranted) of Switzerland as an island of stability in a world of economic fluctuation and uncertainty, best typified by its banking secrecy laws. The role of neutrality herein is implicit rather than explicit, yet its significance for Switzerland's influential financial position is assumed almost universally; one is seen to justify the other.

The connection between neutrality and wealth is less direct in the Swedish case, since its monetary and fiscal policies are much less conducive to the inflow of foreign currency (only in late 1984 were foreign banks even allowed to operate in Sweden); Sweden's large public sector also differs substantially from Switzerland's strongly laissez-faire, hands-off approach to government. Even so, Sweden's independence from power blocs and its lack of a modern colonial empire has helped open Third World markets, and neutrality is often cited as a rationale for reaching out to the developing countries. Sweden, in fact, set a number of "firsts" in its levels of development aid, including being the first (noncolonial) country to surpass the OECD target of .7 percent of GNP, and later to surpass the 1 percent level suggested by the United Nations; and by 1979 it was in the forefront of debt relief for developing states, itself unilaterally writing off much of the debt owed by especially poor countries. These achievements have been directly related to its political neutrality and progressive profile. Even so, both neutral states have been harshly criticized by Marxist writers for their central role as developed, capitalistic powers (Ziegler 1978; Hermele and Larsson 1977).

Both states' low-tariff, aggressively adaptive economic strategies imply a high degree of responsiveness to outside economic developments. Although political neutrality has helped open world markets for both states, their dependence on trade also increases their sensitivity to international developments largely beyond their control, and particularly would render them susceptible to economic disruption and hardship in the event of an international economic embargo (a point illustrated by their difficulties during the Allied blockade of Germany in the two world wars)—again with implications for the economic sanctions problem. This issue was at least part of the neutrals' rationale for refusing to accept full EEC membership, opting instead for the European Free Trade Association (EFTA) and, in 1972, limited free trade agreements with the Common Market.

FACTORS DIFFERENTIATING SWEDEN AND SWITZERLAND

Neutrality and Nation-Building: an Interdisciplinary Approach

While these similarities are helpful as descriptive devices and attest to their comparability within the context of the collective security problem, taken alone they provide little clue as to how and why Swedish and Swiss policies toward sanctions may differ. Clearly other factors also require examination, even though, of course, every state's foreign policy is considered, in its own way, unique and indigenous to the national experience.

One potentially useful approach centers on locating relevant explanatory factors operative at the domestic, rather than the international (systemic) level. Despite the importance of domestic political influences on foreign policy formulation, however, such endogenous factors are often overlooked in favor of emphasizing geopolitical, strategic, and other external constraints on foreign policies of smaller, particularly neutral, states. There is a marked, though understandable, tendency for academic analysts to assume that neutral policies are determined essentially by the international rules of the game as established by the larger powers.[5] This tendency, however, often leads writers to understate the importance of those domestic factors which may encourage continuity in a neutral state's foreign policy.

In the present examples, it is a striking coincidence that the strongest tradition of neutrality has emerged in the two states which represent the European extremes in their degree of cultural and political centralization. The Swedish polity is characterized by ethnic, religious, and linguistic unity, which in turn has been reflected in a highly centralized state administrative structure. Switzerland, on the other hand, is well known for its political decentralization and fragmentation, stemming from its cultural multiplicity. It is axiomatic to describe Switzerland as a "microcosm of Europe" (e.g., Steiner 1974, xi), due to its wide diversity of peoples—entailing three official and four national languages, two confessional groups, and twenty-three cantons wielding considerable autonomy—within a small area. This sharp contrast in their degree of internal unity requires closer examination, in light of the importance attributed by both governments to maintaining a domestic concensus behind foreign policy.

The problem of determining neutral states' adaptation to collective security systems can thus be usefully addressed by focusing on the degree of state unity as an independent variable. A strong case can be made for an interdisciplinary approach to foreign policy studies, specifically by linking the study of state and nation-building processes (utilizing the work of such writers as Rokkan, Tilly, Seton-Watson, Anderson, and Deutsch) with traditional international relations literature. This approach can thereby cultivate what should be a fertile middle ground for studies of foreign policy. Indeed an interdisciplinary approach is particularly relevant to the field of foreign policy analysis due to its important bridge-building function, noting from William Wallace that "foreign policy is that area of politics which bridges the all-important boundary between the nation-state and its environment—the boundary which defines the nation-state, within the limits of which national governments claim supreme authority" (1971, 12). The increasing emphasis in international relations literature on a linkage approach to foreign policy studies, weighing both internal and external variables, would also appear to substantiate the utility of the present approach for studies of neutrality. Equally, one writer has recently suggested that our understanding of the relative usefulness of international sanctions would be increased by further study of the domestic political pressures within the states actually imposing sanctions (Lenway 1988, 425).

One early suggestion for a broader approach to foreign policy studies was made by Roy Macridis, who attempted to link the study of international politics with comparative politics, in order "to combine the study of objective factors in foreign policy with the study of processes by which decisions are reached and policies implemented" (1958, 5). Peter Hansen (1974, 149) similarly argues for a broader framework for analyzing the foreign policies of smaller states (with specific reference to Denmark), by "extending our efforts beyond the level of the international system into the national foreign policy context." Hans Daalder (1973, 27), in his important work on consociational systems in smaller states, has suggested that the nature of the élite culture within national societies is an important independent variable in determining how political conflicts are resolved, and he applied the principle to a comparative study of Switzerland and the Netherlands. In taking these cues, this study will apply this approach to the foreign policy process, by focusing on Sweden as the contrast with Switzerland. A particularly important factor here is the nature of the foreign policy élite culture within the two countries, and its relevance to the adaptability of neutrality.

At this point we can identify two basic preconditions for the establishment of a consistent overall strategy toward the sanctions question. First, since 1918 each government has confronted the problem of modifying its traditional approach to neutrality in order to accommodate the duties of international organizations. Second, each government faced the task of building domestic political support for that shift in national policy. In the following two sections, these two problems will be approached in reverse order: first I shall examine the historical development of political opinion formulation on foreign policy in the two countries, then I shall consider each state's specific conception of neutrality.

Neutrality as Swedish State Policy

Swedish state sovereignty was achieved in 1523 upon the demise of the Union of Kalmar, which had united the three Scandinavian countries under the Danish Crown since 1397. One source dates Sweden's cultural unification as early as 1134, with the uniting of the Svea and the Goths under King Sverker (Seton-Watson 1977, 69). Swedish nobleman Gustav Ericsson Vasa, in alliance with the Hanseatic League, succeeded in driving out the forces of Christian II of Denmark and was elected as the first Swedish king upon the founding of the modern Swedish state. Thereafter Vasa used his position to consolidate power, aided by the creation of a hereditary monarchy in 1544 (Anderson 1974a, 174), in order to impose "a widespread dissemination of the Swedish nation" (Mayer and Burnett 1977, 23).

Probably the decisive act of unity was his forcible imposition of the Lutheran Reformation upon the Swedish realm beginning in 1527, usurping the power of the clergy and effectively removing religion as a potential source of internal conflict. This event was followed by the rapid secularization of society and the dissemination of the Swedish language. S. M. Lipset and Stein Rokkan (1967, 14) have underscored its significance by positing the resolution of the Catholic-Protestant issue as the first and most important of the four critical junctures for centralizing European states in the late Middle Ages. Marxist historian Perry Anderson asserts that "the Vasa Reformation was undoubtedly the most successful economic operation of its kind accomplished by any dynasty in Europe" (Anderson 1974a, 173), particularly insofar as the Crown also sharply reduced the privileges of the landed aristocracy, with the important result that the Swedish élite was urban- rather than rural-based, centered in Stockholm. The school system was then incorporated into the state, so that the central authorities also held the tools for mass education (Lipset and Rokkan 1967, 15). The rapidity and conclusiveness of this process was aided by the relative decentralization of the "four-estate" system (*rikets ständer*) in Sweden. Still another factor was the existence of clearly defined physical boundaries to what became Sweden's national territory, which encouraged the rapid assimilation of territories later captured from Denmark (principally the southern Skåne region).

Sweden's religious and linguistic unity, enforced by the Crown, thus combined with its natural ethnic homogeneity to produce a highly unified Swedish nation at the very time that central Europe became engulfed in conflict by the mid-sixteenth century. This factor enabled successive Vasa kings to lead Sweden on a course of military adventurism, and the great power era was characterized by Sweden's maintenance of a Baltic empire far out of proportion to its indigenous capabilities (Barnes 1974, 252). The timing of the great power era was also very important, for it allowed the monarchy time to reinforce national unification prior to the next set of challenges, stemming from the advent of mass political participation within the democratic framework (Rokkan 1973b, 94).

This unification in turn helped prevent revolutionary breaks with the past, laying the groundwork for subsequent, relatively steady constitutional development and modernization following the collapse of the empire after 1718. Royal predominance in foreign affairs was reasserted by King Gustaf III after the unusual but temporary "era of liberty" (*frihets tiden*) from 1719 to 1772 (characterized by quarrels between the "Caps" and "Hats" factions over relations with Russia), and remained intact even following the constitutional crisis of 1809 and the changeover of the monarchy from the Vasa to the Bernadotte line. The modern constitution of 1809 limited the Crown only through a Council of Ministers (which, together with the four estates, retained the power of the purse), and through a so-called "secret committee" (*hemliga utskott*), which, however, met solely at the King's discretion (Elder 1953, 195).

The important long-term result of this early centralization was that the formulation of Swedish foreign policy has remained the prerogative of a relative few in Sweden; during the nineteenth century policy was made by the monarchy and its central core of advisors (a group of conservative élites), and by the Ministry of Foreign Affairs (*Utrikesdepartementet*, or "UD," formed in 1840 out of the old King's Office for Foreign Correspondence), and later by elected governments.

Despite the advent of full parliamentary rule and the gradual eclipse of royal discretion in foreign affairs by World War I, the foreign policy-making machinery in Sweden has remained centralized. Power is invested mainly in the prime minister (*statsminister*) personally, and within his foreign affairs ministry, an important institution which retains much autonomy in conducting Swedish foreign policy; the UD has even been likened to a "kind of superministry of foreign affairs."[6] The long (forty-four-year, 1932–76 and again from 1982), nearly unbroken era of Social Democratic control over the government has merely perpetuated this historical tendency. Here the linkage between Sweden's cultural unity and the centralization of the foreign policy process assumes importance; the élite and the population at large have internalized basically the same value system. There is a high degree of citizen consciousness of, and orientation to, the system, meriting for Sweden Almond and Verba's description (1963) of the participant political culture.

The effect of these developments has been to reduce to a minimum the domestic constraints on Sweden's modern foreign policy process. The existing societal norms have tended to remove foreign policy from the arena of normal party infighting and political strife. Successive Swedish foreign policymakers have been able to formulate policy with much greater sensitivity to changes in the external balance of power. As a result, Sweden's neutrality has been less a fixed, static orientation than one which offers considerable leeway in external affairs. Within this national context, neutrality has been basically a policy of state, only gradually resorted to by the twentieth century; the completion of the state- and nation-building processes in Sweden long predated, and remained wholly autonomous from, the development of neutrality policy.

Neutrality and Swiss National Unity

In marked contrast to this continuous history of dynastic consolidation in Sweden, the Swiss political system is characterized by considerable fragmentation and decentralization, low on the scales of both "state-ness" and "nation-ness." For centuries many factors have thwarted the drive toward centralization, among them the existence of alpine barriers between the mountain valleys as well as between the city-republics which later developed in the less mountainous crescent stretching from Bern in west-central Switzerland to St. Gallen in the northeast. Thus the local areas, the cantons and smaller communes, were able to retain their own social and economic structure and political autonomy even during the rise of powerful European nation-states (Deutsch and Foltz 1966, 49). Perry Anderson asserts that the Swiss peasantry alone in Europe was able to defy the feudal class completely (Anderson 1974b, 203, n. 15).

Another factor inhibiting the development of a strong center was Switzerland's location in the heart of the European mainland, with few natural external barriers (other than the Upper Valaisan Alps from Italy and the Rhine from Germany). This fostered the development of a unique "polycephalous city network" (Daalder 1973, 16) with Zürich, Schaffhausen, St. Gallen, and Basel all astride key east-west trade routes; each was subject to strong intercity economic competition from the others, yet there was a common emphasis on moderation and compromise with the surrounding areas (Deutsch and Weilenmann 1965, 405). This competitive arrangement also prevented the patrician-ruled (and largest) city of Bern from exerting its influence further than its own hinterland. The cities' strength was further checked by a deep rural/urban cleavage, which for centuries necessitated parity in the number of city and rural cantons within the Confederation to keep an uneasy equilibrium. In addition, the flow of trade through some of the principal north-south mountain passes connecting central Europe with Italy (San Bernardino, St. Gotthard, Simplon) further prevented centralization and created the conditions for what Karl Deutsch has called the "pass-state" (1966, 30), by which Switzerland differed little from other nearby regions which never achieved and sustained sovereignty, such as Dauphiné, Savoy, and Tyrol (Anderson 1974b, 52, n. 2).

This strongly decentralized structure was reinforced by the sharp divisions engendered by the Reformation and Counter-Reformation. The extreme particularism of the Confederation was transposed onto the religious plane on the basis of the *cuius regio, eius religio* principle established by the Peace of

Augsburg in 1555, whereby each sovereign canton maintained the right to determine its own religious policy. Even the Protestant movement within the country was split between Zwinglian (centered in Zürich) and Calvinist (based in Geneva and influencing western Swiss cantons). These divisions, reinforced by the death of Ulrich Zwingli in 1531, the second Peace of Kappel that year, and later (1598) by the Borromean League linking the Catholic areas, continued to fester for centuries; as late as 1847 a civil war was fought over the religious issue (the *Sonderbundskrieg*), after which Protestant dominance in Swiss politics was assured for the rest of the century. In addition, the coincidence of religious and political (cantonal) boundaries often crosscuts the three language areas (German, French, and Italian), creating a complex matrix involving linguistic, ethnic, and religious elements (Lipset and Rokkan 1967, 42).

The result of these profound divisions in terms of foreign policy was the problem of reconciling the competing external obligations of the various quasi-sovereign cantons. The rudimentary political arrangement binding the various rural communes, valley-republics, and cities developed organically into an institutionalized system of political cooperation, in its modern form termed "amicable agreement" (Steiner 1974) or "consociational democracy" (Lijphart 1969, 212). Common agreement on foreign policy served as a means of preventing outright foreign takeover, and Swiss federal government became "a system of treaties and arrangements chiefly touching on foreign relations" (Vincent 1904, 9–10). In earlier times the quasi-sovereign cantons were linked mainly through their common pursuit of military spoils, as with the 1393 *Sempacherbrief*. Later the policy of neutrality was gradually resorted to as a means of sustaining mutual accommodation, particularly given the common practice of groups of cantons allying with neighboring powers, as between the Catholic cantons and the French Crown through the Perpetual Peace of 1516 and 1521 (later solidified through the 1715 *Trücklibund*) and the Eternal Compact or *Erbvereinigung* between some Swiss-German cantons and Austria. The Swiss Diet was forced to reconcile these contradictory positions by playing off the powers against each other, whereby neutrality served as a kind of lowest common denominator between the various cantons (Bonjour 1946, 18). Conversely it was often in the interests of nearby powers to keep Switzerland neutral, due to the strategic advantage of having one less border to defend.

Another peculiar feature of early Swiss decision-making was a form of contractual neutrality, anchored in a series of federal papers (*bundesbriefen*) through which new cantons, starting with Basel and Schaffhausen in 1501 and Appenzell in 1513, pledged to "sit still" in disputes involving the other cantons. Through this policy of *Stilsitzend*, a policy of de facto neutrality was imposed upon each incoming member of the Confederation. The establishment of this form of neutrality through internal treaty in fact considerably preceded the later (1674) emergence of neutrality as continual state policy. When the differences became too great, a formal division was occasionally necessary;

for example, the canton of Appenzell split into half-cantons (Inner- and Aus-ser-Rhoden) in 1597 over foreign policy differences.

Swiss neutrality hence emerged as both a feature of the European balance of power, recognized formally in 1815, and as a means of maintaining the domestic political equilibrium by neutralizing the differences between the cantons (the internal balance of power); it played a pivotal role in the Swiss state-and nation-building processes, first by promoting internal stability as a basis for integration, and later by protecting the nascent state from involvement in surrounding national and religious wars (Holt 1978, 9). It is often argued that neutrality plus federalism have made Switzerland a nation (Petitpierre 1970, 179). The significance of neutrality as a common bond, holding a fragile Swiss nation intact, is an age-old argument by Swiss officials, even up to the present when these historical cleavages have been greatly modified. Thus neutrality, so rooted in the Swiss national fabric, has assumed normative implications; Masnata (1963, 25) has even ascribed a "quasi-mystical" status to neutrality among the Swiss populace; and a quiescent neutral policy is often said to be the best means of maintaining national unity (J. Freymond 1963, 150; Steiner 1974, 68).

The particularist traditions of Swiss political culture have also spawned a perennial and profound distrust of centrally held authority, both internal and foreign, which has affected Swiss foreign policy formulation. The government or Federal Council (*Bundesrat, Conseil fédéral*) is a collegial seven-member body with a weak, annually rotating presidency. In fact, the presidency was traditionally tied to the Swiss Political Department (in 1978 renamed the Ministry for Foreign Affairs, or DFAE), which intermittently until 1920 resulted in the yearly displacement of the foreign minister (B. Freymond 1982, 474); this process unquestionably limited the government's ability to formulate a coherent, long-term foreign policy strategy other than passive neutrality. The politically institutionalized restrictions on Swiss foreign ministers (who even in their own domain are often no more than first among equals within the cabinet), and on federal government generally, have important foreign policy implications, particularly as no Swiss foreign policy élite can be said to exist (Daalder 1973, 26–27), although of course there have been exceptions (viz., Foreign Ministers Numa Droz, Arthur Hoffman, and Giuseppe Motta). Along with the individual cantons, Switzerland's bicameral Federal Assembly (*Bundesversammlung, Assemblée fédérale*) has been yet another restraining influence on the Federal Council, leading to Mayer and Burnett's provocative conclusion that "in effect, Switzerland is not governed" (1977, 203). The highly developed Swiss institutions of semi-direct democracy (the initiative and referendum) impose further limitations on governmental leeway, and represent the clearest expression of a tendency to regard the people as sovereign and the government as mere representatives. The importance of popular opinion has actually increased during this century with two extensions of the system (1921 and 1977) to include provisions for public referenda on certain foreign treaties (Malinverni 1978); both extensions have also been directly connected with the League and UN questions in Switzerland.

These factors suggest an important pattern of linkage between the historical processes of national consolidation and the development of neutrality in each state. Although a widespread consensus supports the continuation of neutrality in both countries, the nature of that support varies markedly. In Sweden cultural unity and political centralization long predated neutrality; in Switzerland the policy of neutrality itself coincided with, and fostered, internal consolidation. As a result, shifts in the focus of neutrality tend to carry greater domestic political implications for Switzerland than for Sweden. In turn, these general factors would appear to have important bearing on each state's attitude toward collective security, in light of the suggested linkage between the level of centralization in the nation-state (and its foreign policy decision-making machinery) and the state's degree of receptivity to new international developments. The relative importance of these domestic factors for the specific sanctions problem will be considered in the four case studies themselves.

The Swedish and Swiss Doctrines of Neutrality

Quite apart from these nation-building factors, the two states can be differentiated, secondly, by their respective interpretations of neutral rights and duties, and their individual designations of neutrality as state policy. Sweden's general description is freedom from alliances (or non-alignment between the power blocs) in peacetime, aiming at neutrality in wartime; the Swiss consider their policy to be one of perpetual or permanent neutrality. These general descriptions in turn generate other important points; for example, Switzerland's permanent neutrality is widely held to constrain the Federal Council from playing an active international role, which results in a conservative or insular—or even parochial—outlook toward international politics. Sweden, on the other hand, is considered freer to determine its own political line of action, and hence its policy is more pragmatic and utilitarian. Indeed, Sweden and Switzerland are often cited as the two extremes on the European neutral scale of rigidity, by which the policies of other neutral states (particularly Austria) are often measured (Stadler 1981, 18). One Swedish writer asserts that Swedish neutrality policy is more "extroverted" while Switzerland's is "introverted" and "almost anxiously doctrinaire" (Edberg 1951, 197). Peter Lyon has succinctly expressed these differing tendencies:

Public discussion of foreign policy in Sweden concentrates almost exclusively on adjusting and justifying Sweden's "alliance-free" policy, and the Swiss remain true to their national custom of not discussing among themselves why they are neutral, while assuring other people that Swiss neutrality is unique, internationally beneficial, deserves respect, and is not susceptible to being duplicated on the international plane. The Swedish concept of non-alignment is liberal and pragmatic; the Swiss is conservative and impermeable. (Lyon 1963, 164)

One distinction between the two countries is the degree to which their policies are based on law. The argument that Swedish neutrality is flexible while Switzerland's is inflexible or rigid tends to rely on two important assumptions: first, that Swiss but not Swedish neutrality is a constitutional principle and an integral part of the domestic legal code, and hence unalterable without formal amendment to the constitution; and second, that Switzerland's permanent neutrality is based upon international (great power) recognition/guarantee, while Sweden's is externally unrestricted. Both of these assumptions require examination.

On the first issue, neutrality is mentioned twice in the Swiss federal constitution, in Arts. 35 (5 & 6) and 102 (8 & 9), establishing respectively the duties of the Swiss Federal Assembly and the Federal Council in the formulation of Swiss foreign policy. Even so, neutrality appears to hold a tangential rather than a central constitutional position; it is an implied norm, a general feature of the document, but not an explicitly formulated principle (thus differing substantially from Austria). In addition, Art. 2, which specifies the primary goals of national policy, calls for the "maintenance of the Fatherland's independence externally, peace and order internally; protection of the freedom and rights of its citizens and promotion of their common welfare," without mentioning neutrality (although it was mentioned in Art. 2 of the original constitutional project of 1832, then subsequently dropped). This relative lack of specificity seems to flow, paradoxically, from the very longevity of neutrality as a feature of Swiss national life, the influence of which has been so ubiquitous that no explicit constitutional guarantee was thought necessary (particularly since the modern Swiss constitution was written in 1848, decades after Swiss neutrality was first recognized internationally).

Thus in terms of foreign policy, the constitution limits the Swiss government only insofar as it cannot completely renounce neutrality without a mandatory constitutional referendum, the same as with every constitutional change (which has occurred more than eighty times since the document was ratified). Pointet adds that this constitutional flexibility prevents Swiss neutrality from being reduced to a simplified formula and remains a "living conception" (1945, 61). The Swiss government itself explicitly confirmed this interpretation of neutrality after World War I (1919 League Message, 47); and the point was illustrated further when in 1919 the Swiss Assembly first stipulated that entry into the League of Nations required a formal constitutional amendment, then later (and under political pressure) withdrew this stipulation.

The "legality" of Swiss neutrality refers, secondly, to its international recognition by the European powers after the Napoleonic Wars. The first stage was the Declaration of Eight Powers on the Affairs of the Helvetic Confederation of 20 March 1815, by which they agreed "that the general interest demands that the Helvetic states should enjoy the benefit of a perpetual neutrality." Following the Swiss Diet's formal acceptance of this Declaration (27

May), it was confirmed through Article 84 of the Treaty of Vienna of 9 June, then finalized through the Treaty of Paris of 20 November 1815, signed by Austria, Russia, Prussia, Britain, and France. Through these agreements, Switzerland was formally recognized as a neutral state; however, the powers did not bind themselves to intervene (either individually or collectively) on behalf of Switzerland in case its territorial integrity was threatened, and they subsequently found no opportunity to do so (Halperin 1966, 62, 65).

In addition, the 1815 Acts by no means created a new international régime for Switzerland; they merely confirmed and perpetuated a state of affairs in existence for nearly three centuries, and thereafter, as before, Switzerland maintained its independence through its own efforts (Wicker 1911, 3). Surely the fact that a Swiss diplomat (Pictet de Rochemont of Geneva) personally wrote the agreement demonstrates that Switzerland was not submitting to any great power restriction; in fact the agreements were considered a triumph for Swiss diplomacy. Switzerland thus has a recognized, not a guaranteed status; it is a "perpetually neutral" but not strictly a "neutralized" state (as, for example, Cracow in 1815, Belgium in 1839, and Luxembourg in 1867); and in 1917 the Swiss government rejected a proposal by Britain, France, and the United States to establish a vague "reserve protector status" for Swiss neutrality. Nonetheless there has been some academic discussion over whether this recognition was coupled with a latent great power guarantee, due to the vague wording of the 1815 Act.[7] With this peculiar and indeed unique international status, the Swiss have come to consider their situation as the best of both worlds, distinct from both ordinary neutrality and neutralization; repeated great power recognition has legitimized its international position, and yet the absence of formal guarantees by those same powers has prevented external legal restrictions on its maneuverability.

In contrast, Sweden's policy of "non-alignment in peace aiming at neutrality in war" suggests a lack of legal underpinnings. One of the primary concerns of successive Swedish policymakers has been to retain maximum freedom of action and to avoid all obligations which would hinder Sweden's ability to remain neutral in the event of a major crisis (*DSFP* 1961, 119). Neutrality is rooted neither in the Swedish constitution (*Regeringsformen*, or "Instrument of Government") of 1809, which was drafted long before neutrality developed, even intermittently, into a doctrine of state, nor in any convention of international law. Adam Roberts thus asserts that Swedish policy is one "for" neutrality rather than one "of" neutrality (1972, 69); Verdross wholly dismisses the Swedish formula as "a mere political maxim that can be repealed at any moment by a unilateral disposition ... without constituting the violation of any international obligation whatsoever" (1958, 477). There is indeed a history of failed attempts to neutralize Sweden through great power guarantee.[8] A legislative addition to the constitution (Art. 74) in 1894 implied that neutrality would be pursued in any future war except in self-defense; this is sometimes regarded as the nearest equivalent to a unilateral declaration of

Sweden's permanent neutrality, but it is not recognized as such in international law (Undén 1939, 28).

From the foregoing we can deduce that Swiss neutrality is more formally grounded in law than is Sweden's; Swiss neutrality has a legal basis in both wartime and peacetime, but Swedish neutrality only during wartime (the Hague rules). Nonetheless, these conceptual differences between the two states are rather less decisive than they first appear. It does not follow, for example, that Switzerland's peacetime policy is legally restricted as a result; on the contrary, both states' policies stem ultimately from their own free choice, and are only restricted by their individual perceptions of what constitutes allowable neutral activity (Hakovirta 1980, 44). The crucial point here, however, is that the legal underpinnings of Swiss neutrality, combined with its historical importance as an element of national cohesion, have produced an element of psychological restraint on Swiss foreign-policy makers. For example, the Swiss assume an obligation to practice a perennially "cautious and prudent foreign policy" (1969 UN Report, 22), espousing only modest aims.[9] On the other hand, Swedish policymakers have come to assume a much wider mandate for "pursuing an active and independent foreign policy" (Karin Söder, speech to the UN, 21 Sept. 1977), whose level of activity shifts considerably according to the prevailing balance of power, and is "conditioned by [its] geographical situation between the two power blocs" (*DSFP* 1961, 118).

The distinction between the two countries is also illustrated by the differing degrees of clarity in their official policy descriptions. Switzerland's perpetual neutrality is based squarely on the notion of impartiality (*FF* 1955, 1:332–33). However, Sweden's official formulation, non-alignment aiming at neutrality in wartime, raises problems of interpretation, even by textbook writers on Swedish government (e.g., Board 1970, 189), due to its vagueness and negative implications; it denotes situations which Swedish governments strive to *avoid* (political and military alliances, wars), yet offers no clue as to what goals Sweden strives *for* in its everyday conduct (Zartmann 1954, 156–57). Thomas Hart (1976, 30) notes that a general uncertainty lingers in Sweden concerning the actual role or meaning of neutrality within its overall foreign policy schema. Notably, Hart himself uses the terms *neutrality* and *non-alignment* interchangeably in his text, as have even top Swedish foreign ministry officials (*DSFP* 1967, 35; Nilsson). Swedish Prime Minister Tage Erlander once candidly admitted that Sweden's official policy description was "in fact, an inadequate and one-sided definition of Sweden's general aims and attitude on foreign policy" (*DSFP* 1961, 117). The irony of this situation is highlighted by the long period during which neutrality has served as a basis for Swedish policy. Nonetheless the Swedes seem to regard their longstanding, demonstrated intention to avoid wars and alliances as more indicative of their true intentions than static legal formulae; and Swedish policy is considered, with reason, to be clearly recognized and accepted abroad.

Thus in Sweden a high degree of political centralization and a loose definition of neutrality suggest a liberal and pragmatic policy; in Switzerland, however, a federalist state structure and a legally based neutrality policy have produced a basically conservative outlook. At this point we can take the analysis one step further, by drawing possible inferences of cause-and-effect regarding the collective security problem. It is proposed that Sweden's flexible formulation of neutrality has not been a major psychological barrier to new international undertakings. Such flexibility would also predispose Sweden (or more precisely, its policymakers) to adapt more readily and successfully to the requirements of international organizations, and also to pursue a more consistent overall policy of accommodation within them. On the other hand, Switzerland's attachment to a cautious, permanent neutral policy would appear to represent a more formidable obstacle to the formulation of a coherent and consistent sanctions strategy. The validity of these points must of course be measured in relation to specific developments within the League and UN systems. In addition, they by no means negate the importance of the common background factors discussed earlier, which also suggest some important areas of policy convergence relative to the collective security issue.

NOTES

1. Compare the USSR's prewar hostility toward neutrals (Lyon, 1963, p. 20), with its much more hospitable attitude after 1945 (Tarschys, 1971, pp. 66–71).

2. Both countries maintain a soldier-to-population ratio of about 1:10; see *The Military Balance 1981–82*, pp. 45–46; also Petitpierre, 1970, p. 174.

3. For examples of violations of arms sale legislation and the issues they raise, see Howe, 1980, pp. 708–9; Sampson, 1977, p. 301; *TG*, 14 January 1983, p. 1; *NZZ*, 6/7 November 1983, p. 17.

4. See for example, FF 1981, Vol. 2, pp. 981–98; Petitpierre, 1970, p. 179; Bindschedler-Robert, 1975, p. 687; Kunz, 1953, p. 288; Forsythe, 1977.

5. See Rothstein, 1968, p. 244; Handel, 1981; and particularly Morgenthau, 1939, p. 480.

6. Sundelius, 1984, p. 116. See also Håstad, 1957, p. 100; Board, 1970, pp. 193–95; Birnbaum, 1965, pp. 6–31; Carlgren, 1982, pp. 455–70.

7. Most writers generally agree that Swiss neutrality has only a recognized international status (e.g., Belin, 1956, p. 21, n. 14; Pointet, 1945, pp. 52–53, n. 41). However, some writers have referred mistakenly to Switzerland as "neutralized"; e.g., Webster, 1934, p. 134; Boczek, 1969, pp. 73–74; Black et. al., 1968, p. 3 and *passim*; and even the editorial board of the *International Law Quarterly*, 1947, p. 14.

8. Edberg, 1951, p. 197; Undén, 1939, p. 27. As recently as 1963, Sweden's parliamentary foreign affairs committee repudiated suggestions for a great-power guarantee for Sweden's neutrality (*DSFP*, 1963, pp. 147–52).

9. Jacques Freymond, 1963, p. 155; Lasserre, 1977, p. 106; and especially André Gorz, quoted in Ziegler, 1978, p. 129. Swiss Foreign Minister Pierre Aubert claimed that "we are active, but we are discreet" (interviewed on Radio Suisse Romande, 29 December 1982).

Part II

The League, the Neutrals, and the Italian Sanctions Operation

3

The Italo-Abyssinian Crisis and Neutrality

BACKGROUND AND THE LEAGUE'S MEASURES

Italy's military invasion of Ethiopia* in October 1935 was the culmination of a series of repeatedly frustrated colonial aspirations in northern and eastern Africa, factors which can only be summarily examined here.[1] By the 1880s Italy possessed minor colonies in the Horn of Africa, including barren Eritrea to the north of Ethiopia, although it was not until 1911 when Italy, seizing Libya from the decrepit Turkish empire, attained a foothold across the Mediterranean. In 1887 Italy had received from Emperor Menelik I (finalized through the Treaty of Uccialli of 1889) a vaguely defined protectorate over parts of Somaliland, to the southeast of Ethiopia, an agreement which had been communicated to, and accepted by, the main powers (Rowan-Robinson 1936, 99). However, the fertile Abyssinian plain, reputedly containing many of the raw materials lacking in Italy, had remained an elusive goal. Then in 1893 Menelik had unilaterally renounced the treaty with Italy, firing patriotic Italian sentiment; and in 1896 Italian Prime Minister Francesco Crispi had sent an expeditionary force to conquer Ethiopia, which was dealt a humiliating defeat at Adowa by the forces under Emperor Menelik II. This ignominious loss to a much weaker, indeed feudal state (coupled with charges of Ethiopian liquidation and even mutilation of the two thousand captured Italian troops) remained a bitter memory for all Italians, and provided fuel for propaganda for the fascist régime which took power in 1922 (Joll 1976, 90–91).

---

* In keeping with common usage, the terms "Abyssinia" and "Ethiopia" will be used interchangeably in this text.

Another central aspect of the situation was Italy's continual maneuvering for great power status. Its prewar agreement with Germany and Austria-Hungary within the Triple Alliance was one means of securing it; another was through the race for colonies in Africa. Here again Ethiopia was a key consideration, as it generally lay outside the sphere of European colonial contention and was apparently susceptible (and open) to Italian influence. Indeed, a December 1906 tripartite agreement between Britain, France, and Italy had established zones of influence in North Africa for each power, with an assumption that Ethiopia remained within the Italian sphere. In July 1924 Britain had ceded to Italy the Trans-Jubaland region adjacent to Italian Somaliland; and under an Anglo-Italian agreement the following year, Britain acknowledged Italy's exclusive right to extend its economic influence in eastern Ethiopia proper (including the right to construct a rail line from Eritrea to Somalia, east of the Ethiopian capital, Addis Ababa).

Even so, this great power agreement was far from amicable, for Italy remained hostile, particularly toward the French, due to lingering resentment over France's seizure of Tunisia (only 100 miles from Sicily) in 1881. The war years stirred further Italian resentment, for neither Britain nor France fulfilled all of its their pledges, made through the secret Treaty of London of April 1915, to grant Italy liberal concessions from the Habsburg and Ottoman Empires (Tyrol, Istria, Trieste, the Dodecanese Islands, North Dalmatia except Fiume, and parts of Albania) in return for Italy's entry into the war against Germany. By that time (1915) Benito Mussolini, then a journalist and editor of an openly promilitarist newspaper, *Popolo d'Italiano*, had become a notable figure in Italy; and his championing of the interventionist cause on the side of France and Britain came into serious conflict with Ethiopia, which due to the influence (and excesses) of Lij Yasu, heir to Menelik II, simultaneously grew markedly more pro-German, pro-Turkish and Islamic (Moseley 1964, 77–80). Ras Tafari, Ethiopian regent after deposing Lij Yasu in 1916, was instrumental in preventing an outright Italian wartime occupation of Ethiopia, further increasing Italian hostility. The perception of economic requirements, principally the need for additional land (colonies) to mitigate Italy's worsening overpopulation problem, has also been cited as an important immediate factor behind Italy's invasion (Joll 1976, 358–59), although the significance of the economic factor has also been sharply disputed (Taylor 1961, 118–19). By the early 1930s the Italian government believed that a convincing politico-military victory over Abyssinia would serve several purposes simultaneously: it would satisfy the desire to avenge Adowa; it would vent Italy's pique at having been allegedly cheated by its erstwhile allies, France and Britain, as well as by Ethiopia; it would galvanize Italian nationalism as a means of averting the rising tide of domestic criticism of the Italian government; and it seemed to promise immediate economic relief. A crucial underlying assumption was that Italian expansion into Abyssinia would not be opposed by the main powers in the League.

Italy's aspirations to control Ethiopia had also been hindered by the latter's accession to the League in 1923, ironically with Italy as a principal backer, and

Britain among others opposed due to primitive conditions there. Ethiopia had since established a reputation as a loyal League member, and as such had retained the support of many of the smaller powers in the League Assembly. In August 1928 Mussolini and Ras Tafari (who in 1930 became Emperor Haile Selassie I) had signed a bilateral Treaty of Friendship, Cooperation and Arbitration at Addis Ababa, by which they agreed to submit all mutual disputes to the League's arbitration and conciliation procedure. Ethiopia also enjoyed the distinction of being one of only two independent black African nations and League members (the other being Liberia) and for having successfully protected its territorial integrity from invasion for centuries; and Emperor Selassie enjoyed a relatively prominent personal standing in the Assembly.

Advance preparations for an Italian invasion of the territory commenced from November 1932, led by Emilio de Bono (Italian minister for the colonies) and Marshal Badoglio (Mussolini's chief of staff), leading to the important Wal-Wal incident of 5–6 December 1934, in the long-disputed region between Italian Somaliland and the Ogaden province of Ethiopia. During the next six months Selassie made three unsuccessful appeals to the League to bring about a solution to the growing crisis, but before as during the embargo, great power maneuvering prevented an early solution. The French had been widely suspected of appeasing Mussolini, and it has been suggested that their foreign minister, Pierre Laval, on a secret trip to Rome in January 1935, agreed to prevent the severance of Italy's oil imports in the event of a crisis. At the Stresa Conference of April 1935 the British and French raised no objections to Italian advances in East Africa, which Mussolini interpreted as tacit approval of his policies (Taylor 1961, 120). Paradoxically, growing disagreement between Britain, which under the new government led by Stanley Baldwin grew (in word if not in deed) more favorable to collective security, and France, which feared that isolating Italy would cause a breakup of the trilateral, anti-German "Stresa Front" and lead to Italy's repudiation of the 1925 Locarno guarantees pertaining to the Franco-German border, continued to hinder decisive League action.

Italy's invasion of Abyssinia commenced on 2 October, while the League Council was preparing a report on the dispute. On 7 October the Council determined that Italy had "resorted to war in disregard of its covenants under Article 12 of the Covenant of the League of Nations." Two days later the League Assembly overwhelmingly agreed, with fifty of the fifty-three delegations present besides Italy assenting to economic sanctions (*OJ*, SS 151:72, 87, n. 1). This concurrence gave the operation considerable respectability—F. P. Walters asserted that "no great international dispute has ever been the subject of a clearer verdict" (1952, 653)—and it provided the League with an unparalleled opportunity to reassert its authority, on the wane since its inability to censure the Japanese invasion of Manchuria and the failure of the Disarmament Conference of 1932–34.

Despite the strong international support for the operation, the Assembly's vote had no legal effect due to its non-unanimity, and thus it did not automatically result in the application of obligatory sanctions under Art. 16 (Wright 1936b, 47). Rather, the League followed the procedure laid down in its important 1921 interpretive resolution of Art. 16,[2] whereby it established (10 October) a Coordination Committee to recommend to member states specific punitive measures to be implemented against Italy. This committee was actually an extension of the Assembly itself, comprised of all fifty states which originally had supported the October 9 resolution. The actual sanctions measures themselves, however, were formulated by a smaller Committee of Eighteen and its accompanying subcommittees dealing with, respectively, economic measures, financial measures, and mutual support, the proposals of which were then adopted by the larger group as recommendations to the League membership. All the sanctions were formulated between 11 and 19 October 1935, whereupon the committee adjourned; it reconvened from 31 October to 2 November to consider the various governments' responses (screened by the legal subcommittee) and to establish specific dates for the entry into force of the various measures. All the measures adopted were officially in place by 18 November.

The Coordination Committee recommended the imposition of four sets of sanctions measures against Italy: an arms embargo, a prohibition on certain financial dealings (including a credit stop), a complete ban on Italian imports, and a partial ban on exports to Italy. The prohibition on the export of arms to Italy (Proposal I), adopted on 11 October, contained four specific measures: (1) that League members which prohibited or restricted the export, re-export, or transit of arms, munitions, or implements of war to Ethiopia agree to lift the prohibition immediately; (2) that member states agree to prohibit the export, re-export, or transit to Italy of all arms, ammunition, and implements of war listed in the annex;[3] (3) that states ensure that all implements of war exported to other countries were not re-exported to Italy, either directly or indirectly; and (4) that these measures would apply also to contracts in the process of execution. Each government was then requested to inform the committee, through the League's secretary-general, "within the shortest possible time" what steps it had taken in conformity with these recommendations (*OJ*, SS 145:14, 32; SS 150:2).

Second, the committee adopted Proposal II (14 October), recommending certain financial and economic reprisals against Italy, including the following: (1) all loans to or from the Italian government, and all subscriptions to loans issued in Italy or elsewhere by or for the Italian government; (2) all banking or other credits to or for the Italian government, or the execution of existing contracts providing for loans to the Italian government; (3) all loans to or for any public authority, person, or corporation in Italian territory and all subscriptions to such loans issued in Italy or elsewhere; (4) all banking and other credits to or for any public authority, person, or corporation in Italy and further execution of contracts to such persons; (5) all issues of shares or other capital flotations for any public authority, person, or corporation in Italy and all subscriptions to such issues of shares or capital flotations in Italy and elsewhere. Governments were asked to take all measures necessary to prevent these transactions, either directly or through intermediaries. The committee "invited" each government to implement these measures immediately on the basis of existing legislation, or if new legislation was needed, to complete it by 31 October 1935 (*OJ*, SS 145:16, 45, 122; SS 150:4).

In an accompanying resolution concerning outstanding claims (2 November), the committee held that outstanding Italian debts to League member states, on clearing or other agreements, were to remain valid at their present level, even if Italy offered payment in kind (*OJ*, SS 146:12, 34, 52; SS 150:5). Also at that time, 18 November was established as the deadline for implementing the credit and financial stop. The Committee of Eighteen then passed Proposal IIA (6 November) regarding clearing agreements (*OJ*, SS 146:48, 65, 76; SS 150:5); it provided that member states should prohibit the acceptance of any new deposit of lira into Italian clearing accounts in payment for member states' exports to Italy, and suspend the operation of all clearing or payment agreements, by the same date (18 November). It further proposed that states take necessary steps to ensure that the purchase price of Italian goods already exported, but for which payment was still outstanding, would be placed in a national account to settle legal claims arising from the export of their products.

The banking and financial prohibitions contained in Proposal II were, however, only indirect measures designed to reduce Italy's long-term purchasing power by preventing the purchase of goods on credit. Largely on Anthony Eden's initiative, the committee then undertook to directly restrict Italy's foreign trade (70 percent of which went to League members), in the belief that this stoppage would deprive Italy of foreign exchange with which it could purchase vital war materials. Proposals III and IV, both adopted on 19 October, respectively banned the importation of all Italian goods and the export of certain key products to Italy. Proposal III included "all goods (other than gold or silver bullion and coin) consigned from or grown, produced or manufactured in Italy or Italian possessions, from whatever place arriving"; this included goods grown or produced in Italy which had also been partially manufactured (but only up to 25 percent of their total value, the so-called "value-added exemption") in another country. The prohibition also applied to existing contracts, although this was later modified.[4] However, goods actually en route were exempted from the prohibition (for a transit period to be determined by the individual governments) as well as the personal belongings of travelers from Italy. The measures were to be effected by 28 October (*OJ*, SS 145:20, 65, 105, 115; SS 150:6). Later (through Proposal IIIA of 6 November), the Committee of Eighteen also exempted the flow of educational materials (*OJ*, SS 146:50, 73; SS 150:8). The measure was further mitigated by the exemption of foreign exchange from the shipping and tourist industries and also by emigrants' re-mittances, all of which helped undercut the total import embargo (RIIA 1938, 88).

The complete prohibition on all Italian imports was considered the most far-reaching of the sanctions imposed against Italy, a view supported by Italy's aggressive response: it called Proposal III "more than an economic measure; [it is] a veritable act of hostility which amply justifies inevitable Italian coun-termeasures..." (Houghton 1936, 100). Proposal III also raised a number of sensitive legal questions, primarily concerning the execution of existing con-tracts—private contracts, commercial treaties, and treaties of friendship and nonaggression—which would be broken through a sudden stoppage of im-ports from Italy. However, the legal subcommittee of the Committee of Eigh-teen, to which these questions were referred, fully upheld the legality of Pro-posal III, since the sanctions had been lawfully enacted by the League, and since Italy, as a party to the Covenant, was legally obligated to accept the de-cisions relating to sanctions against it (*OJ*, SS 150:6–7).

The League's prohibition on certain selected exports to Italy (Proposal IV) mainly covered materials regarded as vital for waging war, including rubber, bauxite, aluminum, iron ore and scrap iron, chromium, manganese, nickel, tin and tin ore, and several rare metals. Member governments were also re-quested to prevent the direct or indirect re-export of these goods to Italy from any other country. Contracts in the course of execution were also subject to the ban, although goods en route to Italy by 19 October (the date of Proposal IV's adoption) were exempted. Later, the committee set 18 November as the deadline for implementing Proposals III and IV (*OJ*, SS 145:24, 78, 87, 100, 112; SS 150:9–10). Also the Committee of Eighteen, through Proposal IVB (6 November) extended the ban to cover also the re-export or indirect supply of embargoed goods to Italy from other countries, through tighter surveillance of the final destination of all goods included on the export ban list (*OJ*, SS 146:47, 64, 75; SS 150:10).

Despite these precautions, however, the partial export embargo was char-acterized by inconsistency. For example, it included iron ore and scrap iron, yet left out finished iron and steel products. Similarly, it prohibited the export of tin ore to Italy, but not tin plate (RIIA 1938, 198). There was also some inconsistency between the complete import ban and the partial export ban; however, the League members were unable to control trade in some vital prod-uct-areas, especially iron and steel and oil. Later, a multitude of problems arose when attempts were made to extend Proposal IV to include an oil em-bargo.(N.B.: The applicability of these measures to Swedish and Swiss trade will be discussed in chapters 4 and 5 respectively.)

The final measure, adopted as Proposal V by the committee on 19 October, provided for mutual assistance among member states in case of difficulties for any state due to the imposition of the blockade. Proposal V was based in Art. 16(3) of the Covenant, and also in a Finnish proposal of May 1926 for League provision of aid to small states victimized by aggression (which had led to the League's Convention on Financial Assistance of October 1930); it supplemented the requirement for individual states to impose sanctions with a collective (though vague) guarantee that no sanctioning state should suffer undue financial losses because of the embargo. Proposal V followed an earlier (14 October) Declaration of Mutual Support, and held that states should (1) ensure that no state should be deprived of the benefits it might have received under a most-favored-nation clause; (2) attempt to replace goods, formerly imported from Italy, with those from other sanctioning states; (3) negotiate with states that suffered serious losses in trade, to increase the flow of goods between them; and (4) abstain from making demands for the application of a most-favored-nation clause in cases of privileges granted under (2) and (3) above. The Committee of Eighteen also asserted that it would consider still other measures of mutual support (*OJ*, SS 145:25, 70, 132; SS 150:11). Even so, attempts to aid states that most needed it (particularly Rumania and Yugoslavia) were meager at best. In addition, the League rejected a specific Ethiopian request (4 November) for mutual support, since the 1930 Convention on Financial Assistance, which would have provided guarantees for the servicing of loans, though not the principal, to the state concerned, had never entered into force (RIIA 1938, 89–90).

These recommended measures achieved widespread, but not total, compliance from the League membership. Three states other than Italy refused to cooperate from the outset, Austria, Hungary, and Albania; Guatemala and the Dominican Republic hesitated at first, then accepted the recommendations; Paraguay later refused to participate fully; Ecuador lifted its sanctions early; and Luxembourg and Switzerland only partly accepted them (*OJ*, SS 151:86, n. 1). In a preliminary report of 2 November, the Coordination Committee reported that a total of fifty-two states accepted in principle Proposals I and III, fifty accepted Proposal II, fifty-one Proposal IV, and thirty-six Proposal V (*OJ*, SS 146:8, 45; SS 150:9–10; SS 151:86–90). However, on 12 December, the Committee of Experts charged with determining the progress of the operation reported considerable variance between professed intent and actual deed; as of 11 December, only fifty states had actually implemented the arms embargo, forty-three states Proposals II and III, and forty-five the partial export ban—though forty-six had taken steps to provide mutual support (*OJ*, SS 147:12–18). The refusal by some states to implement the embargo fully was sharply criticized by Maxim Litvinov, the Soviet delegate and chairman of the Committee of Eighteen (*OJ*, SS 151:36).

Although the Italian invasion was widely condemned as an act of aggression and a gross violation of the League Covenant, the entire conflict was marked by an inability of the international community to respond in kind with a total blockade. Part of the reason was that the 1921 resolutions had interpreted the Covenant's sanctions provisions as "essentially economic in character" (*OJ*, SS 6:25–27), thereby virtually excluding from the outset political, and especially military, pressure. A total blockade was also not instituted due to the nonmembership of Germany and the United States, and although neither state capitalized on the League's action to their own trade advantage, American oil exports to Italy rose substantially. Notably, two other potentially effective, yet nonforcible, measures of punishment—the severance of diplomatic relations with Italy, and the closing of the Suez Canal to Italian shipping en route to Abyssinia—were both rejected at the outset as being too harsh (Walters 1952, 662–63). Other types of contact, including tourism and transport, were left similarly unrestricted.

Two additional problems jeopardized the efficacy of the embargo. One was the considerable delay between the outbreak of hostilities and the actual implementation of the blockade. The embargo was staged rather than automatic, for states were given until 18 November to implement Proposals III and IV (including goods in transit by that time), which enabled Italian stockpiling of goods and foreign currency. This delay considerably cushioned the effects of sanctions once in place; one authoritative source held that the full effects of the embargo were not felt until the end of 1935, nearly three months after the invasion (RIIA 1938, 101).

The second, more general factor was the prevailing attitude in the League Assembly that "business as usual" with Italy should continue despite the embargo: "there was anxiety not to suffer, or inflict, more loss and disturbance than was strictly necessary" (Walters 1952, 656–58), which would also leave open the possibility of a negotiated settlement. The sanctions were to fulfill a moral purpose only, to show that a blatant violation of the Covenant could not go unpunished; certainly the League did not aim to punish the Italian people or bring down the fascist system (Baer 1976, 7). This in turn limited the overall objective of the operation, which aimed primarily to stop the hostilities and repair the damage done by them (Wright 1936b, 48).

The League's main subsequent difficulty was its inability to extend Proposal IV to include an embargo on oil products, pig iron, iron and steel, and coal and coke to Italy, even though its impending implementation had actually been announced by the Committee of Eighteen as early as 6 November (*OJ*, SS 146:46, 61, 68; SS 150:10). The potent combination of Italian threats of retaliation, nonmembership of key oil producers (notably the United States), and mainly the parallel Anglo-French efforts to keep Italy allied within the Stresa Front, effectively terminated any possibility of tightening the embargo. The most poignant reminder of this aim was the abortive scheme between Samuel Hoare and Pierre Laval in December 1935, through which the two foreign ministers agreed to allow virtual Italian annexation of the southern half of Ethiopia. It is important to note that even as late as 1936 an Italo-German axis was by no means inevitable, highlighting the powers' dilemma.[5] Here was a key paradox of the operation: even while Britain, with French acquiescence, initially instigated sanctions (enabling Samuel Baldwin's reelection on a shrewd platform of "all sanctions short of war"), the political need to avoid a full break with Italy prevented the imposition of the very measures which conceivably could have enabled the operation to succeed.

The League's ineffectiveness was underscored by its inability to respond to Italy's diplomatic bluffing and increasingly drastic methods of warfare under Marshal Badoglio, including the indiscriminate use of mustard gas against the civilian population and its repeated bombing raids against Red Cross facilities. The rapid deterioration in Ethiopia's military situation was however overshadowed by the League's preoccupation with Germany's occupation of the Rhineland in March 1936. During the first week in May Addis Ababa fell and Emperor Selassie fled to London, although as a symbolic (if lame) gesture, sanctions remained in place until 15 July (Walters 1952, 683–84).

GENERAL ASPECTS OF THE CRISIS PERTAINING TO NEUTRALITY

An assessment of the attitudes of the neutral states toward the Italo-Abyssinian affair must first distinguish between the two major aspects of the crisis. One was the legal state of war entered into between Italy and Ethiopia; the other was the dispute between Italy and the League of Nations arising from the ensuing sanctions operation. Although these two aspects of the case were of course directly connected (the first giving rise to the second), they must for the moment be regarded, in relation to the theory of neutrality, as separate components of a general international crisis. Indeed in this crisis neutrality was applicable in certain respects but not in others: it was at once a theoretically and legally possible position relative to the war itself, whereas in regards to the League's enforcement operation it was considered a politically untenable position. This dichotomy in fact illustrated one of the chronic shortcomings of the League of Nations system, namely the disjunction between its "automatic and complete" enforcement mechanism, seemingly designed to operate indiscriminately against any aggressor without considering the extenuating political circumstances of a conflict; and the political character of the organization, by which sanctions were much more likely to be applied against some states than others (Hoffmann 1967, 154–55). However, in this event the formal, legalistic basis of Art. 16 resulted in serious difficulties for neutrality.

On the first point, several aspects of the dispute suggested that neutrality was still a possible, if limited, option for states. One factor was the League's failure to achieve the universality which had been considered an essential prerequisite for a bona fide collective security arrangement. Although the League had partially overcome its limited original membership by the entry of the Central powers during the mid-1920s, this positive development had been reversed subsequently by the notice of withdrawal by Japan (1932) and Germany (1933) and by Italy's increasingly contemptuous attitude toward the organization. The accession of the USSR in 1934 had again partially mitigated this trend, but its closer relations with France, combined with Germany's non-

membership and increasingly aggressive bearing, foreshadowed the one development most feared by neutrals since the outset of the League: the establishment of power blocs alongside or even within the League, or worse still, the
decline of the organization itself into a security alliance ranged against Germany. The League's inability to achieve universal membership also represented a major setback for one of the main and long-standing aims of the traditionally neutral member states; accordingly they continued to regard
neutrality as an important fall-back position.

The League's membership problem also tended to justify the view that the
League was acting as something less than an impartial upholder of international law and justice. The sanctions were of course directed against Italy in
the immediate event, and moreover they were widely considered to be the appropriate international response to an obvious act of aggression. More important for the longer term, however, was the view held by some, especially in Britain, that the operation was primarily a trial or test-case for the system, in
anticipation of a future sanctions operation against Germany. Thus even if the
League's nonuniversality itself did not directly cause the sanctions to fail, it
nonetheless was a very important long-term factor in the post-1936 trend for
the smaller European states in reasserting their neutrality while extricating
themselves from their League obligations.

Another factor potentially allowing for a neutral attitude was Italy's great
power status, coupled with its demonstrably hostile attitude toward the
League. Many smaller states feared that an embargo would lead to Italian retaliation; it was significant, but hardly surprising, that the only member states
which refused outright to participate in the sanctions operation—Austria,
Hungary, and Albania—were all in the immediate geographical vicinity of Italy (although political compatibility was another key reason, especially for Albania, Italy's client state). This consideration was crucial for those (neutral)
states intent on avoiding entanglement in future great power conflicts. The
possibility of a major confrontation was real enough in relation to the balance
of forces; although some fifty states concurred with the League's resolution
labeling Italy the aggressor, Britain essentially led the operation through Stanley Baldwin's (and Anthony Eden's) decision to take a resolute stand against
Italy in the autumn of 1935, with France a much less enthusiastic partner. One
analyst thus concluded that "the case of collective sanctions vs. Italy was in
essence the case of Great Britain and France vs. Italy. This was a far cry from
the ideal prerequisite of a concentration of overwhelming power which no prospective lawbreaker would dare to challenge" (Morgenthau 1960, 394).

The factor most relevant to neutrality was the straightforward fact that the
Italo-Abyssinian dispute involved a war in its classical sense, meaning a military duel between two recognizable belligerents. A number of states, including
two League members, asserted that this situation also enabled a neutral posture, even though the war was undeclared and one participant had been identified as the aggressor. The legal régime established by the League Covenant

had undermined certain aspects of the laws of neutrality; even so, the Hague neutrality conventions themselves remained in force, and several interwar treaties had cited the Hague Conventions as a valid source of law (for example the Hague Rules on Aerial Warfare of 1923, and the Havana Rules on Maritime Neutrality of 1928).

Still another factor pertaining to neutrality was the possibility of war arising from the sanctions operation itself. This posed a delicate yet potentially menacing problem for neutrals, notwithstanding the major powers' refusal to contemplate military sanctions. Italy had indeed threatened retaliation against any state levying an oil embargo; and such retaliation could conceivably escalate and embroil, or at least endanger, the European neutral states. Muriel Grieve points out that in this case sanctions could hardly have been considered a substitute for war, and could have become, on the contrary, a prelude to it (1968, 433). The heavy concentration of British naval forces in the Mediterranean during this period also lent credence to this view (Marks 1976, 41). Furthermore, the specter of a future Franco-British military campaign against Germany, utilizing the League's sanctions weapon, compounded these fears both during and after the Italian operation. (In fact, one of the founders of the League, Lord Robert Cecil, called for sanctions against Germany after its remilitarization of the Rhineland in March 1936). The question of whether sanctions against Italy could have led to a general European war must of course remain speculative; the important point in this context is that the *fear* of war resulting from sanctions was very much alive in the minds of French and British statesmen, which could not but affect the position of states hoping to avoid such a conflict. The very fact that the possibility of war was even mentioned, particularly in relation to the off again/on again oil sanction, is a sufficient indicator of the difficulties for neutral states. As will be shown, these points were much more relevant for Switzerland than for Sweden during the dispute; however, in its aftermath both states expressed the fear that war could result from a future application of Art. 16.

These theoretical aspects must, in turn, be considered in light of the very different practical circumstances of the case. The option of neutrality was regarded by the League itself as both unfeasible and politically (and even morally) undesirable. Again, several reasons were advanced in support of this view, which were accepted by nearly the entire League membership. First, Italy had been deemed the clear aggressor by both the League Council and Assembly. Each state which accepted this designation thus identified itself with a near-unanimous decision that one party was in the right, the other in the wrong. After having accepted such a position at the outset, it would be most difficult politically for any state to attempt to adopt an impartial or indifferent attitude toward the conflict (Woolsey 1936, 258). The League itself also clearly, if indirectly, ruled out impartial neutrality by first applying an arms embargo against Italy; any state following suit would be in direct violation of the Hague neutrality conventions. Arnold Toynbee held that neutrality in the event was thus "inherently impossible" and would even contribute to Italy's war effort (*SIA* 1935, 2:218). A contrary attitude by the League membership would of course have been unrealistic; an international organization which condemned one state as the aggressor and named another the victim in a conflict, could hardly then proceed to accept an impartial attitude by any of its members (Borchard 1936, 91–94).

The League also ruled out the neutrality option in the other major aspect of the conflict, the sanctions operation against Italy. British officials were especially adamant in the view that neutrality was not only undesirable, but was even inapplicable, to a case of (limited) economic sanctions. According to this view, a partial economic embargo did not breach the Hague neutrality rules, which only apply to situations of armed conflict; and most League members accordingly accepted this judgment by rejecting out of hand Italy's claim that all neutral member states were bound to respect the rules of neutrality in applying the embargo (Gihl 1938, 70).

Thus while the status of neutrality retained some meaning relative to the war in the Horn of Africa, it was clearly inapplicable to the League's limited economic embargo which was accompanied by neither political (diplomatic) sanctions nor the threat of subsequent military action. It could be, and was, argued that the imposition of the oil sanction could lead to war with Italy, which the Italians themselves had threatened. Even so, this remained only a theoretical possibility for the future; and the eventual course of the oil sanction debate did not affect, or even pertain to, individual states' responses to the partial measures recommended at the outset of the crisis. Hence from the League's viewpoint, any attempt by states to establish a distinction between the two aspects of the conflict as the basis for a nondiscriminatory policy was false, and it regarded neutrality in all forms as unacceptable. Sweden's and Switzerland's responses to the crisis must be seen in this context; and the wide variance between their respective policies, as will be shown below, highlighted the continuing problems for neutrality posed by the League's coercive mechanism.

NOTES

1. More detailed examinations of the background to the Italo-Abyssinian crisis can be found in: Potter, 1936, pp. 27–44; Baer, 1973, 1976; Rowan–Robinson, 1936, pp. 98–121; Brown–John, 1975, pp. 59–139; Taylor, 1961, pp. 118–27; Walters, vol. 2, 1952, pp. 623–91; Joll, 1976, pp. 90–91, 358–60; RIIA, 1938; Doxey, 1980, pp. 42–55; Wright, 1936b, pp. 45–57; and *DIA* 1935, vol. 2, is devoted exclusively to the crisis.

2. Handed down by the League's Blockade Committee in its report of 4 October 1921 (*OJ*, SS no. 6, 1921, pp. 25–27), which effectively reduced the scope of Art. 16, an interpretation upheld in a 1927 League circular (*OJ*, SS no. 14, 1927). See also Wright, 1936b, pp. 46–47.

3. See *OJ*, SS no. 145, pp. 14, 32; SS no. 150, pp. 2–3. The list was altered slightly through an annex (Proposal IA) issued on 16 October (*OJ*, SS no. 145, pp. 19, 63; SS no. 150, p. 3).

4. On 2 November the Committee exempted from Proposal III contracts which had been paid in full, and in some cases, those in the process of execution; see *OJ*, SS no. 146, pp. 48, 64, 68, 73; SS no. 150, p. 7.

5. See Baer, 1976, pp. 8–9; and Fredrik Hoffmann, 1967, pp. 158–59, n. 7. Both Britain and France justifiably saw Italy as a needed (and seemingly willing) bulwark against German expansion to the south.

4

Sweden and the Italian Operation

ASPECTS OF SWEDEN'S INITIAL ATTITUDE

It was apparent even prior to Italy's invasion of Abyssinia in October 1935 that Sweden would offer unqualified support for an international sanctions operation in case of such aggression. Indeed Sweden (and Scandinavia generally) led an upsurge in support among the smaller League member states for more decisive League action during the summer of 1935. On 29 August in Oslo, following their biennial meeting, the four Nordic foreign ministers (representing Sweden, Denmark, Norway, and Finland) issued a joint declaration of support for all League measures aiming at the preservation of peace and at the maintenance of the legal principles of the Covenant. In a speech in Uppsala two days later, Östen Undén, chairman of the Riksdag's Foreign Affairs Committee, stressed the need for collective action to resolve the dispute: "Peace-loving people insist now not on neutrality in the sense of impartial passivity but the prevention of war or the stopping of hostilities by mutual effort" (Jones 1939, 259–60).

Similar Scandinavian overtures were forthcoming during the sixteenth League Assembly session which commenced on 4 September 1935. The Swedish delegation, led by Foreign Minister Rickard Sandler, argued that the basic League principles must be upheld, and deplored "the fact that the Council was not able to exercise its influence on the course of events at an earlier stage of the dispute" (OJ, SS 138:62). However, he refrained from criticizing the Council directly, and merely expressed the conviction that all states, including Sweden, "should be ready to shoulder their responsibilities in the present grave situation" (OJ, SS 138:63). These statements were indicative of Sweden's official, two-fold position throughout the conflict: support for the principles of the Covenant through the application of sanctions, accompanied by a lack of any pretenses to neutrality in the operation.

One of the most noteworthy and consistent features of Sweden's response was the high degree of political unanimity in favor of a resolute stand by the League. As indicated in chapter 2, this factor was historically rooted, and it had also characterized Sweden's previous attitude toward the organization; nonetheless, this particular dispute had not always engendered complete political agreement. During the earlier (and less urgent) stages of the crisis the Swedish left and right diverged over the League's halfhearted attempts to resolve the dispute: the rightist parties tended to criticize the League directly for its failure to bring about a solution, whereas the left generally blamed Italy's intransigence. However, such interparty differences dissolved rapidly after the outbreak of hostilities in October 1935. After the initial meeting of the Advisory Council on Foreign Affairs (20 October), Social Democratic Prime Minister P. A. Hansson announced that all the main Swedish parties were completely united in the call for sanctions (Jones 1939, 261). His assertion was largely accurate, even though some Conservatives questioned the veracity of such claims to absolute unity. All five parties with Riksdag representation, including the ruling Social Democrats and their Agrarian allies, Liberals, Conservatives, and particularly the Communists (after their abrupt change in heart following Soviet entry into the League in 1934), favored active Swedish participation, with only a few small fringe parties opposed (including the National, National Socialist, Left-Wing Socialist, and Syndicalist factions). For example, the new Conservative leader, Gösta Bagge, asserted at the beginning of October that Sweden must fulfill its duties under the Covenant and apply economic sanctions; however, he also ruled out all participation in a possible military sanctions operation, more explicitly than did the government (Tingsten 1944, 201). Later, the Foreign Minister commended this political unity before parliament (*RP*, AK, 1936, 4:23); indeed the Riksdag was not recalled in special session because none of the opposition leaders even called for an early debate. This interparty unity in turn reflected a consensus of political opinion within the country at large; for example, the Conservative newspapers *Svenska Dagbladet* and *Svenska Morgonbladet*, both of which previously had been rather critical of the League of Nations, were nearly as bitter in their denunciations of Italy as was *Social Democraten*.

There were several major, and closely interconnected, reasons for the broad upswelling of support in Sweden for international sanctions. One was a general determination that the League's earlier failure to resolve international crises must not be allowed to recur. The Swedish government had deplored the failure of the League's Lytton Commission to censure the Japanese invasion and occupation of Manchuria in 1931; even earlier it had expressed strong disappointment over the lack of resolute League action during the Greco-Italian dispute over Corfu. Due to the legacy of these past failures, nearly all Swedes were convinced that the principles of the League must be upheld for once through a definitive stance against Italian tyranny. Foreign Minister Sandler stated in early November that the international mobilization for "collective action in order to build respect for the international legal order is a gain which cannot be measured by the petty yardsticks of the day"; and at that time he made his well known statement that "it is not against Italy but against war which the sanctions are directed" (Tingsten 1944, 201).

The Italo-Abyssinian dispute offered a particularly apt opportunity for defending principles of international law; and the government held that "the provisions of the Covenant are equally applicable to great and small, to strong and to weak countries . . . a law which is not applied to all ceases by that very fact to be law" (*OJ*, SS 138:63). This aim was reiterated in King Gustaf's annual Speech from the Throne in early 1936, in which he asserted that the aim of sanctions "is to restore peace and confidence in the international legal order" (Tingsten 1944, 202). Swedish policy throughout the dispute was couched in terms of upholding the principles of the Covenant and international law generally, a tendency reminiscent of the strong utopian element of Swedish (and particularly Social Democratic) policy throughout much of the League era.

Sweden was, however, equally concerned about the ongoing power realignment in Europe, and its consequences for the Nordic balance of power. Whereas the Social Democrats' earlier, idealistic hopes for international solidarity (culminating in its steps toward unilateral disarmament of the mid-1920s) had been facilitated by Sweden's geopolitical insulation, the deterioration in its strategic situation by the 1930s forced a reconsideration of many previous assumptions. Indeed Sweden had already taken steps toward providing for a more adequate national defense system. The work of the Swedish Defense Commission, begun in 1930, was completed in August 1935, just two months prior to the Italian invasion; and its formal report, issued that November, strongly recommended a renewed program of *upprustning* (rearmament). The Social Democrats and the opposition parties agreed readily to support these recommendations, thereby extending the earlier political consensus on foreign policy to include defense issues as well, although this trend had begun during 1931–32, in conjunction with the international disarmament conference in Geneva.

Against the backdrop of the world crisis, the first of what became a series of annual conferences between the Nordic foreign ministers was held in 1932, which produced plans for greater intra-Nordic economic cooperation (Tham 1948, 44). Sweden's attitude in fact signified a major turnabout in the great power–small power balance within the League, two groups which had been described as, respectively, the "producers" and "consumers" of security (Zimmern 1936a, 366). The traditional attitude of the consumers (i.e., the smaller and weaker states, including Sweden) had been one of opposition in principle to sanctions obligations which would restrict their freedom of action and damage their long-term security prospects. This view had contrasted sharply with that of the producers, mainly France and its eastern allies, which had championed the extension of sanctions obligations and a general strengthening of the League's security mechanism. By 1935, however, this situation had been reversed: many smaller powers now urged the League, especially Britain and France, to resolve the conflict, if necessary through enforcement action. Most Swedes now perceived that their future security prospects hinged directly on the League's ability to confront and thwart a great-power threat: a threat against not only a smaller League member state but even against the very principles of the Covenant.

A third major reason for the coalescing of support in Sweden behind a forceful League stance was a widely held antipathy toward the Italian fascist system. Sweden's attitude was in fact marked by overtly political and ideological factors which no amount of legalistic phraseology could disguise, even though Sandler expressed the official Swedish view of the conflict in a curiously evenhanded manner (*OJ*, SS 138:63), and in spite of his earlier insistence that the sanctions were directed against war and not against Italy. Anti-Italian sentiment ran deep in the Swedish political debate. Much earlier the Swedish government, represented by SAP leader Hjalmar Branting, had made its first impassioned plea for League intervention during the Italian invasion of Corfu in 1923, a stand which even at that time had engendered near-universal support within the country (Bellquist 1929, 255). The Corfu crisis, coming shortly after Mussolini's march on Rome and his seizure of power, had convinced most Swedes of Italy's hostility toward the established international order, and indeed had "aroused a more lively discussion than almost any other incident in the history of the League" (Tingsten 1944, 64). At that time *Social Democraten* called Mussolini "the universal enemy" and claimed in the strongest terms that Italy's intransigence had been even worse than Germany's violation of Belgian neutrality at the outset of World War I. In addition, the gradual termination of the long-running disarmament debate in Sweden was directly linked to the perceived menace to world peace from Mussolini's Italy (Tingsten 1973, 550–51).

Antipathy toward the Italian régime was closely related to the increasing predominance of social democratic thought in Sweden. The SAP had been returned to office in 1932 under a new generation of leadership, including Prime Minister P. A. Hansson, Foreign Minister Rickard Sandler, and Finance Minister Ernst Wigforss, although from early 1933 it depended on the tacit support of the Agrarian League (under their so-called *kohandeln*, or "cow-dealing" arrangement). The SAP nonetheless retained its association with the international workers' movement established by the earlier leadership of August Palm and Hjalmar Branting. Within the League Assembly, it associated closely with the other European socialist parties. Its close ties with international labor ideologically predisposed the SAP to oppose the Italian fascist dictatorship; fascism was indeed considered antithetical to all the values for which the SAP and international socialism stood. The SAP had asserted frequently that the ideals of social democracy could serve as the major guiding force behind a stronger League of Nations; for example, in 1926 *Social Democraten* wrote that "Social Democratic governments can provide perhaps the only lasting guarantee for the development of the League into a power which no Mussolini would dare to defy" (quoted in Tingsten 1944, 71).

Furthermore, these denunciations of the Italian government were not unrelated to the ongoing drive to construct the Swedish welfare state, or *folkhemmet* (home of the people). By the mid-1930s Sweden was widely renowned as a European economic success story despite the worldwide depression (partly due to low trade barriers agreed upon at the Oslo Convention of 1930), and as such was highly praised in Marquis Child's celebrated book *Sweden: The Middle Way*; and the success of the expansionist economic policies instituted by the SAP from 1932 was corroborated by the League's Economic Intelligence Service.[1] The struggle for economic and political equality, which the SAP (and earlier, the Liberals) had waged with the Swedish Conservatives since the early 1920s, was applied even across national frontiers. It became clear that the sanctions question was indissolubly connected with Sweden's desire to see—and if possible contribute towards—a change in the Italian system of government by supporting its working class.

The Swedish Social Democrats were already on record as supporting the use of the general strike as a means of strengthening the League's sanctions system (*RP*, FK 1932, 18:97). In this case, many believed that concerted international pressure on the Italian régime—which was showing definite signs of strain after thirteen years of rule—could only weaken the system, thereby creating the conditions for a renewal of Italian democracy from within. Both the Socialist International and the World Federation of Trade Unions, supported by many Swedes, argued for forceful League action against Italy, combined with support for the Italian workers, to effect a change in the political régime. Some also suggested that a democratic revolution there could provide impetus for a similar process of destabilization within National Socialist Germany. A few members of the Social Democratic press (though not the party apparatus) even issued specific pleas to the Italian workers to rebel, the choice being "democracy or dictatorship"; however, the government, taking a considerably more pragmatic line, completely ruled out material aid in support of any such rebellion. Prime Minister Hansson was scarcely a socialist idealogue (he was in fact a master parliamentary tactician, often accused of a readiness to compromise his socialist principles), and his major collaborators, Sandler, Undén, and Wigforss, were all academicians rather than party activists. In addition, the government showed no signs of preventing Swedish industrial interests from stepping up their supplies to Italy in advance of the invasion of Abyssinia, a development which was reported in the international press (*SIA* 1936, 2:221 n.). Even so, the widespread party support in favor of forceful League action clearly found at least a sympathetic ear within governmental circles, and their activism undoubtedly contributed toward the strong and forthright stand taken by Sweden throughout the conflict.

This manifest hostility toward the Italian government was coupled with traditionally strong antipathy toward the French. The reverse effect of Sweden's close relations with Germany both prior to and during World War I (both between the Conservative government and royal family and the Kaisers, and between the Social Democratic opposition and the German Socialists) was a profound distrust of postwar French intentions. Sweden's strong resentment over the terms of the Versailles Treaty stemmed largely from what it regarded as France's obsession with security. This suspicion of French motives was reinforced by the French occupation of the Ruhr in 1923, an event which provoked fierce public indignation from all points of the Swedish political spectrum. One Swedish analyst has even suggested that French President Raymond Poincaré's low esteem among the Swedish public was comparable to Josef Stalin's (Wickman 1951, 208). Furthermore, many Swedes held the French (Laval) government responsible for the League's failure to resolve the Italo-Abyssinian dispute at an earlier stage.

Swedish attitudes also contained a strong measure of sympathy for the plight of Emperor Haile Selassie and the Abyssinian people. Despite Sweden's geographical removal from the area, the two peoples had developed close ties through Swedish missionaries and other humanitarian groups in Africa since the 1880s, and through significant Swedish economic investment in the region; these ties in fact prompted a visit to Abyssinia by Sweden's Crown Prince Gustaf Adolf in January 1935, during his tour of the Middle East. After World War I the Swedish military had even sent advisors to help train the Abyssinian Imperial Guard (Tham 1948, 243); most of these advisors remained in Abyssinia throughout the 1935–36 war, seriously jeopardizing Italo-Swedish relations and demonstrating Sweden's non-neutral attitude (Halldin Norberg 1977, 146–54). The Abyssinian government also had wanted to include a Swedish (and a Belgian) officer on its delegation to work out with Italy a neutral zone in the disputed Wal-Wal region in January 1936, but Italy rejected the idea (*SIA* 1936, 2:141). Moreover, as recently as August 1935 Sweden had signed a Treaty of Friendship and Commerce with Abyssinia (*DIA* 1937, 1:281). These various factors indicate that Sweden's outspoken support for League sanctions contained two separate elements: while the government couched its policy in detached, abstract phraseology which emphasized the need to defend the principles of international law and justice and basic League principles (*OJ*, SS 138:63), it also held strong political motivations, including deep-seated animosity toward both Italian and French governments, and favoritism toward Abyssinia.

Due to these factors, Sweden never qualified its support for sanctions with a declaration of impartial neutrality. This fact was largely a function of the limited measures called for; the League never even contemplated military action, thus eliminating all possibility of waging war against Italy on behalf of

Abyssinia or (on a loftier note) in defense of the League's principles. Moreover, Sweden considered the Hague rules of neutrality to be inapplicable in relation to the Italo-Abyssinian war itself—even though several states took a contrary view—since the League had condemned Italy as the aggressor.

Sweden's attitude was also affected by its geographical distance from the scene of conflict, which offered protection from possible Italian reprisals resulting from Swedish support for the embargo. Previously within the League, Sweden had objected to sanctions mainly insofar as they could unilaterally jeopardize Sweden's national security, a factor which did not apply in this case. Thus Stewart Oakley (1966, 245) seems quite mistaken in claiming that "fears were expressed in some circles that this [participation in sanctions] might jeopardize Sweden's neutrality." The government's deliberate suppression of neutrality in turn lay the groundwork for its consistent support for League policy during the crisis. Nonetheless, it retained the right to refuse participation should sanctions ever be extended to include military action. Indeed the government indicated that it still considered neutrality to be an important fall-back option in case of a further deterioration of the international political climate.[2]

SWEDEN'S PRE-1935 SANCTIONS POLICY AS A FACTOR

In many ways, Sweden's attitude of cooperation with the Italian embargo represented a logical continuation of its earlier sanctions policy within the League. Swedish policy exhibited a clear trend from considerable scepticism and reserve on the sanctions question in the early 1920s to a much more unqualified acceptance a decade later. In 1918–19 suggestions for an international effort in maintaining the peace were well received in official Swedish circles, due partly to the established tradition of international cooperation in the form of intra-Scandinavian unity, as well as to the strength of indigenous pacifist organizations (associated with the SAP, in government since 1917) calling for greater international solidarity to promote the causes of obligatory "all-in" arbitration and disarmament.

Even so, most early official interest was focused on an international system exercising juridical and administrative, rather than political and coercive, responsibilities, with sanctions only as a last resort. This emphasis was illustrated through a preliminary Scandinavian draft convention (1918), through Swedish statements at the Crillon neutrals' conference of March 1919, and in the government's official proposition advocating Swedish accession to the Covenant.[3] Although Sweden's representatives at Crillon conceded that it was "both just and necessary that economic and military sanctions be employed," it quickly emerged that Sweden desired to limit sanctions obligations wherever possible in order to maintain maximum freedom of action. The government was in fact rather critical of the provisions for an automatic and complete blockade, at one point asserting that "the sanctions process . . . is built . . . on a juridical fiction" (Prop. 90, 1920, 56), through its assumption (Art. 10) that an attack on one League member should be considered an attack against all.[4]

On this basis, the government's acceptance of punitive sanctions was only conditional, pending two important reforms of the system which, it argued, would increase the flexibility, and hence viability, of the coercive mechanism. First, it proposed the adoption of a series of punitive measures to be graded into effect by stages, in order to achieve a general "softening" (uppmjukning) of the sanctions provisions, specifically through "definite economic measures which might be employed successively and according to a scale of increasing rigor." Second, it wanted to empower the League Council to delay the implementation of the blockade by an endangered state or states, or even to exempt such states totally from participating, so long as such a delay or exemption did not jeopardize the success of the embargo (Prop. 90, 1920, 159–60). This attenuated Swedish view of economic sanctions indicated a fear of having its own neutrality abrogated as a result of the automatic imposition of a total blockade against a neighboring aggressor.

Meanwhile the government was even more adamant on maintaining full freedom of action on the question of military sanctions.[5] This issue was rather less difficult to resolve, since even the League Council had accepted the non-obligatory nature of League military sanctions as early as March 1919; even so, the far-reaching nature of the League's sanctions provisions was indicated by the strong opposition to Sweden's League membership by its chiefs of staff.[6] One early indication that the government's position was not based on a strict reading of the Hague neutrality conventions was its unequivocal acceptance of the right of passage for League troops as a natural consequence of League membership. This clear deviation from the Hague rules also suggested that the Swedish attitude toward sanctions was flexible, and indicated a willingness to alter its prewar policy in order to accommodate the new duties inherent in the collective security organization; indeed the government agreed that "the obligation to take part in an economic sanctions operation and allow the right of passage implies for member states a renunciation (avrängelse) of the right to neutrality in its previous meaning against a state which breaks the Covenant."[7]

The Swedish political debate over League accession has been called the most vociferous on a foreign policy issue in Sweden since the introduction of bicameralism in 1867 (Håstad 1956, 16), and it sharply divided the Swedish political spectrum. The moderate left (the governing Liberals and Social Democrats in coalition) was highly favorable to League membership, mainly because of what SAP leader Hjalmar Branting called "the germ of an idea which is likely to develop in the right direction" (L of N Journal 1919, 1[8]:296); however, the Left-Wing Socialist Party was vigorously opposed, due to its close ties with the Comintern.[8] Meanwhile, the political right, the

Farmers' Alliance (*Bondeförbundet*) and particularly the Conservative Party, expressed scepticism and even hostility toward the organization. The Conservatives, due to their traditionally close ties with Imperial Germany, considered the League to be a mere cloak for the continued postwar domination of the western alliance; they were also more inclined to protect Sweden's neutrality in the postwar period.[9] The votes of 3–4 March 1920, which resulted in approval for Sweden's League membership, reflected this sharp party-political split.[10]

A far more important development was the rapid and conclusive acceptance of Sweden's League obligations by the political opposition soon after accession. As early as autumn 1920 Sweden could boast near-unanimous political support for the broad aims of its League policies (*RP*, FK 1921, 20:38–51). The most striking single example was the rapid reversal in the attitude of Conservative leader Ernst Trygger, who, after attending the first Assembly session as a Swedish delegate, delivered a remarkable public admission that his earlier opposition to the League had been mistaken (*RP*, FK 1921, 3:2–4). This rapid accrual of all-party support was partly the product of successful steps by the government to eliminate remaining pockets of resistance to the League, including the early designation of inter-party League delegations and the creation in 1921 of an Advisory Council on Foreign Affairs (*Utrikesnämnden*). Herbert Tingsten thus asserted that "in any account of Swedish policy in the League of Nations, it may be treated as an unbroken unity" (1944, 32). This unity was particularly noteworthy in light of the serious, often bitter political differences over domestic issues which arose during the same period, and indeed the 1920s are otherwise regarded as an era of unstable minority parliamentarism in Sweden. Foreign affairs even became a single focus of general political agreement; there was also a distinct inclination for this political opinion to coalesce in times of crisis (Tingsten 1944, 319), a tendency which held very important implications for the Italian dispute.

Sweden's sanctions policy subsequent to League entry continued to be based upon the position set out during 1919–20, which lay the groundwork for a consistent trend toward an acceptance of sanctions. In line with their earlier opposition to an automatic procedure, the three Scandinavian governments in late 1920 proposed a League dispensation for any states requesting permission to continue trading with a state which had broken the Covenant (*OJ*, 1[6]:353–56). It was significant that the League's International Blockade Committee, established to set guidelines for the enforcement mechanism, fully upheld the Scandinavian viewpoint in its important October 1921 report on Art. 16 (*OJ*, SS 6:25–28). Second, Sweden opposed all proposals designed to increase sanctions obligations without simultaneously developing arbitration procedures and encouraging international disarmament, thereby linking the three strands of the security triad in an overall, and more workable, security framework. It also rejected as a "standing rule" all suggestions that military sanctions be made obligatory (Jones 1939, 238). On this basis, in 1923 it rejected the draft Treaty of Mutual Guarantee (adopted as Res. XIV by the Third Assembly) and its related draft Treaty of Mutual Assistance, though it was equivocal on the Geneva Protocol of 1924–25.[11]

However, by the late 1920s, due to further developments in arbitration and disarmament through the Kellogg-Briand Pact and the General Act of 1928[12] and the decision (1931) to convene the long-delayed disarmament conference, Sweden became distinctly more favorable toward sanctions. In 1930 Sweden supported a scaled-down version of the Convention on Financial Assistance to Victims of Aggression, which also gained full bipartisan support in the Riksdag's Constitution Committee (*RP*, AK 1931, 20:3–35). By then Undén even considered the sanctions provisions to be "one of the cornerstones of the League" (quoted in Jones 1939, 242). A further step was taken at the Geneva disarmament conference, when Sweden's Foreign Minister Sten Ramel, in response to a French proposal, agreed to "give unbiased and careful consideration to any proposal intended to reinforce security—for instance, by the organization of an international armed force" (*RP*, AK 1931, 20:35–36). This view was widely interpreted in the Riksdag as an acknowledgement of the need to extend the League's sanctions system following the realization of disarmament (*RP*, AK 1932, 18:2–40), again in keeping with Sweden's earlier attitude. Moreover, these opinions were reflected in Swedish policy during the period immediately preceding the Italian crisis, when Sweden decided to contribute troops to the first international peacekeeping force actually deployed, the League's "police" contingency of 3,300 sent to supervise the Saar plebiscite of January 1935 (Dolman 1979, 62). Sweden's increasing efforts by the 1930s to promote international political cooperation were particularly noteworthy in light of the contemporaneous deterioration of the international political climate, following Japan's invasion and occupation of Manchuria in 1931, and the failure of the disarmament conference (1932–34) to achieve substantive results.

SWEDEN'S IMPLEMENTATION OF SANCTIONS

The government's support for the League's operation was amply demonstrated by its rapid application of the recommended sanctions against Italy. Most of its measures were implemented on the basis of existing legislation (which had been suggested by the League in Proposal II), although the ban on credits was only temporary and was strengthened by full-power legislation passed during the spring of 1936. The first League proposal, the weapons embargo, was implemented in full by governmental decree of 18 October 1935.[13] This measure merely formalized a de facto embargo already in place; through its adherence (despite nonratification) to the 1925 Convention on the Control of the International Trade in Arms, Sweden was preventing all arms sales to countries involved in hostilities, except by governmental permission (which was granted in the case of Ethiopia). This prohibition was particularly important for Sweden; it was the world's fifth leading supplier of arms in 1935 (at that time ahead even of Italy and Germany)[14] in spite of the long-standing antimilitarist posture of the governing Social Democratic Party.

Sweden's implementation of the financial prohibition (Proposal II) required more extensive preparation than did the weapons embargo. The government stated its desire to prevent the granting of loans and credits to Italy (*OJ*, SS 145:51), although it was restricted to temporary measures until formal legislation could be drawn up. In the interim, the government enacted a temporary stop on credits to Italy, on 28 October.[15] It also undertook to prevent the export of all goods sold on credit to Italy, through direct intervention by the Swedish customs authorities. They allowed only for very limited exemptions, such as goods paid for, at the latest, upon receipt by the purchaser; personal goods of travelers in Italy; and goods in transit before 18 November (the date the decree took effect).

The government achieved this ban on banking credits through action by the Swedish *Riksbank*. In addition, the members of the Swedish private banking consortium concluded an informal agreement to prohibit the granting of all credits to Italian nationals, which "would be communicated to the Swedish government, which would officially take note of it" (*OJ*, SS 145:51). This act was significant insofar as it seemed to demonstrate a general willingness within the Swedish business community to comply with the League's measures, since the private banks agreed, without governmental pressure, to refuse credit transactions with Italian officials and nationals, thus apparently depriving themselves of a potential source of income. This ban on credits also compelled the suspension of all clearing agreements with Italy (Proposal IIA), thereby preventing Italy from paying for goods in lira.[16] Even so, Italy's general lack of creditworthiness at the time, indicated by its difficulties in securing loans in the City of London and other international capital markets (Doxey 1987, 30) undoubtedly mitigated the effect of the Swedish credit ban; thus a more sceptical interpretation of this move could be that it was actually in the bankers' interest to forswear business with a potential defaulter.

The 1936 Law on Financial Sanctions

Although these ad hoc measures were sufficient to halt Swedish-Italian financial dealings, the government eventually bolstered its authority through passage of a full-power law, enabling it to decree a general prohibition on credit if called upon to do so by the League under Art. 16 of the Covenant.[17] Although this proposal created much political opposition over the desirability of such an extension of governmental authority (*RP*, AK 1936, 22:8–35), the new law concerning the full credit stop was finally enacted on 24 April 1936,[18] and the accompanying decree specifically prohibiting credits to Italy on 30 April.[19]

The 1936 credit law was a significant step for Swedish relations with the League, since it provided the first legal authorization for the Swedish government to implement League recommendations concerning sanctions unilaterally (i.e., without prior parliamentary approval). Up until this point, Sweden's application of Proposal II had been grounded in previous legislation which did not refer specifically to the League. This new legislation was also significant in contrast to the attitude of previous Swedish governments, which had resisted efforts by the League to induce member states to prepare sanctions legislation in advance (*SOU* 1970, 19:33); furthermore, the Social Democratic Party, which now proposed this legislation, had been among the strongest opponents of an extension of the government's authority on this issue (*RP*, AK 1936, 4:58; Undén).

The new law indicated two major changes in Sweden's sanctions policy: first, it increased the government's competence vis-à-vis parliament during sanctions operations; and second, it provided general authority, being applicable to future League embargoes as well as the Italian operation. In addition, the government considered the new legislation to constitute another step away from the pre-1918 policy of integral neutrality which, it asserted, was only "justified during a period when war was regarded as a legal duel between states"; but in relation to League actions the idea was "certainly absurd [sic] to observe complete neutrality toward both parties ... without considering that the members of the League should react against the aggressor" (*RP*, AK 1936, 22:18; Undén). Hence Swedish officials regarded the law both as an extension of Sweden's international duties, and as a further derogation of impartial neutrality in a sanctions operation.

On the other hand, the government (partly for political reasons) deliberately de-emphasized the significance of the law. One mitigating factor was its late (April 1936) enactment, which meant that the law held few implications for the Italian crisis itself. Second, Foreign Minister Rickard Sandler argued that the new law was operative only under the terms of Covenant Art. 16, and not Art. 17, pertaining to enforcement against nonmembers, which appeared to rule out Swedish participation in a future sanctions operation against Germany. His third and main point was that the law was applicable only if the League came to a unanimous recommendation on sanctions; this view in fact appeared to backtrack from his earlier view that each member was bound individually to sanction an aggressor, and indicated a step away from Sweden's unilateral support for sanctions the previous October (*RP*, AK 1936, 22:8). The main exponent of the bill, Undén, added that the new measure applied only to the severance of financial credits, and that the government was already empowered to apply import and export prohibitions on its own; thus the measure could not lead, as some opponents suggested, to Swedish participation in a League-sponsored "hunger blockade" (*RP*, AK 1936, 22:15–18).

The impact of the bill was also mitigated by the fact that Sweden was only one of some ten states which passed such legislation, and indeed its law was

TABLE 4-1
Swedish-Italian Annual Trade, 1933-36

Year	Total Swedish Imports from Italy (in 1000s SEK) (1)	Total Swedish Exports to Italy (in 1000s SEK) (2)	Overall Trade Balance (in 1000s SEK) (3)
1933	16,906	24,976	+ 8,070
1934	18,906	30,977	+ 12,071
1935	22,862	29,916	+ 7,054
1936	8,816	19,579	+ 10,763

Source: Sveriges Officiella Statistik, Handel, Berättelse för år 1933, 1934, 1935, 1936; pp. 396-97 (1933); pp. 433-35 (1934); 444-46 (1935); 452-53 (1936).

arguably the weakest of the ten, insofar as it (1) covered only one proposal (II) rather than all; (2) was temporary rather than permanent (set to expire on 28 February 1937); and (3) was the only one which did not refer directly (but only by inference) to the Italo-Abyssinian dispute (Highley 1938, 159).

Sweden and the Economic Embargo

The Swedish government also declared its willingness to implement Proposals III and IV by whatever date the Coordination Committee recommended (OJ, SS 150:264). Accordingly, it enacted both decrees four days prior to the committee's 18 November deadline. The prohibition on imports from Italy included the import of all goods produced fully or partially (over 25 percent) in Italy or consigned from there, except for the goods exempted through Proposal IIIA. In addition, it gave Swedish customs officials considerable leeway to refuse goods from any source, if such goods were suspected of Italian origin (Art. 2). The only exception applied to goods already exported from Italy by the date the decree entered into force (18 November), and to goods fully paid for by 19 October (the date the League adopted Proposal III); (SFS 1935, 560:1213–14; OJ, SS 150:267).

Regarding the total embargo, Sweden faced the prospect of losing Italy as a supplier of goods, since it agreed to Proposal III in full. Sweden's imports from Italy totaled some SEK 22.9m during 1935 (from table 4-1); for the first half of 1935 (January–June), which corresponded with the main part of the sanctioning period the following year, that figure stood at SEK 12,559,000. The monthly breakdown of imports from Italy during the year leading up to sanctions is given in table 4-2, col. 1. An analysis of the figures shows the generally nonessential nature of these imports, of which approximately 50 percent were food products, and the remainder other goods including yarn and silk, sulphur, and nonelectrical machinery.

The government applied the embargo on selected exports to Italy (Proposal IV) on the basis of a list of embargoed materials drawn up in accordance with Swedish customs regulations (*SFS* 1935, 561:1214–15). It also prohibited the export of these goods to countries other than Italy if they were believed to be destined for Italy (indirect supply being the subject of Proposal IVB), and required Swedish exporters to declare that they did not foresee the re-export of their goods to Italy. Sweden's exports to Italy consisted mainly of three products: paper pulp (56 percent of the total in 1934); iron and steel (14 percent); and machinery (10 percent). Sweden in fact supplied 37 percent of all Italy's paper pulp imports in 1934, although Italian imports of finished paper products from Sweden fell sharply from 31 percent in 1934 to just 11 percent in 1935. At the same time, Italy's imports of Swedish electrical generators and motors rose from 14 percent to 21 percent in the year preceding the embargo, which the Swedish statistical commentary interpreted as a new development in Italy's trade policy (most likely in conjunction with its war preparations); (*OJ*, SS 150:270).

It was significant that none of these three products were subject to the partial export ban in Proposal IV, given that the export earnings they generated were important to the Swedish economy. This factor no doubt eased Sweden's decision to comply with the operation. The main Swedish exports which were covered by Proposal IV included iron-based products. In 1934 Sweden exported to Italy some SEK 0.18m worth of iron ore, and SEK 0.12m worth of iron alloys. Indeed an important indication that the export embargo did not threaten Sweden's economic well-being was the dichotomy between Sweden's very low total of iron ore exported to Italy, in contrast with its overall position as one of the world's leading iron ore exporters, at the time accounting for some 5.6 percent of the world's total output (RIIA 1938, 45). During the embargo, Italy's iron ore requirements were filled by the USSR, Algeria (then a French colony), and Spain (*SKM*, 23[18]:648).

A relatively more important export category was that of pig iron (*tackjärn*), which earned Sweden a total of SEK 607,752 in 1935. Pig iron was designated by the League (through Proposal IVA), along with oil products, to be sanctioned if international conditions warranted it; this deferred decision resulted from a lengthy League committee debate concerning which categories of iron (iron ore, scrap iron, pig iron, and iron and steel products) to include in the original Proposal IV (see *OJ*, SS 145 and 146). The Swedish delegate suggested that Sweden "would take the necessary steps [to embargo pig iron] as soon as there appeared to be a possibility of adopting effective measures" (*OJ*, SS 146:63); and subsequent figures showed that Sweden did in fact restrict severely its export of pig iron to Italy. Thus the export embargo applied to Sweden only to the amount of about SEK 0.3m (or nearly 1m if pig iron is included), but the import embargo covered nearly SEK 23m worth of imports from Italy (as totaled from the previous full year).[20] Finally, Sweden (in coordination with the other ex-neutral states, particularly the Low Countries) demurred from taking a leading role in the oil embargo controversy, since it was not itself an oil producer; it did appear, however, that Sweden supported the oil sanction in principle and was willing to cooperate should it be imposed (*RP*, AK 1936, 4:25).

Even so, Sweden's general support for sanctions was excepted by its attitude on the question of mutual support. The government merely gave notice of receipt of Proposal V, stating that no decree was necessary for its implementation (AKU 1935:83–84). Foreign Minister Sandler insisted that Sweden alone would determine what type of aid to give to states damaged by the imposition of the embargo, if any, and the manner in which it would be delivered. This view was rather more in line with Sweden's previous insistence on freedom of action than with its more recent policy of support for sanctions, and accorded with its earlier rejection of the draft Treaty of Mutual Guarantee (1923) and the Treaty of Financial Assistance (1928).

These measures significantly reduced Sweden's level of imports from Italy, although the reciprocal effect on Sweden's exports to Italy did not occur. The government later released figures showing a precipitous decline in Italian imports, but not a complete shutoff. Table 4-2, col. 2, clearly shows this trend; Swedish imports from Italy declined from SEK 2,518,000 in November 1935 to a (temporary) low of only SEK 107,000 in March 1936 (also *RP*, FK 1936, 36:4); in June, the last sanctioning month, this level fell to just SEK 75,000.

All this trade must however be accounted for, given Sweden's unquestioned acceptance of Proposal III. The figures for January–June 1936 show that nearly two-thirds of all Sweden's imports from Italy consisted of food and food products, an even higher percentage than before the embargo; this category of imports accounted for SEK 644,000 out of the SEK 1,002,000 registered. The remainder consisted of nonelectrical machinery (SEK 168,000), spun products including cotton, wool, and other textiles (SEK 148,000), and limited amounts of other goods (e.g., glass, chemicals). The Swedish trade authorities later explained that this trade consisted of goods arriving in Sweden prior to the date the embargo took effect (18 November 1935), which were exempted from the restrictions, along with goods imported on long-term contracts paid for in full by that date. This explanation, however, seems inadequate in itself; while it could explain imports registered two or three months after the embargo had been imposed (allowing time for national distribution of products), it would appear less plausible concerning the continuation of some imports even in June 1936, nearly seven months later. The perishable nature of many of these products (fruits and vegetables) would also seem to cast doubt on this explanation, unless they were dried goods rather than fresh (a distinction which was not made in the statistics).

An overall comparison with other leading sanctioning states may be useful here. According to a comparison in the Swedish statistics (*SKM*, 23[18]:651),

TABLE 4-2

Sweden's Monthly Trade with Italy, 1934-36

Month	Total Import Value (in 1000s SEK)		Total Export Value (in 1000s SEK)	
	1934-35 (1)	1935-36 (2)	1934-35 (3)	1935-36 (4)
Oct	1,622	2,032	2,595	2,258
Nov	2,037	2,518	2,079	2,526
Dec	1,434	979	4,379	2,645
Jan	1,898	395	2,757	1,991
Feb	2,544	168	2,326	2,265
Mar	2,573	107	1,988	1,397
Apr	2,155	108	2,490	2,111
May	2,001	149	2,190	2,043
Jun	1,388	75	2,943	1,633
		post-sanctions		post-sanctions
Jul	1,621	297	1,768	1,377
Aug	1,925	400	2,890	1,186
Sep	1,317	431	2,824	1,115
Oct	(2,032)	1,684	(2,258)	1,184
Nov	(2,518)	1,792	(2,526)	2,432
Dec	(979)	2,353	(2,645)	1,661

Source: *Sveriges Kommersiella Meddelanden*, utgivna av Kungl. Kommerskollegium, årgang 1935, 1936, monthly.

both Britain and France reduced their imports from Italy even more sharply than did Sweden. Whereas Sweden's level of December 1935–June 1936 was 14.3 percent of the level during the corresponding period the previous year, France's was only 12.3 percent; the UK's was much lower still, at just 2.5 percent of its previous level; and Britain's very low total (0.1m for January–June 1936) was the closest any state came to severing its trade with Italy completely. Thus Sweden's declared support for the sanctions operation was not entirely corroborated by its actual trade performance.[21]

Nonetheless it remains arguable that this continuation of trade was not particularly significant or revealing, since the Swedes did in fact sharply reduce the level of their Italian imports. Whereas its level of November 1935 was 25 percent higher than the corresponding month the previous year, the June 1936 figure (the last sanctioning month) of SEK 75,000 was just 5 percent of that of the previous June. The paucity of this level by the end of the sanctioning period, particularly in products which were clearly nonessential to Sweden, should indicate that Sweden had little motivation to mislead the League through the continuation of a very small, and declining, level of imports from the target state. In addition, table 4-2 indicates a gradual but clear resumption of the normal pattern of Swedish-Italian trade in the months following the lifting of the sanctions, which illustrates the effect of the restrictions imposed in November 1935. In addition, table 4-1, col. 1, shows that Sweden's imports from Italy were on the increase from 1934 to 1935, leading up to the sanctioning period, which highlights the subsequent reductions brought about during the crisis itself.

On the other hand, table 4-2, col. 4, shows that Swedish exports to Italy during this period declined only marginally, further distorting Sweden's already substantial trade surplus with Italy (as shown in table 4-1, col. 3). This existing surplus had eased the initial difficulties for Sweden in applying the embargo, especially the prohibition on the granting of credit to Italy. Although most of its exports to Italy were not subject to the embargo, it would be instructive to see those figures as well. Sweden's exports to Italy fell only modestly, from SEK 19.1m from December 1934 to June 1935 to 14.1m from December 1935–June 1936. Of these exports, paper pulp fell slightly, from SEK 13.1m to 11.2m; and iron and steel from 2.8 to 2.4m. This latter figure is no doubt the more significant, since iron and steel products were not embargoed in spite of their obvious usefulness in a military campaign. In vivid contrast, France's exports of iron and steel to the Italians fell very sharply during the embargo, from FFr 72.6m to just 10.9m, a seven-fold drop (this again according to the Swedish statistics; *SKM* 23[18]:650). Here again, Sweden's compliance with the spirit, if not the letter, of the embargo appeared to be less than complete. The only nonembargoed product which Sweden did limit sharply was electrical machinery sold to Italy, which fell from SEK 1.8m in the previous period to just 0.4m during the sanctioning period.

Sweden's yearly export of pig iron, which as indicated earlier was not included in the original list of Proposal IV but was targeted as a future sanction, also showed a very sharp drop: from over SEK 600,000 worth of pig iron exported to Italy in 1935, the total for all of 1936 came to just SEK 55,400. Even so, Italy could dispense with those Swedish exports without great difficulty, and some experts questioned whether Italy's steel works could utilize foreign-produced scrap iron or pig iron. In all, Sweden's total exports to Italy during the embargo were 73.8 percent of the corresponding period the previous year; in contrast, the Swedish source lists France's total exports to Italy at just 25.4 percent of the previous period, and Britain's at only 7.1 percent (*SKM*, 23[18]:651). All of these measures (except the full-power law of 24 April 1936) were, however, repealed by Sweden in July 1936, after the League recommended a lifting of the embargo.[22]

The government coupled these measures with a memorandum to the League Council (23 December 1935), which deplored the refusal of some states to implement the sanctions fully (*AKU* 1936:19, n. 2). Sweden's willingness to apply sanctions despite its neutrality, and its pointed criticism of other states for failing to do likewise, also achieved some international notoriety. During the initial (January 1936) Riksdag debate on the dispute, the government referred, with apparent satisfaction, to a dispatch from *The Times* of London, commenting on Sweden's unilaterally forceful stand:

It is not without hesitation that the Swedish people, for which neutrality has received the sanctity of tradition, is taking part in the first attempt to check aggression through collective action.... Despite the temptations of neutrality ... Sweden is willing to take its full part in the collective defence as it is defined in the League of Nations Covenant. This decision marks an important turning point in the history of Swedish foreign relations. (*RP*, AK 1936, 2:6)

Despite such indications of a new departure for Swedish neutrality, the balance of evidence indicates that its policy accorded with its gradual but consistent trend during the 1920s and 1930s toward fuller acceptance of sanctions duties, even in a nonuniversal League. On the other hand, it remains arguable that such rosy accounts of absolute Swedish compliance with the operation were somewhat overstated, as indicated by the preceding discussion and by the actual trade figures.

THE POLITICAL DEBATE IN SWEDEN

In accordance with the strong domestic unity in Sweden in favor of sanctions, all political parties supported in principle any joint Franco-British effort to resolve the conflict outside the League's aegis. Although the Swedish delegate to the Committee of Eighteen refused to comment on the ongoing French peace initiative (late November 1935) before the League Council had examined it in detail, he also held that all member states would be obliged to apply sanctions if such an agreement called for it (*AKU* 1936:86).

However, once the details of the Hoare-Laval plan were released in December, the Swedish condemnation was swift and vigorous. Great Britain bore the brunt of Swedish criticism, primarily because the Baldwin government had been vigorous in its defense of the Covenant. The French government, on the other hand, received rather less criticism, since it had already been suspected of intentionally pacifying Mussolini. Accordingly most Swedes applauded the subsequent rapid collapse of the plan (and particularly Hoare's resignation as British foreign secretary) even though its long-term effect was to eliminate any remaining possibility of levying the oil embargo, which the Swedish government appeared to favor. Thereafter, especially in light of the failed sanctions operation, the Swedish debate was drawn toward further discussion of the future viability of the League itself.

The Swedish Red Cross Bombing Incident

The Riksdag's vociferous reaction to the Italian campaign was compounded by what appeared to be an act of direct Italian retaliation against Sweden. In a particularly tragic incident, Italian war planes bombed a Swedish Red Cross ambulance while on duty in Ethiopia, on 30 December 1935 (after a preliminary raid on 22 December, near Dolo). The ambulance was at the time in operation at Malka Dida, in the westernmost sector of the southern Abyssinian province of Borona and attached to Ras Desta's army. Several of its attendants were injured, and one (a Dr. Lundström) was killed in the attack, along with several patients. This act, quite apart from its direct contravention of the 1929 Geneva Red Cross Conventions, violated all accepted international norms of wartime conduct. The resulting political fallout was particularly great in Sweden, due to its strong humanitarian tradition (the Swedish Red Cross had been in fact second in the field during the conflict); the reaction, especially in the press, was sharp and even violent (see Tingsten 1944, 204–7). The Swedish government held that the attack was purposeful, in order to silence Sweden's denunciations of the Italian government and its outspoken support for the League's operation. The state-controlled Italian mass media's defense of the bombing fueled Swedish animosity further.

The attack immediately provoked a formal protest by the Swedish foreign minister to Italy's ambassador in Stockholm, who expressed his government's sorrow over the "accident." His apparent contrition, however, was contradicted by a communiqué issued by the Italian Press and Propaganda Ministry, which declared the bombardment to be "fully justified" since Abyssinian commanders allegedly took refuge with the Swedish Red Cross whenever Italian planes appeared. Thus not only did the Italians offer no formal apology, but the Italians (specifically the under-secretary of state for foreign affairs, Signor Suvich) even, in return, accused the Swedish Red Cross of engaging in unneutral activity by harboring the leaders of belligerent forces, and repudiated the "deceived" Swedish public outcry (AKU *Den Svenska Röda-Kors-Ambulansen* 1937:15–18). Thus the act was justified as an act of reprisal against Swedish aid to Abyssinia, even though the government never admitted directly that the Swedish ambulance (which the ICRC confirmed was well marked) was the actual target of the bombing mission. Although this was the worst such incident, Italian forces attacked other Red Cross facilities as well, including Egyptian, American, British, Abyssinian, and Sweden's again, on 17 March 1936 (*SIA* 1936, 2:411–12).

The incident was brought up for League examination in April 1936, when both Italy and Ethiopia assured the Council of their desire to observe the 1929 Geneva Convention Relative to the Treatment of the Wounded and Sick in the Field. According to Art. 30 of this Convention, the parties to a dispute were to launch an investigation of any violations. However, no such study was ever undertaken; indeed the League Council never even called in officials of the International Red Cross to testify on the issue, despite the fact that the League's secretary-general had specifically requested such an inquiry on 8 April (AKU 1936:4–5).

The Riksdag Debates

The Riksdag *remiss* debates of January 1936, held in the immediate wake of the Red Cross incident, reflected the Swedish outcry over Italy's provocation. Virtual unanimity (apart from the extreme left) greeted Foreign Minister Rickard Sandler's first Riksdag address on the crisis of 18 January, in which he asserted that there was "no other way to go" but to continue applying pressure against Italy. He also specifically saluted the support of governmental policy by the political right, even calling it "a position [which deserves] a special honor. It is a circumstance which gives Swedish foreign policy in this affair a steadfastness which it otherwise could not possess" (*RP*, AK 1936, 4:23).

Conservative leader Gösta Bagge agreed that "Sweden must fulfill its obligations according to the Covenant. . . . It is both our country's duty and it lies in our obvious interest that we seek to contribute . . . to the advantage of peace and justice in the world." However, he also stressed that Sweden should not "take an especially conspicuous and leading place in the formulation of sanctions," with apparent reference to the oil embargo; and he considered the operation to be an important test case for the League, whose "future credibility would be largely determined" by the consequences of the operation (*RP*, FK 1936, 3:2–3). Slightly more scepticism was expressed by Liberal leader Felix Hamrin who, while agreeing that "we stand by our word" on Covenant obligations, also criticized the League for its inability to achieve results (*RP*, FK 1936, 3:14). This general agreement was also shown by the unanimous rejection by the Constitution Committee of an extremist (Nerman-Lindhagen) motion for Swedish withdrawal from the League, although its curiously unenthusiastic support for League membership as an alternative to isolation was roundly criticized by the Hansson government.[23]

Another feature of the debate was a widespread acknowledgment that Sweden's neutrality had been indelibly altered as a result of its League membership. It was noteworthy that King Gustaf, in his annual Speech from the Throne in early 1936, failed even to mention neutrality in connection with Sweden's response to the operation (*BRP* 1936, 1 Saml., 1). The January 1936 debate was in fact the first substantive discussion of neutrality policy since Sweden's League accession in March 1920 (Tingsten 1944, 210), which in itself indicated Sweden's continuing inability to establish the precise implications of its neutrality in relation to League membership.

Nearly every deputy, including the Communist Party's representatives, agreed that neutrality no longer implied a legally based policy of abstention and detachment. Agrarian leader K. G. Westman asserted that the doctrinaire, pre-1914 neutrality had "been shot in the side"; significantly, he also ruled out neutrality in case war erupted as the result of a League sanctions operation, although on this point he was inconsistent (*RP*, FK 1936, 3:36–38). Foreign Minister Sandler added that Sweden's neutrality had been undermined through participation in this limited operation (*RP*, AK 1936, 4:21–27). He saw only two possible means of avoiding economic sanctions obligations, both of which he regarded as totally unrealistic: either to deny the existence of the conflict, or to withdraw from the League. Notably, he failed to even mention a third alternative, that adopted by the Swiss Federal Council: to consider the dispute a classic case of war and thereby avoid full participation in sanctions by attempting to treat each belligerent equally. He also acknowledged that this attitude represented a distinct shift from his view expressed as recently as 1934 during the disarmament conference, when he had said that "responsible governments have an elementary duty to reserve for themselves the right to choose the path of neutrality" (*RP*, FK 1936, 3:79–80).

The Gradual Reassertion of Neutrality

This interparty agreement on Swedish policy during the winter was however gradually superseded by a tendency toward more open disagreement during and after the parliamentary round of April–May 1936. This trend was due largely to frustration at the League's inability to prevent an Italian military victory, which in turn increased the political controversy over the government's extension (April 1936) of its authority to impose sanctions (*RP*, AK 1936, 22:8–35). Moreover, the government was weakening due to an unrelated domestic issue (pension reform) and was in fact well on its way toward a June resignation. Direct criticism of the League itself was much more marked, particularly from the Conservative and Agrarian benches, whereas the SAP government and Liberals generally refrained from taking a definite stance until the international situation was more clarified.

The debate was prompted by a 25 April interpellation by Bagge (*RP*, FK 1936, 27:39–41) for the government to clarify its position in the wake of the operation, particularly in light of the gap between the "high expressions and formal obligations, and on the other side, the naked reality" that Italian aggression had succeeded. The following month he specifically proposed a reduction in the League's authority on security issues, mainly through "a thorough reinvestigation (of Art. 16) which . . . must first be aimed at the abolition of the present sanctions system" (*RP*, FK 1936, 36:14–15). Even so, he favored other reforms geared to make the League a more effective, if limited institution, envisioning it as primarily a forum for international debate and as a means of strengthening international law on the basis of sovereign equality of all states; these points thus underscored the remaining Swedish unity on hopes for eventual League reform. On the other hand, the government was more equivocal as to Sweden's future obligations. While Sandler strongly (and quite naturally) defended Sweden's full application of the embargo, he was loathe to "draw any generalized conclusions on the effectiveness of economic sanctions in other cases." He would only rule out two extreme solutions for Swedish policy, either a "desperate withdrawal" from the League, or continuing as if nothing had happened. The Liberals meanwhile adopted a "wait and see" attitude (*RP*, FK 1936, 36:1–28).

The parties also differed on the question of reasserting Sweden's traditional neutrality in response to the League's decline. For example, the Conservatives and Agrarians were forthright on the need for Sweden to "fall back on its hard-won neutrality in situations which are forthcoming" (*RP*, FK 1936, 36:15; Bagge). Westman argued for greater isolationism: "so long as Sweden is left in the League of Nations, our country ought to observe neutrality in its old meaning . . . and our position in the League of Nations a . . . functional addition to this foundation" (*RP*, FK 1936, 36:26). Westman's views were also significant insofar as he would be named Sweden's foreign minister during a short-lived Agrarian minority government under Axel Pehrsson-Bramstorp in summer 1936 (the so-called *semesterregeringen*, or "ninety days" government), when Sweden would take its first substantive steps away from its League obligations.

However, for its part the government's deliberate suppression of neutrality during the crisis now gave way to uncertainty and confusion over whether, and how, to reassert neutrality in light of the League's decline. According to Sandler, neutrality could no longer be measured directly in terms of Sweden's international security obligations: "at the present time it is going through a strong process of fermentation, from which new contents will come but which nonetheless is still not crystallized" (*RP*, FK 1936, 36:10–12). He argued that a policy of isolated neutrality would no more guarantee Sweden's security than would remaining a League member, although he did support the idea of increasing collaboration with the other ex-neutral member states. Östen Undén, in rejecting Bagge's proposal to work for an abrogation of Art. 16, queried whether isolated neutrality was any solution for Sweden's situation, and even whether it was a valid formulation in its own right: "neutrality policy is . . . no formula which holds good for eternal time without reference to developments in other fields" (*RP*, FK 1936, 36:33). Thus Swedish officials evidently did not consider a reassertion of neutrality to be merely the direct inverse of League duties, and during 1936–37 neutrality was still considered reconcilable with a limited sanctions operation; as we shall see in chapter 5, this sharply contrasted with Switzerland's post-sanctions policy.

The government also signaled its intention to work for positive League reform through its assumption of a second nonpermanent Council seat in September 1936 after a decade-long absence, which it held until 1939. Sweden's delegate to the Committee of 28, Östen Undén, continued to argue that the security mechanism was not necessarily ill-construed, but that the organization lacked sufficient political and moral force to uphold its aims (*AKU* 1937:46–47). This attitude indicated a general refusal to accept the League's failure in 1935–36 as conclusive; on the contrary, it signaled a hope that the League would regain, perhaps even surpass, its earlier influence (Tingsten 1944, 239). The government also forwarded a number of concrete and useful suggestions for reforming the Covenant, as in its August 29 response to a League circular (sent in July) soliciting such suggestions.[24]

In 1937–38 the Swedish debate mirrored Margaret Doxey's point (1987, 31) that the post-sanctions League debate consisted mainly of sterile discussions over whether sanctions were obligatory or voluntary. The government's inability to articulate a clearcut sanctions policy paradoxically increased as the debate progressed, illustrated by the widespread confusion as to the extent of Sweden's League obligations during the Riksdag debates of May 1937 (*RP*, FK 1937, 33:19–25; AK, 34:51–57). The problem was directly attributable to the Hansson government itself, particularly Sandler (compounded by his notoriously vague and rhetorical style of speaking) to formulate a coherent League policy, even though the Social Democrats, along with their Agrarian allies, enjoyed a massive (236-seat) Riksdag majority after the September 1936 elections. Two points are worth noting. One, as indicated above, was the increasingly imprecise meaning of neutrality for Sweden. In the debates the term "neutrality" was used almost interchangeably with other circumlocutions such as "freedom of action," "freedom of alliances," and even "independent policy," with none used with much authority or precision (Tingsten 1944, 214–15). However, this obscurity could also be interpreted as a product of Sweden's lingering faith in collective security even during the League's decline.

On the second point, after mid-1936 the government tended to regard sanctions as not compulsory under all circumstances. The first indication of this attitude was through Sweden's association with the Geneva Declaration by seven smaller League states (the Nordic countries, Spain, Switzerland, and the Netherlands), which represented a collective expression of doubt as to the viability of Art. 16 (*OJ*, SS 154:18–20). At that time the government also completely ruled out the idea of compulsory military sanctions. In May 1937 Sweden attempted to increase its freedom of action further, by considering mutual assistance and the right of passage as military sanctions, hence optional (*RP*, FK 1937, 33:22–23; Undén). By the end of 1937 the government regarded Sweden as free from all mandatory obligations under Art. 16, including economic sanctions. In January 1938 Undén told the League's Committee of Twenty-Eight that Sweden regarded Art. 16 as "de facto suspended," since sanctions had not been used in many cases where warranted, and then only in an "incomplete and hesitating manner" (*AKU* 1938:8). Yet even this assertion did not indicate an outright refusal to participate in sanctions; it was only a frank declaration attesting to the League's own shortcomings. Sweden did not repudiate its League obligations; it merely recognized that the League had failed of its own accord.

The government's view of neutrality implied an increasingly political and security-related policy of state which could enable Sweden (and Scandinavia) to avoid a future war (La Ruche 1953, 53–59), accompanied by Nordic cooperation on security issues. This led to the ambitious (but unrealized) Stockholm Plan of January 1939, involving a revision of the 1921 Åland Convention and a joint Fenno-Swedish defense of the Åland islands in case of war. This point was in fact closely related to Sweden's refusal to repudiate Art. 16 altogether, since it considered the possibility of cooperating in sanctions in defense of one of its neighbors (especially Denmark or Finland). In May 1938 a Nordic statute of neutrality was enunciated (Podelford 1938, 789–93); and on 24 July the so-called Oslo Powers (the four Nordic and the three Low Countries) together asserted that "the system of sanctions has acquired a non-obligatory character, (which) applies not only to a particular group of states, but to all members of the League" (*OJ*, SS 183:38; Sandler).

As such, this was not a reversion to a Swiss-type isolated neutrality; on the contrary, it was evidence that the government desired to uphold basic League principles even while protecting Sweden's national security (Ørvik 1971, 187). For its part, the League (due to vetoes from France and the USSR) refused to recognize Sweden's unilateral proposal for an optional sanctions system in early 1938. Later (autumn 1938) these two states also rejected a Swedish proposal that neutrality "be considered fully compatible with a loyal interpretation of the duties of League members"(*AKU* 1938:26), which sharply contrasted with Switzerland's simultaneous success in obtaining special League recognition of its neutrality. Due to this failure, increasing demand for a formal release from sanctions obligations was voiced in Sweden, under the threat of withdrawal from the organization. The idea of repudiating the League altogether continued to be an issue amongst the Conservatives well into 1939,[25] though the SAP government continued to reject the idea.

NOTES

1. Particularly due to the devaluation of the krona in 1932, and increased public works projects instituted by the Social Democrats. See *World Economic Survey*, 1935–36, pp. 136–37; *Monetary Review*, 1935–36, pp. 164–65.

2. In a speech of 3 May 1935, Sandler stated that "governments should retain the right to choose the path of neutrality" (*DIA*, 1937, vol. 1, p. 159); see also La Ruche, 1953, p. 53.

3. "Kungl. Maj:ts Proposition no. 90," *BRP*, 1 Saml. 10 Band år 1920, pp. 1–244. This document also included the Scandinavian draft Convention of 1918, addended to Prop. 90, 1920, pp. 224–42, and summarized in Würtemburg, 1923, pp. 210–13; and in Jones, 1939, pp. 37–40.

For Sweden's instructions to its delegation at the Crillon Conference, see Prop. 90, 1920, pp. 18, 156–62; also Miller, 1928, vol. 2, pp. 592–645, Doc. 25; and Trygger, 1923, pp. 430–33.

4. The government added that sanctions would probably be impossible to realize in practice against a distant power, and were unrealistic and even dangerous when applied against a neighboring great power (Munch 1923, p. 176; Trygger 1923, p. 430; Prop. 90, 1920, p. 56). It also held that a blockade against a nonmember would be inconsistent with the prevailing principles of international law (Prop. 90, 1920, pp. 84–98, esp. p. 93).

5. At Crillon Sweden had argued that, for states not voting for military sanctions, such measures would remain optional (Munch 1923, p. 175); and it fully assumed its own military freedom of action in the 1920 bill (Prop. 90, 1920, p. 111). See also Miller 1928, vol. 2, pp. 308, 643.

6. See Prop. 90, 1920, pp. 98–102, and Annex 8, pp. 202–12 (Chief of the General Staff); and pp. 102–5 (Chief of the Naval Forces).

7. In addition, from the outset Sweden, unlike Switzerland, determined that no constitutional addition pertaining to League accession was necessary; Särskilda Utskottets Utlåtande no. 1 (1920), *BRP*, 11 Saml., pp. 13–14; also *RP*, FK, 1920, no. 19, pp. 23–4 (Adelswärd); and Bellquist, 1929, p. 281.

On the other hand, Swedish neutrality remained possible in an "allowed" war (Prop. 90, 1920, p. 62).

8. *RP*, FK, 1920, no. 13, pp. 18–23 (Lindhagen); AK, 1920, no. 18, pp. 4–11 (Vennerström).

9. For the Conservatives' views, see *RP*, FK, 1920, no. 18, p. 16 (Trygger); also their minority report in the Riksdag's Committee of 24 on 1 March 1920, Särskilda Utskottets Utlåtande no. 1 (1920), *BRP*, 11 Saml., pp. 25–43; also in Trygger, 1923, pp. 434–39.

10. The votes were: 152–67 in the Lower Chamber (*RP*, AK, 1920, no. 24, p. 24); and 86–47 in the Upper Chamber (*RP*, FK, 1920, no. 20, pp. 60–1).

11. See *RP*, FK, 1925, no. 3, pp. 7–8, 30 (Trygger); p. 9 (Ekman); p. 14 (Unddén); and AK, 1925, no. 4, pp. 6–7, 89–90 (Lindman); also see "Rapport du Comité d'Experts chargé par le gouvernement Suédois de l'Examen du Protocole dit le Genève," 1925, esp. pp. 120–25. The government's main fear was a possible new obligation to apply military sanctions.

12. Indeed it was a Conservative government which not only proposed acceptance of the General Act, but even helped draft it; Kungl. Maj:ts Prop. no. 108 ar 1929; KU 1929, no. 8; *RP*, FK, 1929, no. 19, pp. 102–13, esp. 102–3 (Foreign Minister Trygger).

13. *SFS* 1935, no. 537, pp. 1107–9; see also Sweden's letter of 18 October 1935 to the League declaring its acceptance of Proposal I; *OJ*, SS no. 150, pp. 261, 262–64.

14. After Britain, Czechoslovakia, France, and the United States. During 1935 Sweden exported a total of nearly \$3.3m worth of arms, or some 7.7 percent of the world's total arms trade (RIIA, 1938, p. 25, table).

15. *SFS* 1935, no. 551, p. 1175. The measure took effect on 31 October. See also *OJ*, SS no. 150, pp. 264, 266.

16. *SFS* 1935, no. 562, p. 1216. See also Sweden's letter of 4 November; *OJ*, SS no. 150, Coord. Comm. Doc. 82/q, comm. no. 9, p. 265.

17. See *OJ*, SS no. 150, p. 270. The official bill (Kungl. Maj:ts Prop. no. 67 år 1936) was deposited on 7 February, and the Legal Committee expressed its opinion on it on 2 April 1936; Lagrådets utlåtande no. 29; *RP*, AK, 1936, no. 22, p. 7.

18. *SFS* 1936, no. 123, pp. 191–92. For an English translation, see *OJ*, SS no. 150, pp. 271–72. Although the law was set to expire on 28 February 1937, it was revoked in August 1936 after the League recommended the lifting of sanctions against Italy.

19. *SFS* 1936, no. 139, p. 231. It took effect on 1 May and, as with law no. 123, its expiration date of 28 February 1937 was cut short, in August 1936.

20. These figures are taken from *SKM*, vol. 23, no. 18 (30 September 1936), pp. 646–51; and vol. 23, nos. 15–16 (August 1936), p. 574); *SOS*, Handel, Berättelse för år 1936, pp. 100, 452–54.

21. *SKM*, vol. 23, nos. 15–16 (August 1936), pp. 574–79; and vol. 23, no. 18 (September 1936), pp. 646–51; *SOS*, Handel, Berättelse för år 1936 av Kommerskollegium, pp. 452–53.

22. Done through decrees of 8 July 1936: *SFS* 1936, no. 455, p. 855, removing the prohibition on credits; and no. 456, p. 856, removing the import and partial export ban. Both entered into force on 15 July.

23. KU Utlåtande no. 308, 1936, p. 1; and the ensuing debate in *RP*, FK, 1936, no. 10; AK, 1936, no. 10.

24. *OJ*, SS no. 154, pp. 18–20; also NFs Sjuttonde Ordinarie Möte, Aktstycken, 1936, pp. 119–21; *RP*, UU no. 4, 1937, p. 7.

25. See for example the Foreign Affairs Committee report of spring 1938, which contained four dissenting (Conservative) members; *RP*, UU utlåtande no. 5 år 1938, pp. 8–9, reservations by Hammarskjöld, Domö, Bagge, and Andersson. Also *RP*, FK, 1938, no. 40, pp. 33–87; and *RP*, AK, 1938, no. 41, pp. 13–41. Even some Liberals and Social Democrats held this view: *RP*, FK, 1938, no. 4; *RP*, AK, 1938, no. 4.

5

Switzerland and the Italian Operation

The Swiss government's position relative to the Italo-Abyssinian crisis was particularly sensitive due to the two separate aspects of the general conflict discussed in chapter 3: the war itself and the sanctions operation that followed. Unlike Sweden, which from the start ruled out neutrality in any form, this distinction was very important to the Swiss government in determining the extent of its compliance with the League's operation. In connection with the African war, the Federal Council considered itself obligated to apply the Hague rules of neutrality and to adopt an impartial stance, since the League in 1920 had guaranteed the continuation of Switzerland's military neutrality as a League member. Yet on the other hand, Switzerland's League membership compelled it to forgo all notions of equal treatment and act in solidarity with the participant states. These two conflicting factors created an acute dilemma for the Swiss government in its attempts to balance its neutrality with a demonstration of international solidarity, and resulted in an amalgamated Swiss response encompassing only partial adherence to each of its sets of responsibilities.

FACTORS INFLUENCING THE SWISS ATTITUDE

From the start Switzerland's difficulties in the crisis were greatly complicated by its historically close relations with Italy. Most League member states (including Sweden) had little to fear from an embargo against Italy, due to their generally insignificant levels of trade with it and their geographical distance from the region in dispute. The scenario was, however, fundamentally different for the Swiss, due to what their foreign minister, Giuseppe Motta, called

Switzerland's "truly exceptional situation in the present conflict" in a special letter (28 October) to the League's secretary-general (*OJ*, SS 150:272). The Swiss government's technical advisor on League matters, Walther Stucki, pointed to three general but significant circumstances particularly facing Switzerland in the conflict: (1) its geographical proximity to the great power being embargoed; (2) the existence of a large Italian-speaking minority within Switzerland; and (3) the necessity of promulgating official Swiss decrees in the Italian language (Italian being one of three official languages of the Swiss Confederation) (*OJ*, SS 145:108–9).

In his representations to the initial meeting of the Committee of Eighteen on 11 October (*OJ*, SS 145:41), Motta particularly stressed the importance of the long common border separating the two countries to the south and east, which in several places favors Italo-Swiss communications. The easternmost Swiss canton of Graubünden sweeps to the southeast in three separate valleys, each of which extends into Italy's physical territory; of the 160,000 residents of canton Ticino, some 35,000 were Italian citizens and most of the rest Italian-speaking Swiss; and canton Valais also borders Italy in the south (although the Monte Rosa alpine chain in the Upper Valais precludes normal land transportation between the two countries in that region). Motta thus argued that this proximity, and particularly the common linguistic heritage, increased the risk for Switzerland in particular.

These geographical and cultural ties had also fostered close commercial and financial links between the two countries, which suggested that a severance of most or all of Swiss trade with Italy would threaten Switzerland's own economic and even political security. Switzerland's situation in this specific crisis in fact largely paralleled the conditions which originally facilitated the development of its permanent neutrality: its centrally located, acutely exposed position in the heart of Europe, adjacent to the major European powers and heavily dependent on economic interaction with them. The importance of Italian commerce to Swiss economic life was particularly strong due to their long common border and to Switzerland's strategic position astride several of the major Alpine passes linking Germany with Italy. This factor had intensified in importance after the conclusion of the tripartite Gotthard Convention of 13 October 1909 between Italy, Germany, and Switzerland, which legally bound the Swiss government to protect the flow of north-south trade through the St. Gotthard Pass (*SIA* 1936, 2:87).

Furthermore, the cultural and linguistic ties between Italian-speaking parts of Switzerland and Italy had fostered the growth of numerous Swiss firms, many based in the Lugano region, with subsidiaries in Italy. These transnational commercial linkages had led to significant crossborder migration of Swiss and especially Italian nationals, accounting for the thirty-five thousand Italian citizens living in the Ticino alone, with others commuting daily from Varese and Como to jobs in Lugano and Chiasso. In addition, the Swiss banking system was a key repository of Italian gold stocks, which further exposed the Swiss role during the crisis itself.

TABLE 5-1
Swiss-Italian Annual Trade, 1933-36

Year	Total Swiss Imports from Italy (in millions SwFrs) (1)	% of Total Swiss Imports (2)	Total Swiss Exports to Italy (in millions SwFrs) (3)	% of Total Swiss Exports (4)	Overall Trade Balance (in millions SwFrs) (5)
1933	133.8	8.39	80.1	9.40	- 53.7
1934	116.1	8.09	76.1	9.01	- 40.0
1935	91.3	7.11	72.8	8.93	- 18.5
1936	83.5	6.59	61.6	6.99	- 21.9

Source: *Statistique Mensuelle du Commerce extérieur de la Suisse*, 1933-36, Appendice: Tableau Annuel (Berne: Publie par la direction général des douanes fédérales, 1934-37), pp. 190-91 (1934); 190-91 (1935); 192-93 (1936); 198 (1937).

Official League statistics corroborated the Swiss government's repeated claims that its economic health, already tenuous, would suffer through participation in a blockade of Italian commerce. According to the sub-committee on economic measures established by the League's Secretariat, Switzerland was Italy's second largest trading partner within the League (and fourth largest overall), more significant even than France; in 1934 its share of Italy's total exports was 8.11 percent, compared with 11.5 percent to the United Kingdom and 7.7 percent to France, although Germany at 12.1 percent and the US at 9 percent ranked higher in importance (*OJ*, SS 145:95). Italy, meanwhile, was Switzerland's third largest supplier (well below Germany and France); and Switzerland was the fourth largest supplier of goods to Italy (after Germany, France, and the UK).[1] That said, however, table 5-1 (cols. 1–4) indicates that the flow of Italo-Swiss trade had decreased during the period of 1933–35 (immediately prior to sanctions), in both directions, and both in gross amount and percentage terms; the decline was probably due to the continued contraction of overall economic activity in Switzerland during this period (see table 5-1).

The significance of these Italo-Swiss commercial and financial linkages can be further gauged in relation to Switzerland's weak overall economic performance during the early and mid-1930s. The country's traditionally liberal free-trade policy, necessitated by its dearth of indigenous raw materials, had been endangered by the European drift toward economic protectionism and autarky since 1930 to mitigate the effects of the worldwide depression. The League's Economic Intelligence Service corroborated the detrimental effects of the economic depression in Switzerland, which indeed were more severe there than in most other European countries due to the consequences of the prolonged application of a deflationary monetary and fiscal policy. Unlike most other states, where expansionist economic strategies helped offset the worst of the economic downturn, Switzerland during the same period experienced a continuing contraction in economic activity, high interest rates, high and rising unemployment, and severe budgetary and trade imbalances; these problems were exacerbated by Switzerland's refusal (prior to 1936) to leave the old Gold Bloc and devalue its currency *(World Economic Survey* 1935–36, 136, 297). All this contributed to a temporary but destabilizing flight from the Swiss franc and the withdrawal of foreign bank deposits on an unprecedented scale during the second quarter of 1935 (during which time Swiss gold reserves fell by SwFr 513m) in the run-up to the so-called "Crisis Initiative" of 2 June 1935. This initiative, a Socialist (and widely considered inflationary) proposal to raise a large state loan for financing various public projects, was defeated in referendum, thereby stemming the outflow of currency from Switzerland and setting a precedent for future economic policy *(Monetary Review* 1935–36, 68). These factors clearly predisposed Switzerland against the adoption of any measures which would place additional burden on its economic performance.

Yet another factor for Switzerland was the traditionally close political relationship between the two states. Although normalized at the end of World War I, Italo-Swiss relations became increasingly strained by the 1930s, due to outright Italian provocation. Most of Italy's demands centered on the status of the Ticino, the southernmost (and only entirely Italian-speaking) Swiss canton. The Ticino was hardly a disputed border area (such as, for example, the Alto Adige, formerly the Austrian South Tyrol and since 1919 a German-speaking part of Italy; indeed, it had joined Switzerland through forced annexation as early as 1478, and thereafter had remained loyal to the Confederation (Steinberg 1976, 9). The Swiss therefore grew uneasy over Italy's insistent claims that the area was a natural part of greater Italy. In 1921 the Italian government began offering special scholarships to Swiss Ticinese students to study in Italy, and distributing school cartographical maps including Swiss-Italian regions as part of Italian territory; and in the debate in the Italian Chamber of Deputies of 21 June 1921, the Fascist deputy (Mussolini) declared that Italian unification would be incomplete until the Ticino was officially incorporated (Bonjour 1978, 97).

These political difficulties were temporarily ameliorated by the conclusion in 1924 of an Italo-Swiss bilateral Treaty of Conciliation and Judicial Settlement of Conflicts, which Motta had praised as a model instrument for the pacific resolution of international disputes, and Mussolini as a treaty effective "in perpetuity." Swiss officials even proclaimed Italo-Swiss relations as a model for two states with differing social and political systems (Rigonalli 1983, 146). However, relations became strained further during the latter half of the 1920s, as a result of numerous minor crises (border incidents, the temporary detention of Swiss journalists based in Italy, the prevention of liberal Ticinese societies from meeting on Italian soil). Another serious problem was the increasing level of activity by indigenous fascist groups in Switzerland, fed by cultural propaganda and the secret flow of illicit funds from Italy (supporting such publications as the journal *Adula*), encouraging irredentist claims in Switzerland (Rigonalli 1983, 145). Motta first met Mussolini in Rome in 1934 during the Holy Year celebrations and insisted that Switzerland would not tolerate any overt threats to its neutrality and sovereignty (Bonjour 1970: III, 153–54). However, this merely increased Italy's intransigence, and from that point the incorporation of the Ticino became a stated aim of Italian foreign policy (Bonjour 1978, 97–98); nonetheless Italy's primary security concern lay to the east of Switzerland, particularly to the Brenner Pass in Austria.

Italy also criticized the Swiss authorities for what it described as Swiss "oppression" of 45,000 Romansch (an ancient Latin-based dialect) speakers in the eastern canton of Graubünden. These problems arising from their common linguistic heritage were not merely transitory; partly due to the continuing Italian threat to Switzerland's territorial and cultural integrity, the Swiss government in February 1938 established Romansch as the fourth national (though not official) language of Switzerland through a constitutional addition (Art. 116) (Wiskemann 1967, 273–74).

Due to these overt threats from the south, Switzerland remained conspicuously silent during the League debates on the Italo-Abyssinian dispute during the autumn of 1935. League historian F. P. Walters (1952, 650–51) asserts that only Spain and Switzerland, of all the states previously expected to support League action against Italy, declined to adopt a clear stand. There is in fact evidence suggesting that the Federal Council, in the immediate prewar period, actively opposed the growing movement within the League Assembly to sanction Italy in case of war (Stettler 1977, 224–26). This attitude was indicated through incriminating private correspondence between Giuseppe Motta and the Swiss minister in Rome (Wagnière) in July 1935, in which Motta accepted the view that Italy had a right to pursue economic and political expansion in Abyssinia (Rigonalli 1983, 151).

The Swiss particularly feared the possible escalation of a limited embargo into overt League military intervention (*BS*, CN 1936:599). Military sanctions would not only risk direct Swiss involvement and threaten its neutrality, but such an operation would moreover be directed from the League's headquarters on Swiss territory, against a neighboring state. Swiss Defense Minister Rudolf Minger even argued that economic sanctions alone could lead to war with Italy (Stettler 1977, 220). The Swiss thus began to regard the Covenant's distinction between military and economic sanctions, earlier so clear and apparently protective, to be increasingly artificial and dangerous (Zahler 1936, 756–57); they feared a slow but inextricable involvement in hostilities against a great-power neighbor with whom it was vital to retain at least passably good relations, particularly with Germany threatening from the north. Their exposed situation was also reflected in Minger's activism for a stronger Swiss defense policy, which resulted in public approval, through a mid-1935 referendum, of an increase in the defense budget to SwFr 235 m. Switzerland's reticence in the dispute therefore reflected both present and future concerns: probable damage to the Swiss economy resulting directly from participation in an economic blockade, and also a possible future involvement in actual hostilities.

THE INITIAL SWISS RESPONSE TO SANCTIONS

These various concerns were well reflected in the Swiss government's equivocal initial response to the crisis. On the one hand, its first reaction to the Council's designation of Italian aggression (5 October), which paved the way for the implementation of sanctions, was to declare itself bound to the Council's determination:

The Swiss delegation . . . has tacitly associated itself with the findings of the States Members of the Council. This opens the way to the sanctions provided for by Article 16 of the Covenant. . . . The Swiss Confederation will not fail in its duty of solidarity with the other Members of the League of Nations. Respect for undertakings assumed and the observation of treaties freely concluded are maxims which, so far as it is concerned, admit of no discussion. Its policy has always been and will always be honorable, clear and straightforward. (*OJ*, SS 138:106; FF 1935, 2:927–28)

This statement strongly implied that the government accepted, in principle, the obligation to apply any economic and financial measures which the League might impose against Italy. In addition, Motta also implied that Switzerland's consequent participation in a limited sanctions operation was fully consistent with its status as a neutral member of the League:

Hitherto, no one, apart from one of the parties directly concerned, has alluded to sanctions involving the use of force in the strict sense of that term. The Swiss delegation takes note of this important fact. The other category of sanctions is that of economic and financial sanctions. By their nature and purpose, such sanctions are not designed to be and, in our eyes do not constitute hostile acts. They aim at exercising moral, and particularly, material pressure on one of the parties in order to induce it to restore peace. (*OJ*, SS 138:106–7; FF 1935, 2:928)

These assertions seemed to indicate that the government accepted the view that the situation did not warrant an impartial attitude. Despite the clarity of this initial statement, however, the Federal Council then proceeded to assert that the Confederation's traditional status of neutrality would be the guiding principle for Swiss policy in the crisis:

The limits of our obligations are determined by our neutrality, which, in our opinion, constitutes a fundamental principle and at the same time a vital interest. We do not consider ourselves bound to take part in sanctions which, by their nature and effect, would expose our neutrality to real dangers—dangers which we must judge in the full exercise of our sovereignty. (*OJ*, SS 138:106)

Motta's lengthy statement quickly betrayed a latent "conflict of conscience" between two equally desirable aims: defending Swiss neutrality and fulfilling its League obligations (Bonjour 1978, 99). His assertion that economic and financial sanctions by their nature "do not constitute hostile acts" seemed tantamount to admitting that they were compatible with neutrality. Also Switzerland, along with Sweden, associated itself with the League's operation through its acceptance of membership on the smaller Committee of Eighteen, which actually formulated the sanctions recommendations. This position was however contradicted by Switzerland's declared intention to avoid all sanctions that "would expose our neutrality to real dangers," which suggested only partial acquiescence in the League's operation. These conflicting signals tended to confuse rather than clarify the Federal Council's position in the crisis, despite Motta's insistence that the statement of 9 October was the result of "repeated examination and reflection" (*BS*, CN 1936:648).

The Swiss government did not immediately clarify the ambiguities of Motta's 9 October statement, due to its delay in responding to the League's first request for information on applying the embargo. The stated reason for this delay was a problem in determining which branch of government, the Federal Council (according to Art. 102 [8 & 9] of the Swiss constitution) or the Federal Assembly (according to Art. 85[6]) had ultimate constitutional authority to formulate Switzerland's League policy. The Swiss parliament debated this issue at length in January 1936, indicating that a lack of political unity continued to hinder the formulation of a clearcut sanctions policy by the government (*BS*, CN 1936, 602–55). Even so, this delay seemed clearly to be tactical, and it probably reflected official indecision on the sanctions question. Notably, later (in its December 1935 report to parliament on the dispute), the Federal Council back-tracked on this point, asserting that "the circumstances were not, in our view, of a nature which would justify a convocation of the Federal Assembly in an extraordinary session"(*FF* 1935, 2:948).

The government's initial hesitation was also partly attributable to the equivocal personal attitude of the influential, long-time foreign minister, Motta, who was primarily responsible for formulating and articulating Switzerland's position throughout the conflict. Any discussion of Swiss policy during this period must begin with and revolve around Motta's position, because of his high domestic and international profile; indeed subsequent to the crisis Motta felt obliged to deny insinuations that Swiss policy had been his own personal creation (*BS*, CN 1937, 126). His competing loyalties in the dispute—specifically his genuine desire to uphold the Covenant's principles, Switzerland's neutral tradition, and its close ties with Italy simultaneously—all contributed to the political disunity which arose over Swiss policy in the crisis. Although Motta, in his dual capacity since 1920 as both Swiss foreign minister and League delegate had attained the reputation as a strong, occasionally eloquent defender of the principles of the Covenant, the fact remained that he was a Swiss-Italian from the Ticino (formerly an Airolo innkeeper), and, moreover, a staunch Catholic. In that capacity he made no attempt to hide his cultural sympathy for Italy, at one point even calling the embargo "vulgar" (*BS*, CE 1936, 34–35), notwithstanding his occasionally ostentatious praise of both Britain and France,[2] his fluency in both their languages, and his proclivity for speaking officially in French rather than Italian. It would seem rather more difficult to argue that his cultural ties to Italy translated directly in political favoritism, although Christopher Hughes asserts that even his commitment to the precepts of liberal democracy were suspect (1975, 162). These factors suggest that Switzerland's assertions of neutrality were not only based on valid legal obligations; they also appeared as a deliberately ambiguous posture designed to limit punishment of Italy as much as possible.

There were, furthermore, earlier indications that Motta did not regard Abyssinia as an equal League partner. For example, in 1923 he had recommended (in vain) that Abyssinia's impending entry into the League be postponed due to its "underdeveloped social state" (*BS*, CN 1936, 649). Although Britain and several other states had voiced similar arguments (due to lingering slave practices in the territory), this position was clearly inconsistent with his continual and outspoken advocacy of universal League membership.

This point was also related to the complex and rather indeterminate nature of Italo-Swiss political relations during the crisis itself. The Swiss government was subjected to verbal abuse from Italian authorities from the moment it assented to the League's determination that Italy was the aggressor, including a direct threat from Mussolini that he would refuse to recognize Swiss neutrality any longer (Bonjour 1978, 99). The Italians demanded in return that the Swiss adopt the same attitude as Austria, Hungary, and Albania (the three states which refused to apply sanctions outright), even though Switzerland did not ideologically support the Italian fascist régime as did these others.

It remained, of course, difficult to gauge the degree of sincerity in Mussolini's veiled and obscure threats of reprisal, as well as the extent to which they influenced Swiss policy. However, this threat apparently referred only to Switzerland's attitude toward a possible future extension of the embargo (particularly the oil sanction) and not to the original measures imposed. In private exchanges between Swiss officials and the new Italian minister in Bern, Tamaro (who replaced Dino Marchi at the outset of the crisis in October 1935), the Italian government was in fact considerably more congenial than Mussolini's blustering otherwise suggested (Rigonalli 1983, 152–53); and later, Motta freely told the Swiss *Ständerat* that "Italy at no point considered our attitude inamicable" (*BS*, CE 1936, 34). Nonetheless, throughout 1935–36 the Swiss Federal Council reported numerous minor incidents including border violations and injudicious activity by Italian journalists in Switzerland, which worsened the political atmosphere between the two countries; at one point the Federal Council protested to the Italian government "to put an end to this campaign directed against the integrity of our country" (*RCF* 1936, 77–78). And surely the fears of Italian retaliation expressed by both French and British officials were even more justified in the Swiss case. Due to this vague politico-military threat, the Swiss government held that Italian policy potentially jeopardized Switzerland's political as well as economic well-being. Thereafter the government's overriding, and fully comprehensible, aim was to facilitate the general aim of the League's operation (to reduce Italy's capacity to conduct its military campaign), while simultaneously limiting the damage to Switzerland itself as much as possible.

SWITZERLAND'S PRE-1935 SANCTIONS POLICY AS A FACTOR

Switzerland's equivocal position during the Italian affair was also largely attributable to the peculiar nature of its pre-1935 relations with the League, whereby it gradually retreated from its initially favorable attitude. From the start the Federal Council (led by the foreign policy inner sanctum of President Gustav Ador, Economics Minister Edmund Schulthess, and above all Foreign Minister Felix Calonder) waged an uncommonly vigorous campaign to secure Switzerland's accession.[3] However, it also emphasized the need to secure League guarantees of protection of the sovereignty of member states, from as early as the March 1919 Crillon neutrals' conference (Miller 1928, vol. 2, Doc. 25, 45).

In its important August 1919 message formally proposing Switzerland's accession, the government in fact endorsed Swiss entry with no neutrality reservations, coupled with an express refusal to participate in all League military activity.[4] Indeed it considered economic sanctions to be fully compatible with neutrality; moreover, this acceptance of economic sanctions (even more unqualified than the Swedish government's) was regarded as a necessary bow to the principle of international solidarity.[5] The government in fact asserted that League membership would mean "a whole-sale departure from the neutral policy hitherto followed by us" (1919 League Message, 40). It held, with reason, that Switzerland's continued credibility could only be ensured through the precise establishment of its position in advance: participation in all economic sanctions and abstention from all military sanctions. This position would thereby "form an absolutely constant factor in strategic calculations" (1919 League Message, 127), and also would eliminate the possibility of a gradual acquiescence in a sanctions operation (41).

This straightforward official position was, however, subsequently undermined by significant opposition from the Federal Assembly as well as from different political factions in the referendum campaign. Even while generously approving the general proposition for Swiss membership (128–43 and 33–6 in the two chambers), the Assembly opposed the specific terms of (Swiss) accession, on two points. First, it assumed the task of nominating and instructing the Swiss delegation to the League, which directly threatened the Federal Council's constitutional policymaking authority. Second, it hinged its consent upon the entry of all five major powers (known as the "American clause," after the only remaining main power nonsignatory).[6] These conditions were later dropped or modified, but only after the Federal Council had stiffened its attitude toward the League, specifically by requesting a special League dispensation for Swiss neutrality, to placate the domestic opposition.

The League Council fully complied with the Swiss request for special recognition of its neutrality through its important Declaration of London of February 1920. The Council, even while confirming the general principle that a policy of neutrality was incompatible with League membership, "recognizes that Switzerland is in a unique situation, based on a tradition of several centuries, which has been explicitly incorporated into the Law of Nations," a status which had also been reiterated through Art. 435 of the Versailles Treaty. On this basis the League formally exempted Switzerland from all obligations to apply League military (but not economic) sanctions:

Switzerland recognizes and proclaims the duties of joint liability ... including therein the duty of co-operating in economic and financial measures ... against a convenant-breaking state ... but will not be obliged to take part in any military action or to allow the passage of foreign troops or the preparation of military operations within her territory. (*OJ*, March 1920, 2:57–58)

The Declaration had crucial consequences for Switzerland's entire policy orientation as a League member, and indeed it formed the crux of a curious paradox for Swiss policy. The intention was to establish the basis for Switzerland's shift from "integral" to "differential" neutrality, and thereby to bridge the dilemma between neutrality and League membership; however, it actually reinforced rather than relaxed the neutrality/sanctions problem for Switzerland, by strengthening its resolve to defend its traditional neutrality even as a League member. Whereas it seemingly ruled out the possibility of Swiss equivocation by establishing its prior course of action in crises, in fact it predisposed the government to adopt an ad hoc, case-by-case method of examining the major issues before the organization, judging each situation carefully in order to determine whether taking a stand would conflict with its guaranteed neutral status; if it suggested a dilemma, Swiss abstention almost invariably followed. This attitude tended to prevent the formulation of a coherent overall strategy toward contentious League issues.

Moreover, the Declaration sowed the seeds of a discernible gap between word and deed, whereby the government was unable to back up its utterances of international solidarity with concrete steps toward its realization. Switzerland remained hesitant to adopt an active political role within the League; for example, it never agreed (unlike Sweden) to serve on the League Council in a nonpermanent capacity, despite its favorable position and high profile as host country for the organization (headquartered in Geneva). The government showed this reluctance in a number of specific situations: in its hesitating position during the Vilna dispute of 1920–21, when it eventually refused to allow an international contingent to cross its territory en route to supervise a League plebiscite there; in its subsequent attempts to associate itself with the efforts within the League to restrict the applicability of Art. 16; through its abstention on the draft Treaty of Mutual Assistance in 1922; through its rejection of the 1928 draft Treaty of Financial Assistance to Victims of Aggression; and especially by its refusal to participate (and moreover its unusual prevention of Swiss nationals from participating) in the work of the League's preparatory commission for the Saar plebiscite in 1934.[7]

Another key factor impinging on the government's ability, and will, to cooperate with League activities was the strong and continuing public hostility toward the League. Indeed the League issue engendered profound differences of political opinion within Switzerland, and the League was opposed by elements on both left and right while favored by the "soft center." One major source of hostility was the Socialist Party, the largest parliamentary faction following the 1919 elections, which remained implacably opposed to the League until Soviet entry in 1934 (Masnata 1963, 127). Moreover the bitter legacy of the 1918 general strike, instigated by the Socialists (with the support of the major Bolshevik leaders exiled in Switzerland until 1917 [Senn 1971]) left many Swiss with a profoundly anti-socialist, antiforeign, and even xenophobic attitude, paradoxically at the very time when the League was being established to promote international solidarity. Most of the other parties however were deeply split on the issue, and in fact most of the opposition was culturally based rather than (political) party-based, which revealed the existence of much deep-seated, structural opposition to the League, and even to the very notion of international political cooperation. As a result, much of the anti-League campaign was conducted as an emotional polemic against all forms of international activity, in contrast to the generally reasoned Swedish debate; these ingrained attitudes also proved much harder to eradicate in subsequent years.

Several lines of cleavage divided the Swiss polity on the League issue. The most prominent of these was the linguistic (French vs. German) division, partly a legacy of the serious divide (*graben*) which developed within Switzerland during World War I, threatening its political unity and even wartime neutrality. Many Swiss-Germans opposed the League due to the allegedly harsh treatment of Germany in the Versailles Treaty and its exclusion from League membership; not surprisingly, the Swiss-German population was also most inclined to defend Switzerland's integral neutrality against League encroachment. In vivid contrast, the great majority of French- and Italian-speaking Swiss were highly favorable to League membership.[8] A second element of national division was confessional, due to the suspicion of many of the *Katholisch-Konservativ* (K-K) forces, particularly in the old Swiss heartland of the *Waldstätte*, or "Forest Cantons," that the League was inherently liberal and anticlerical. Thus the religious cleavage was in turn related to a third basis of profound division, the localist/centralist divide, whereby the smaller, rural (and generally conservative) cantons tended to oppose the League both for its centralist tendencies and for its seeming threat as a foreign institution with coercive powers, especially one stationed on Swiss territory; this was particularly the case with the rural peasantry, whom one deputy (Herr Müller) described accurately as "the great mass of silent adversaries" (quoted in Rappard 1923, 404).

Due to these many elements of national division, the Swiss project for adhesion (including the very favorable terms of accession granted by the League: express recognition of its neutrality, exemption from military sanctions, and designation of Geneva as the host city) was nearly defeated in the 1920 referendum. Though popular approval was more than sufficient—the proposition was supported by 56.3 percent, or 416,870 votes to 323,719 opposed—the issue was nearly defeated at the cantonal level (eleven and one-half to ten and one-half), with the peculiar circumstance that a shift of only two hundred votes in the small half-canton of Appenzell Ausser-Rhoden would have defeated the entire League project. This result clearly indicated the strong undercurrent of domestic Swiss hostility to the acceptance of new international obligations. Moreover, popular control over Swiss foreign policy was extended the very next year (1921) through an important extension of the system of semidirect democracy to provide, for the first time, for an optional referendum on certain international treaties, through a revision of Art. 89(4) of the federal constitution (Mowat 1923–24, 93). The government's subsequent caution on important League issues, particularly those relating to the enforcement weapon, was largely attributable to this widespread, ingrained hostility toward the League idea.

SWITZERLAND AND THE ARMS EMBARGO DEBATE (PROPOSAL I)

The dilemma inherent in Switzerland's stated intent to act in solidarity with the League even while maintaining its neutrality in the crisis was clearly revealed through its response to the League's initial measure (11 October), the arms embargo against Italy:

The Government of the Confederation has decided to prohibit, as from October 31st, 1935, the exportation, re-exportation and transit to Ethiopia and to Italy of the categories of arms, munitions, and implements of war. . . . In view of Article 9 of the Hague Convention of October 18th 1907, concerning the rights and duties of neutral Powers and persons in case of land warfare, and in view of our Statute of Neutrality, we cannot forgo the embargo on arms, munitions, and implements of war destined for Ethiopia. (*OJ*, SS 150:272)

The official decrees implementing these measures were promulgated the following day in the Swiss legal code.[9]

Switzerland's dual embargo against both belligerents was applied also by another neutral member state, Luxembourg;[10] also the United States, under recent neutrality legislation, applied basically the same measure, as did Germany. In itself, this decision indisputably accorded with a strict interpretation of Hague Convention V of 1907, since the Italo-Abyssinian conflict constituted a "war" by all definitions of the term. The government indeed held that this dual prohibition was not only permitted by the laws of neutrality, but was even required by the League's Declaration of London of 1920, which had guaranteed Switzerland's military neutrality.

On this point differences of opinion arose over how the arms embargo should be classified. The Swiss foreign minister held for example that Switzerland was "neutral in the military sphere and in those subjects which were closely akin thereto" (*OJ*, SS 146:36); hence he apparently regarded the arms embargo as a military sanction, which allowed for an assertion of the duties of neutrality. On the other hand, as discussed in chapter 3, the Italo-Abyssinian war hardly seemed conducive to an invocation of the Hague rules, being undeclared and involving a straightforward violation by one of the parties of both the League Covenant and the Kellogg-Briand Pact. Nearly all the delegations at Geneva agreed that the laws of neutrality were irrelevant in a limited sanctions operation (Gihl 1938, 70). In addition, the arms embargo was not a military sanction in the precise meaning of the Covenant, since it called for no armed enforcement action by member states, and particularly since Britain and France continually ruled out all possibility of individual or collective military retaliation. Even more importantly, the Swiss government itself had recently set a precedent for participating in an international arms embargo in contravention of the Hague neutrality rules; only the previous year (1934), during the Chaco War between Bolivia and Paraguay, Switzerland had acted in full conformity with the League, by first levying a dual embargo against both states, then unilaterally lifting it against Bolivia while maintaining it against Paraguay when the latter refused to adhere to a Council recommendation to resolve the dispute.[11]

Switzerland's decision on Proposal I aroused a storm of League criticism, partly because fifty-two of the fifty-four member states accepted it, which tended to isolate the Swiss position. The general hostility also stemmed in part from the manner in which the Swiss measure was implemented, whereby the only *unilateral* Swiss action was to embargo arms to Ethiopia, which directly contravened the spirit of Proposal I. The Swiss dual embargo thus gave the unfortunate impression that, under the guise of a strictly impartial attitude,

Swiss policy would in fact unilaterally harm the Ethiopian cause in a patently unneutral manner—by aiding a state in conflict with the League—thus contradicting a long-standing element of Swiss foreign policy (Miller 1928, 1:304).

In League debate, the French delegate Coulondre held that Switzerland's legal argument based on the Hague Conventions "ran counter to Art. 16 of the Covenant, and the London Agreement between the League Council and Switzerland with regard to the Confederation's entry into the League" (*OJ*, SS 146:39). The French were particularly concerned with Switzerland's sensitive strategic position conducive to international transit (in this case, of arms destined to Italy), by which Swiss territory could be used by other states to circumvent the arms embargo (*FF* 1935, 2:939). These criticisms later aroused much resentment within the Swiss Federal Assembly (*BS*, CN 1936:595–656); even so, this (French) view was supported in its entirety by the delegates from Poland (Komarnicki), Rumania (Visoianu), the Soviet Union (Antonov), and the United Kingdom (Malkin). Each speaker, through his agreement to disagree with the Swiss view, feared what Mr. Komarnicki called "the very serious doubts which might arise if the attitude taken by the Swiss Government were to constitute a precedent.... No interpretation laying down a general principle conflicting with Art. 16 could, of course, be tolerated by the League" (*OJ*, SS 146:39). The respected Greek jurist, Nicholas Politis, provided the most penetrating critique of the Swiss position in asserting that "one of the fundamental principles of neutrality had been abandoned by Switzerland herself when the latter agreed to examine, in common with the other Members of the League, the question of the responsible party in a case of breach of the Covenant" (*OJ*, SS 146:42).

In a lengthy reply to these charges (*OJ*, SS 146:40–41), Motta argued that Swiss policy had successfully "brought her loyalites to the League into harmony with her fundamental and traditional conception of neutrality." Nonetheless, his refusal to "permit a distinction being made between Ethiopia and Italy" seemed to directly contradict his earlier (9 October) "tacit association" with the League's ruling of Italian aggression. The international pressure brought to bear did however appear to have some effect: the Federal Council later admitted the possibility of allowing limited transit of arms to Ethiopia, and thus "to some extent mitigate the general rule by means of exceptions." On a related point, Motta displayed the somewhat naïve view that specific League proposals to ban the sale of chemical weapons to Italy should be rejected, since the use of such weapons was already in violation of existing international law (specifically the 1925 Protocol outlawing the use of poison gas)—apparently failing to consider the possibility that Italy could follow its blatant violation of the League Covenant with further acts of contempt for international law (*OJ*, SS 146:63).

Moreover, Swiss policy indicated an avoidance of the difficult moral issues of the crisis. Specifically, the Swiss *Nationalrat* Commission refused to condemn Italy's bombing of the Swedish Red Cross facilities in late December 1935 (*BS*, CN 1936, 653–54); this silence was particularly surprising due to the predilection of Swiss officials to draw parallels between the principles of the (all-Swiss) ICRC and Switzerland's perpetual neutrality. In this case, however, the government's refusal to express any judgment on even the most blatant infringement of international law was clearly inconsistent with its own tendency to justify various facets of its own neutral policy through references to international legal principles.

The debate over Switzerland's dual arms embargo was in fact largely academic, since Switzerland was a very minor source of arms to both belligerents. Its overall share of world arms exports stood at around 1 percent, with less than a half-million U.S. dollars' worth of sales annually (RIIA 1938, 25, table), and Italy's share for all of 1935 amounted to only SwFr 88,000. These low figures indicated that no action (or inaction) by the Federal Council could alter the strategic balance of the war. Even this fact, however, indicated an inconsistency in the Swiss viewpoint: whereas the government cited its peripheral importance on the arms question as a reason for not fully complying with the League's measure (*OJ*, SS 146:41), it subsequently refused to implement the proposed economic embargo fully because of its significant level of trade with Italy. The attitude of Switzerland (and Luxembourg) was also important as regarded future League action, particularly if at a later point one of them prohibited the sale, export or re-export of arms to a (European) victim of German aggression, such as France.

SWITZERLAND AND ECONOMIC SANCTIONS (PROPOSALS II–IV)

Switzerland's international credibility in the operation was damaged further by its attitude toward the recommended economic and financial measures. Whereas the dual arms embargo was at least theoretically justifiable on the grounds of its military neutrality, Switzerland's refusal to apply the full trade embargo could not be explained in reference to the Hague Conventions, and in fact it represented a straightforward breach of its obligations undertaken in 1920. In general, the government applied only those economic sanctions which would not damage Swiss interests, and refused or only partially implemented those that would. Switzerland implemented Proposal II, but with two important reservations; it refused to implement the import ban (Proposal III), opting instead to freeze Swiss imports from Italy at the previously attained level; however, it readily agreed to apply Proposal IV (the partial export ban).

Switzerland's position on Proposal II, the credit ban, indicated this general bearing. The Swiss delegation argued that the close financial relations between Swiss and Milanese banks and firms rendered Switzerland, much more than most other countries, susceptible to major losses due to the stop on credit (*OJ*,

SS 147:42–44); this may well have been Motta's rationale for refusing Switzerland's appointment to the financial sub-committee of the Committee of Eighteen (Highley 1938, 168). Also, Motta told the League Assembly that Switzerland did not consider itself duty-bound to enforce the financial sanctions within its own borders, and that the measure applied only "in effect, from territory to territory" (*FF* 1935, 2:930); this apparently referred to the government's inability to prevent all financial transactions between private Swiss firms and Italians resident in Switzerland.

Thus Switzerland's decree enacting Proposal II[11] contained two important loopholes. First, according to Art. II of the decree, "Should the application of the provisions of Art. I entail serious consequences for branches, agencies, or participations of Swiss firms in Italy, the National Bank may authorize certain limited loans" (to individual Swiss firms). This would allow, for example, such firms to pay their employees in case of nonpayment by Italy upon delivery of goods, due to the severance of credit. The second exception was Switzerland's refusal to implement Proposal IIA, which requested states to suspend all clearing agreements with Italy by 18 November. This request was in fact contradicted (though under clearly exceptional circumstances) when the two countries signed a special, bilateral clearing agreement on 9 December. Both these exceptions later engendered considerable League criticism.

The Swiss government was more cooperative with the League regarding the embargo on selected exports to Italy (Proposal IV). The Federal Council complied fully with the export ban, subjecting the export of all embargoed products to an authorization of the Swiss directorate-general of customs.[12] The government admitted that this compliance was possible since the export prohibition scarcely affected "Switzerland as a whole [since it] does not export to Italy any goods that Italy could not dispense with easily."[13]

As noted in table 5-1, total Swiss exports to Italy in 1935 came to SwFr 72.8 m. Manufactured goods accounted for two-thirds of the total (67 percent), raw materials for 23 percent, and foodstuffs for 10 percent. The main manufactured goods exported to Italy included machinery (SwFr 10.2m, up from 7.8m in 1934), clocks and watches (10.3m), pharmaceuticals (3.7m), dyes (3.7m), and iron-based products (3.4m). While none of these important Swiss exports were subject to the embargo, several other Swiss exports were, including such metals as scrap iron and waste from iron workings (SwFr 2.93m), aluminum (0.6m), nickel (0.54m), tin (0.23m), zinc (0.19m), and minute amounts of ferro-chrome. In addition, farm livestock was included in the embargo on transport animals; this category covered some SwFr 4.3m in Swiss exports to Italy (though down from 6.5m in 1934), and the Swiss agreed to sever this trade (*OJ*, SS 147:40–41). No iron ore was produced in Switzerland. Swiss exports covered by Proposal IV thus totaled approximately SwFr 9m out of 72.8m, or about one-eighth of its total exports to Italy;[14] this was a much higher figure (in both absolute and percentage terms) than that for Sweden.

Switzerland's response to the total ban on Italian imports (Proposal III) was much less cooperative, due to a number of factors. Indeed the Swiss held it to be "obvious" that an outright acceptance of Proposal III was "absolutely impossible," since it would result in the total severance of their (significant) level of trade with Italy, and would increase Swiss unemployment by about ten thousand people (*OJ*, SS 146:57; 150:273). One potentially serious problem was the permanent residence of some thirty-five thousand Italian citizens in Switzerland, whose civil liberties and freedom of movement would have to be restricted in the event of a total trade prohibition, since this would require the forcible prevention of most personal intercourse between the two countries. Moreover, such a ban would be especially unfair to Switzerland, since the League had refused to ban personal travel to and from Italy. In this case, the Swiss argued, even preferential treatment by League members in the form of mutual support would be inadequate to compensate for its loss of the Italian market (*OJ*, SS 150:273).

Yet another problem was the government's difficult task in preventing the transit of goods overland to Italy; and it was at least partly due to Swiss protests that the League did not impose a ban on such transit (as through the major Alpine passes). Given Austria's refusal to implement the embargo, and especially as long as free transit across the high seas (and thus access to Italy's many ports) was allowed, the Swiss quite rightly argued that such a ban would have been unfair to them (*FF* 1935, 2:941). Generally, the Federal Council held that Switzerland would suffer "political, intellectual and moral injury caused by a rupture of all economic relations between the Italian-speaking parts of Switzerland and Italy" (*OJ*, SS 150:273). However, the government's claim that it would lose the entire Italian market if it applied Proposal III in full would appear to be exaggerated; as the Swedish case demonstrated (tables 4-1 and 4-2), imports from Italy could be cut substantially without disrupting export trade, even though it might exacerbate existing trade imbalances.

Swiss imports from Italy totaled some SwFr 116.1m in 1934, and 91.5 m in 1935 as shown in table 5-1. The bulk of these imports consisted of foodstuffs (34 percent), manufactured goods (28 percent), and raw materials (16 percent). The main food items were, in order of importance, fruit, wine, meat, and vegetables. The main manufactured goods included silk fabric and artificial raw silk (a total of SwFr7m), automobiles (4.1m), and machinery (1.2m); this last figure showed a steep decline, down from 4.9m in 1933 and 2.7m in 1934, which was much larger in percentage terms than was the overall decline in Swiss imports from Italy. This trend likely represented a shift in Italy's trade priorities, specifically towards an effort to stem the export of machinery in order to advance its own military buildup; and this interpretation is supported by a similarly large and simultaneous rise in Sweden's exports of machinery to Italy, as indicated in chapter 4.

Although it did not implement Proposal III, the Swiss government did not summarily refuse all cooperation with the League by increasing its level of trade with Italy (as did both Austria and Hungary); according to Motta, "Switzerland had no thought of profiting by the common misfortune or of taking advantage of the situation; indeed, the very idea was repugnant to her" (*OJ*, SS 145:41, 116). The Federal Council proceeded to enact measures which would maintain the same "volume [of trade with Italy] it has hitherto attained," measured on a quarterly basis, during the corresponding period the previous year, 1934 (*RO* 1935, 51:743). This policy, called the *courant normale* (literally, the "normal flow" of commerce) was defended as a measure which would facilitate the essential aim of the League—which in this case (Proposal III) was to eliminate Italy's foreign currency reserves. The *courant normale* scheme certainly had no basis in the laws of neutrality, to which the Swiss had strictly adhered by implementing the dual arms embargo, and was merely a political response (Dutoit 1962, 51). The Swiss measure, moreover, lacked the redeeming quality of equal treatment of both belligerents, since it was only applied against Italy.

Walther Stucki, technical advisor to the Swiss delegation, argued that the problems involved in prohibiting both Italian imports (Proposal III) and the issuance of credit (Proposals II and IIA) were closely connected. He held that the Coordination Committee could not, in practice, compel the universal liquidation of clearing debts with Italy, since that would require the transfer of direct payments from Italy; all those states claiming debts from Italians could be repaid with either goods or currency, which would in turn violate Proposal III. In Switzerland's view (in which the French concurred), the call for a suspension of clearing agreements (Proposal IIA) and the total ban on Italian imports (Proposal III) were even mutually incompatible objectives.[15] This problem was even greater in Switzerland's case, since Italy's trade surplus with it was much larger than for most other states; as table 5-1 shows, the Swiss trade deficit with Italy had amounted to some SwFr 40m in 1934, although that figure had been reduced to an estimated 15–16m for all of 1935 (the actual figure came to 18m). Due to this trade imbalance, he argued, the application of Proposal III would damage the Swiss economy more than Italy's (*OJ*, SS 145:97, 107–108, 116); and this argument was considered valid by a Chatham House report published subsequent to the sanctions operation (RIIA 1938, 192).

In return, Walther Stucki proposed for the other member states what Switzerland itself eventually adopted: a stop on all further direct payments to Italy for its imported goods, in order to reduce their bilateral trade to "compensation transactions" (*FF* 1935, 2:935–36). At this point the linkage for Switzerland in Proposals IIA and III became evident: Motta observed that Switzerland could prevent Italy from obtaining foreign currency through the establishment of a special clearing agreement, which allowed for a continuation of trade even while preventing the direct exchange of currency to pay for it (*OJ*, SS 150:273). This agreement was in fact concluded between Italy and Switzerland, though after extended and difficult negotiations,[16] on 9 December 1935.[17]

The ultimate aim of this complicated agreement was threefold: (1) to reduce, and gradually eliminate, Italy's foreign exchange reserves (accruing partly from its chronic trade surplus with Switzerland) by achieving a balance in their bilateral trade; (2) to prevent foreign exchange payments to the Italians, replacing them with a compensation procedure using goods as payment; and (3) to maintain Switzerland's bilateral trade with Italy at the 1934 level (the most recent year completed with available figures)—that is, the *courant normale*—in order to prevent Swiss circumvention of the League's embargo (*OJ*, SS 147:39–40).

The Swiss also claimed that the agreement would cause the repatriation of Swiss assets (some 20 million francs in commercial claims) held in Italy, which would prevent Italy from using them to purchase war supplies elsewhere (*OJ*, SS 147:40). Deprived of adequate supplies of foreign currency and saddled with an increasingly worthless lira, Italy would be unable to buy war matériel from other sources such as sympathetic nonmember states (Germany, Japan) or from League members refusing to apply the blockade (Austria, Albania, Hungary). Rather than stopping all trade with Italy, the Swiss would bring about an export-import balance, thus depriving Italy of the remaining funds (circa SwFr 15m) due on account of its foreign exchange surplus; after that, their normal pattern of bilateral trade would continue. Due to this particular system of payments, the Swiss even argued that Proposal IIA (the ban on clearing agreements) did not need to be fulfilled (*OJ*, SS 150:276).

The Swiss government vigorously defended these actions as part of a policy which, although different from the League's actions, ultimately accorded with the main aim, which was to prevent Italy from receiving valuable foreign exchange (*OJ*, SS 146:40). Nonetheless these claims were repudiated by many League delegates in the relevant sub-committees.[18] For example, the *rapporteur* for Proposal III in the Committee of Experts, Suetins of Belgium, asserted that the Italo-Swiss clearing agreement contravened the 2 November League declaration aimed at establishing a common front regarding outstanding debt claims by Italians; and he held that the Swiss aim of merely eliminating its trade imbalance with Italy, rather than all its imports from it, represented at best only partial compliance with the League (*OJ*, SS 147:40; 150:5). And despite Swiss assurances, the Committee of Eighteen also criticized Switzerland's loophole in Proposal II, due to fears that it would give the Swiss National Bank far too much leeway in making exceptions to the credit ban, and thus would enable it to circumvent the credit stop.

Another major point of controversy was Switzerland's claim to compensation for any losses suffered by its restrictions on trade with Italy. This attitude was also clearly at odds with Switzerland's earlier rejection of mutual support within the context of League sanctions. The Swiss asserted that Art. 16(3) of the Covenant "entitles Switzerland to seek compensation [*se faire indemniser*] from the other Members of the League for the special sacrifices imposed upon her" (*OJ*, SS 150:273; 146:35). However, the Spanish delegate (de Madariaga) argued that the Swiss claim to "compensation," which presumably meant direct payments by League members to Switzerland, was an exaggeration of the

League's intent in organizing for mutual support (Proposal V), which could provide only for concerted trade concessions and not the direct flow of aid (*OJ*, SS 146:35). When faced with this criticism, the Swiss modified their demand by replacing the verb "entitles" with the phrase "would entitle," to appear as less than a categorical (Swiss) demand for direct payments, admitting that "mutual support was the most that Switzerland could expect" (*OJ*, SS no, 146:35); but even this request (as with those from Yugoslavia and Rumania) was not heeded. Nonetheless the Federal Council repeated its "indisputable right to large compensations" from other member states, in its December 1935 report to a sceptical Federal Assembly (*FF* 1935, 2:934), if Switzerland sustained significant economic losses.

The most straightforward rebuttal of Switzerland's arguments concerned the Swiss claim that, through its limited measures, it was acting in complete solidarity with the League. Swiss policy came under veiled attack from the Rumanian delegate Titulesco, who charged that different categories of states were being created in the conflict: nonmembers, members who refused to cooperate with the League (clearly referring to Switzerland), and those who applied sanctions in full (*OJ*, SS 145:73–74). The French delegation was especially critical of the Swiss attitude:

In the face of public opinion at home, the governments of the other countries could not accept the Swiss statement. They themselves were preparing to make extremely heavy sacrifices which would involve the complete stoppage of Italian imports into their countries and, in all probability, the complete cessation of their exports to Italy . . . But they cannot stand by and allow it to be said that the effect of measures they were taking would in no way differ from the effect of measures under which the existing flow of trade with Italy would be maintained. (*OJ*, SS 146:36)

To this the South African representative (te Water) added that "rightly or wrongly, the impression has got abroad . . . that the Swiss attitude in this matter has been obstructive" (*OJ*, SS 146:36). The President of the International Union of Associations for the League of Nations even suggested that Switzerland's attitude be scrutinized by the Permanent Court of International Justice at The Hague (*BS*, CN 1935:633). There is even some evidence suggesting that Italy used Switzerland, through Ruegger (the new Swiss minister in Rome, who replaced Wagnière in February 1936) and Motta himself, as a lever within the League's Coordination Committee to hinder attempts to bring about the oil sanction, with an overt threat to withdraw from League membership if additional sanctions were imposed (Rigonalli 1983, 154).

Despite these criticisms, the Swiss government maintained that its actions fully accorded with the basic aims of the League's operation. Indeed Motta's lengthy explanation of the Federal Council's view to parliament, in January 1936, reveals a striking failure to address, or indeed even mention, these criticisms of the Swiss position—and even an occasional attempt to interpret a

TABLE 5-2

Switzerland's Monthly Trade with Italy, 1934-36

Month	Swiss Imports from Italy (in SwFrs 1000s)		Swiss Exports to Italy (in SwFrs 1000s)	
	1934–35	1935–36	1934–35	1935–36
	(1)	(2)	(3)	(4)
Nov	8,222	7,660	9,072	6,420
Dec	10,891	6,659	8,319	4,419
Jan	6,351	3,860	5,967	3,501
Feb	7,393	4,399	6,477	5,248
Mar	8,715	4,902	9,000	5,415
Apr	9,267	4,791	7,184	5,289
May	7,910	5,186	4,718	4,965
Jun	7,628	5,634	5,277	4,900
TOTALS:	66,377	43,091	56,014	40,157

Source: Statistique Mensuelle du Commerce extérieur de la Suisse, 1934-36.

point of criticism as an expression of praise for the Swiss attitude (for example, Motta in *BS*, CN 1936, 650). Within the League, Stucki maintained that Article 16 should be observed by all member states, and that "it was very difficult for the Swiss people to understand that their economic neutrality was at an end" (*OJ*, SS 146:58). This was a most curious statement, particularly since the Swiss government itself had asserted continually throughout the League era that "economic neutrality" was a false term which had no basis in international law; it also belied the result of the 1920 referendum, by which the Swiss public, if only narrowly, had accepted the duty to implement economic sanctions against an aggressor. The Swiss also maintained their ultimate independence in determining their degree of compliance with the operation, and questioned the authority of the Coordination Committee to take decisions for the League membership (*OJ*, SS 146:53).

Switzerland's endeavor to maintain its previous levels of trade with Italy actually resulted in a marked, though not precipitous, decline during the sanctioning period. This decrease is shown in table 5-2, particularly in the comparison between cols. 1 and 2. This decline was more attributable to the overall reduction in Italy's foreign commerce during the embargo than to Switzerland's own partial trade restrictions, and reflected a continuation of the downward trend in Swiss-Italian trade even prior to the operation (shown in table 5-1). Despite the government's refusal to implement Proposal III, the level of Swiss imports from Italy dropped nearly one-third relative to the corresponding period for the previous year. Measured in francs, Swiss imports from Italy during the sanctioning period (table 5-2, col. 2) were only 65 percent of the corresponding eight-month figure for 1934–35. Meanwhile the export total (table 5-2, col. 4) was just 72 percent of the previous year; again this was partly due to Switzerland's acceptance of Proposal IV, but it was mainly the result of its overall decline in trade. This trend was corroborated by League figures, computed in old US gold dollars.[19] These figures also substantiated the Swiss government's stated aim to bring about an overall balance of trade with Italy; Swiss imports from Italy during the sanctioning period totalled $8.3m, comparable to the export figure of $7.7m; these figures also substantiated the Swiss government's stated aim of bringing about an overall balance of trade with Italy, although the imbalance was not eliminated altogether. On the other hand, the Swiss banking system played a significant if tacit role in aiding Italy during the crisis, when over a third of all gold exported from Italy went to Switzerland, a total of nearly $35m worth (RIIA 1938, 87, table 1).

THE SWISS POLITICAL DEBATE

The Federal Council's difficulties in the crisis were compounded further by a number of domestic political cleavages which prevented a unified Swiss response. These differences were clearly expressed during the main parliamentary debates on the issue, in January 1936 (*BS*, CN 1936, 595–656, of 28 January; CE 1936, 24–35, 18 January). As in the 1919–20 debate over League accession, at least two lines of political division arose: one between the Federal Council and Federal Assembly, the other between the various linguistic and ethnic subpopulations in the country. Both these elements were exacerbated by the government's lack of effective leadership, due partly to its hesitant response to the League's operation, but mainly due to Motta's inability (because of his known sympathy for Italy and his Catholicism) to exercise the national unifying role he had repeatedly filled earlier in his career, as the most popular federal councillor (Håstad 1936, 719–24). Still another difficulty was the latent opposition of public opinion, which according to Rigonalli favored more support for the Abyssinian cause "in a large majority" (1983, 155).

Taken as a whole, the Federal Assembly took an even more conservative position than did the government on the question of preserving Switzerland's traditional neutrality and independent posture. For example, the National Council's Sanctions Commission approved the Federal Council's basic policy, but asserted that, should the League adopt any further measures, the Federal Assembly, not the Federal Council, would determine Swiss policy.[20] This attempt to usurp authority derived partly from the longstanding, uncertain division of authority within Switzerland over League policy; this uncertainty had, paradoxically, increased since 1920 as the Federal Assembly had been gradually left out of the foreign policy decision-making process in Switzerland (Hughes 1962, 149), highlighted by the Federal Council's successful endeavor since the early 1920s to prevent the establishment of a permanent parliamentary committee on foreign affairs (Håstad 1936, 407–11). As it stood, the Assembly was highly critical of the government's acceptance of the partial export embargo (*BS*, CN 1936, 596–98), in what one deputy derided as the government's *kompromiss-politik*. Equally noteworthy was the Commission's failure to mention the desire, or necessity, of defending the Covenant's principles, apart from a rather desultory acknowledgment that Switzerland should fulfill its contractual obligations. The report thus demonstrated the continuing importance of parliamentary obstructionism as a major impediment to a unified Swiss foreign policy; indeed later in 1936 the Assembly succeeded in forming a foreign affairs committee in the lower chamber.

Divergence from the Federal Council's line was also indicated by three separate parliamentary proposals; two from the leftist parties and one from the far right. The leftist proposals, tabled respectively by Robert Grimm, the longtime Socialist leader, and the Communist deputy (Bodemann), both aimed at fostering closer Swiss cooperation with the League's operation. This bloc of (leftist) parliamentary opposition was very significant, for the Socialists reemerged after the October 1935 elections as the largest single faction, holding 50 out of 187 seats in the National Council (*Annuaire Statistique de la Suisse* 1935, 396); the Socialists' strong position also underscored the political significance of their continued exclusion from the Federal Council by the other parties (their first seat was not granted until 1943), despite their modified party platform of 1935 (Masnata 1963, 127–28). In further testimony to the Socialists' continued political isolation, the Grimm resolution, which closely accorded with the position of many member governments, was largely shunned by the nonsocialist bloc, and both Motta and Vallotton (chairman of the parliament's sanctions commission) rejected it out of hand (*BS*, CN 1936, 651, 653). They especially opposed the second (and relatively moderate) Bodemann proposal that the government associate itself fully with the League's operation (*BS*, CN 1936, 609–610, 618–20); indeed the forceful, even condescending, manner of their rejection was in itself noteworthy (654, 656).

On the other hand, the nonleftist political factions appeared to support a stronger neutral line. For example, the Swiss-Italian population, in 1919–20 heavily supportive of League membership, emerged in 1935 as the strongest supporter of governmental policy, principally due to Motta's influence (*BS*, CN 1936, 624–28; Rusca, 632–34; Bossi). More surprising was the shift in the general attitude of the French-Swiss population, which now appeared considerably more reluctant to support unreservedly the principle of League solidarity. For example, one expressed the common view that a qualitative distinction could be drawn between Swiss neutrality, which was "constitutionally and traditionally our only permanent policy," and "the League of Nations and the engagements that we have with it [which] are in some senses new, and perhaps passing and ephemeral" (*BS*, CN 1936, 620-21; Gorgerat). And although many French-Swiss did retain a measure of their strong early support for the League's principles, "the sympathy that we hold, despite certain disillusionment, for the League of Nations should not close our eyes to the harsh realities" (*BS*, CN 1936, 644; Musy).

Not surprisingly, the strongest arguments in favor of an unambiguous reassertion of Swiss neutrality was expressed by the majority Swiss-German population. Debate centered around an uncompromising proposal by the sole Frontist (extreme rightist) deputy from Zürich, Herr Tobler, for the Federal Council to "take the necessary measures to re-establish the traditional and integral neutrality of Switzerland" (*BS*, CN 1936, 610, 621–24). His obvious, if implied, aim was to induce Swiss repudiation of its sanctions obligations and, ultimately, withdrawal from the League altogether. Many similar, if less categorical, views were expressed by other speakers, and the Tobler motion was in fact much better received by the *Nationalrat* Commission than was the Bodemann proposal, its virtual antithesis.

Two other, closely related points were expressed in the debate. One was the widely held fear of loss of Swiss state sovereignty and political independence due to its obligation to apply League sanctions. It was even argued that Switzerland, due to its special League position, was not unconditionally bound to its Covenant obligations, and even "has the obligation to refuse" any activity conflicting with its special neutral position (*BS*, CN 1936, 617, 643; Gut; Musy). The second major concern was that Swiss acquiescence in a limited sanctions operation could potentially create a dangerous precedent for the future, with particularly stark implications for a possible future embargo against Germany (*BS*, CN 1936, 602–9, 643).

Despite this widespread and forceful defense of neutrality, it was nonetheless clear that few deputies seriously considered an even-handed, impartial Swiss attitude toward the Italo-Abyssinian conflict to be legitimate. Many deputies in fact came out openly in support of the Italian position; one even claimed that "if it were necessary to give up neutrality, it would be easier to do so in support of Italy, cradle of our Latin and Western civilization, rather than in support of Ethiopia, nation of savages" (*BS*, CN 1936, 621; Gorgerat; this strident assertion drew applause from other deputies). In the Council of States, some (e.g., Coulon) similarly assented to Italy's "legitimate need for expansion, which is regarded as bad oil by the powers" (*BS*, CE 1936, 30). Given the sharp political divergence indicated by such statements, Motta's claim that "the conclusion of the debate will be, in effect, that the conduct of the Federal Council is approved by the moral unanimity of Parliament, and, I will add, by the unanimity of the nation" (*BS*, CN 1936, 647) appeared disingenuous.

THE RETURN TO INTEGRAL NEUTRALITY

One of the best indications of the significance of the Italian crisis to Switzerland's security and neutrality was the continuing high priority which the

Federal Council gave to Italy's position as a determinant of Swiss policy even after the crisis. In May 1936 the government departed from its low profile before and during the sanctions operation and became outspoken in favor of an early lifting of the embargo, arguing that "to continue to enforce economic sanctions would be to maintain, to engender, general disturbance, irritation, and insecurity. The Assembly has the . . . duty to declare that there is no longer any ground for applying sanctions" (*DIA* 1937, 2:534). However, Switzerland did not lift its own partial measures until after the League recommended it, and they remained in the Swiss legal code until 8 July 1936 (*RO* 1936, 52:552). At the outset of the seventeenth League Assembly session in July 1936, Switzerland and five other states abstained on the question of allowing Ethiopia to retain its seat (but it did not vote against, as did four other states); and Motta urged that Selassie not be allowed to speak to the Assembly on its opening day (*SIA* 1936, 2:492–93, 525).

Late in 1936, the government stirred a great deal of domestic and international controversy when it undertook unilaterally (23 December) to recognize de jure Italian sovereignty over Ethiopia, on the somewhat spurious grounds of protecting Swiss interests in Abyssinia. This decision was particularly contentious since none of the other powers had yet recognized the Italian annexation (*RCF* 1936, 77–78), and since the Swiss government at that time still refused to recognize the Soviet Union, a League member state; this inconsistency was harshly criticized during the March 1937 parliamentary debate (*BS*, CN 1937, 124). Another curious, if tangentially related, incident occurred in April 1937 when the University of Lausanne in its 400th anniversary celebrations conferred the title of *docteur honoris causa* upon Benito Mussolini (Rigonalli 1983, 157; Hughes 1975, 118). These favors, however, were not returned; the Italians banned the distribution of two Swiss-German newspapers, the *Neue Zürcher Zeitung* and *Der Bund* in Italy, even though both had been rather sympathetic to Italy's position during the 1935–36 crisis (Wiskemann 1967, 305).

Switzerland's relative leniency toward Italy became increasingly unpopular among the Swiss public. By 1937–38 Motta became estranged from the Young Catholic group, centered in Lucerne and ostensibly among his strongest groups of supporters. This group indeed became bitter political opponents of the foreign minister and outspoken in their condemnations of both Italy and Germany, despite Motta's additional prominence as Swiss president for 1937, and the Christian Democrats' acceptance of a second Federal Council seat the following year (Wiskemann 1967, 294). This split between government and people also contributed toward a deterioration in official Italo-Swiss relations. In a 1938 referendum, the public forcefully rejected a minor treaty of May 1937, between the two countries (concerning the use of hydraulic force on the river Spöl); Prof. Guggenheim has asserted that this rejection demonstrated considerably greater public intolerance toward the Italian régime than shown by the Swiss government (1967, 147–48).

Moreover, Italy's withdrawal from the League in November 1937 (carried out despite strong Swiss protestations) was an important catalyst for Swiss attempts to recover their "integral" neutrality. Motta told the National Council on 22 December that "the Confederation must prepare itself henceforth, without hesitation, to make it known that it cannot limit itself to a qualified neutrality, and that its neutrality must be absolute, conforming to the secular tradition, to geography and to the history of the country" (*BS*, CN 1937, 20). During the spring of 1938 the government drafted a special memorandum concerning Swiss neutrality, which aimed at allowing Switzerland "to ask that her neutrality be explicitly recognized within the framework of the League."[21] This request was tantamount to petitioning for a formal renunciation of its political obligations to the League altogether, despite Motta's claim that Switzerland was thereby "rendering an undeniable service to the cause of peace" (*OJ*, May–June 1938, Annex 4029:311–12).

As in 1920, the League complied with the Swiss request. By acknowledging Swiss neutrality as "an uncontested principle of international law," the Council took "note that Switzerland, invoking her perpetual neutrality, has expressed the intention not to participate any longer in any manner in the putting into operation of the provisions of the Covenant relating to sanctions and declares that she will not be invited to do so" (*OJ*, May–June 1938, comm. no. 4058:368–70). One observer considered this formal exemption for Switzerland to represent the first admission by the League itself of the collapse of the legal principles upon which it was founded (Morgenthau 1938, 562); it was also inconsistent with the League's attitude during the Italo-Abyssinian dispute that an attitude of neutrality was unacceptable. This formal recognition by the League merely reiterated Switzerland's special international standing; the League's *rapporteur* (who by happenstance was the Swedish foreign minister, Rickard Sandler) stated at the time that the Swiss exemption was inapplicable to all other neutral states (*AKU* 1938, 24). This act effectively terminated Switzerland's association with all subsequent League activity (*FF* 1938, 2:824); and the Swiss delegation abstained on the League's last substantive action, the expulsion of the Soviet Union in December 1939 after its attack on Finland, even though the Federal Council had attempted up to 1934 to prevent the accession of the USSR.

NOTES

1. *Statistique du Commerce Suisse*, Rapport Annuel, 1935, IIe partie, pp. 12–35.
2. Motta asserted that Italy was the "mother of my language, the mother of law, . . . the mother of arts," and had "brought the most impressive contribution to human civilization that history recognizes" (*BS*, CN, 1936, p. 649). Even in January 1936, immediately following Italy's bombardment of Sweden's Red Cross facilities, he claimed (in most untimely fashion) that "Italy has a great role to play in the League of Nations" (*BS*, CN, 1936, p. 652). For more on Motta's peculiar style, see Håstad, 1936, pp. 282–83.

3. See Foreign Minister Calonder's remarkable speech to the Swiss National Council of 6 June 1918, openly championing the League idea; 1919 Swiss League Message, Annex I, part 3, pp. 145–54; also *International Conciliation*, vol. 1 (January–April 1919), pp. 54–67; and Belin, 1956, p. 33.

4. It asserted for example that Switzerland would "maintain under all conditions a neutral attitude on the military side" of the League, including a refusal to allow the right of passage for League troops, in accordance with Arts. 2 and 5 of Hague Convention V of 1907 (1919 Message, pp. 42–43, 32–33, 61–62, 127–28).

5. Indeed the Swiss accepted economic sanctions from both the legal and the politico-security viewpoints. See Munch, 1923, p. 178; 1919 League Message, pp. 37–38; *FF* 1920, vol. 2, pp. 760–62; *BS*, CN, 1919, p. 788; and *OJ*, May–June 1938, p. 312.

6. "Message Complementaire du Conseil fédéral du 17 février 1920," *FF* 1920, vol. 1, p. 362; Rappard, 1923, p. 391; and "Documents Concerning the Accession of Switzerland to the League of Nations," 1920.

7. See for these responses *FF* 1921, vol. 5, pp. 535–36; *FF* 1923, vol. 1, pp. 21–22; *FF* 1928, vol. 3, pp. 926–27; *RCF*, 1934, pp. 27–28.

8. *BS*, CN, 1919, p. 788 (de Meuron); p. 822 (Bercier). For a general discussion of the debate, see Rappard, 1923.

9. *RO* 1935, 51, pp. 715, 720; *FF* 1935, vol. 2, pp. 965–67; *OJ*, SS no. 150, pp. 273–74 (English translation).

10. For Luxembourg's position, see *OJ*, SS no. 146, pp. 13, 35; esp. statement of Bech.
Switzerland, on the other hand, invoked Art. 9 of Hague Convention V of 1907, as well as its traditional neutral status. See *OJ*, SS no. 146, p. 35; SS no. 150, p. 272.

11. *OJ*, SS no. 133, p. 44; *FF* 1934, vol. 2, p. 520; *FF* 1935, vol. 1, p. 441; *FF* 1935, vol. 2, p. 157.

12. *FF* 1935, vol. 2, pp. 967–69; *RO* 1935, 51, p. 729; *OJ*, SS no. 150, pp. 274–75 (English translation); enacted on 12 November 1935.

13. *OJ* SS no. 146, pp. 272–73; also *OJ*, SS no. 145, pp. 107–08; *FF* 1935, vol. 2, p. 935.

14. *Statistique du Commerce extérieur de la Suisse*, 1935, IIe partie, pp. 217–25; *Statistique du Commerce Suisse, Rapport Annuel*, 1935, IIe partie, pp. 32–35; same for 1936, pp. 32–35; and *Statistique mensuelle du Commerce extérieur de la Suisse*, October 1935, p. 141.

15. *OJ*, SS no. 146, pp. 15–19, 22–26; SS no. 145, pp. 108–9. This contention was supported by the fact that those countries which maintained clearing agreements with Italy prior to sanctions were the main objectors to Proposal III, including (besides Switzerland) Rumania, Turkey and Yugoslavia.

16. This included hot denials by the Swiss delegate, Walther Stucki, of secret bilateral negotiations in Geneva outside the normal negotiating channels; see *OJ*, SS no. 145, p. 100; SS no. 147, p. 39.

17. The clearing agreement provided for reciprocal bank accounts for the settlement of outstanding payments; the aim, apart from preventing direct payments to Italy, was to hold sufficient funds in Switzerland in reserve, to meet outstanding Swiss claims on Italians; most (80 percent) was retained in payment for goods imported from Italy, so as to meet the excess of between SwFr 15–18m. See *OJ*, SS no. 150, pp. 277–78; *RO* 51, 1935, p. 793.

18. See the League debates of 2 November 1935 (in the Committee of Eighteen), *OJ*, SS no. 146, pp. 35–37; and of 11 December (the Committee of Experts), *OJ*, SS no. 146, pp. 39–44. Also *BS*, CN, 1935, p. 633.

19. Whereas during the period November 1934–June 1935 Swiss imports from Italy totaled 12,781,900 gold dollars, the total for the sanctioning period (November 1935–June 1936) fell to $8,321,000. The lowest monthly total came in Jan. 1936 at $745,600, but it thereafter rose gradually to above $1 million in June 1936. Meanwhile Swiss exports to Italy fell from a previous level of $10,782,800 to $7,769,200 during the sanctioning period (RIIA, 1938, p. 103; p. 58, table 3).

20. The *rapporteur*, Vallotton, held that sanctions were "capable of resulting in a general war . . . [hence] the question of [future] competence should be resolved in favor of the Federal Assembly" (*BS*, CN, 1936, p. 599); and this view was reiterated in the Council of States by its *rapporteur*, Piller (*BS*, CE, 1936, pp. 24–25).

21. Letter from Motta to the League's secretary-general, 20 April 1938; *OJ*, May–June 1938, Annex 1706, comm. no. 1, p. 385–86. The memorandum of 29 April, repudiating sanctions in every form, is on pp. 385–87, also in *FF* 1938, vol. 1, pp. 850–53.

Part III

The United Nations, the Neutrals, and the Rhodesian Sanctions Operation

6

The Rhodesian Operation and Neutrality

BACKGROUND AND THE UN'S MEASURES

The Security Council's initial consideration of the Rhodesian crisis followed decades of refusal by successive British governments to countenance international action in the case. From 1899 until 1922, the territory of Southern Rhodesia had been administered by the British South Africa Company, established by Cecil Rhodes after the annexation of the territory by the British Crown. Through the Letters of Patent of October 1923, Southern Rhodesia became virtually a self-governing territory, though still formally under British rule. Then from 1953 to 1963 it was united with two neighboring British dependencies, Northern Rhodesia and Nyasaland, in the Federation of Rhodesia and Nyasaland as a step toward independence; and through its constitution of 1961 it obtained full independence in internal matters, and partly even in foreign policy.

By the early 1960s, however, the political situation in Rhodesia became a major point of contention between the United Kingdom and the Afro-Asian bloc in the General Assembly. The new African members of the UN desired to include Rhodesia in the decolonization movement which had transformed the Assembly's membership roster since the late 1950s; decolonization had been first established as a top UN priority in 1960 through the Assembly's landmark Resolution 1514 (XV), the "Declaration in the Granting of Independence to Colonial Countries and Peoples." The Rhodesian question hinged largely on whether the colony had attained full self-government. For its part, Britain held that Rhodesia's self-rule was "an inescapable constitutional and political fact" (*YUN* 1963, 469), due to its indisputable (if slightly contradictory) situation as a "self-governing colony." In fact, the General Assembly itself had bolstered this interpretation, through Resolution 66(I) of 14 December 1946, in which it did not consider Rhodesia to be non-self-governing (Cefkin 1968, 653, n. 14). On this basis Britain ruled out the applicability of Charter Art. 73 pertaining to self-government for colonial peoples; it also held (prior to November 1965) to a tight interpretation of Art. 2(7), which prevents UN meddling into the internal affairs of its member states, as it considered Rhodesia to be solely the concern of the Commonwealth.

The Rhodesian issue was first brought up for UN debate in the Fourth (Trusteeship and Non-Self-Governing Territories) Committee during the 16th Assembly session in 1961. The following year the Special Committee on the Situation with Regard to the Implementation of the Declaration on the Granting of Independence to Colonial Countries and Peoples (the Committee of Twenty-Four, set up in November 1961 to help implement Resolution 1514), was asked by the Assembly (through Resolution 1745 [XVI]) to consider whether Southern Rhodesia had attained full self-government; in response, the Committee of Twenty-Four (and subsequently, the Assembly as a whole, through Resolution 1747 [XVI]), adopted the view that Rhodesia was not self-governing in the meaning of Chapter XI of the Charter, and was therefore liable to their call for full self-determination (*YUN* 1962, 426). This interpretation was underscored through GA Resolution 1755 (12 October 1962) and 1760 (31 October), the latter of which called on Britain to suspend the (racialist) Rhodesian constitution of December 1961, and to stop the planned general elections there. However, the British refused to acknowledge Assembly competence to deal with the matter.

Similarly, Britain spurned early attempts to bring the Rhodesian case before the Security Council. On 9 September 1963, it vetoed a proposal by thirty-two African states that the Council take up the Rhodesian question in pursuance of GA Resolutions 1745 and 1760. The British view (supported by the French, due to their earlier insistence that the Algerian war was a domestic affair and hence outside UN concern) remained essentially unaltered following the dissolution of the Federation on 31 December 1963, and the assumption of statehood by both Northern Rhodesia (Zambia) and Nyasaland (Malawi), both of which entered the UN in December 1964 (*YUN* 1964, 442–43; *YUN* 1965, 122–23). However, the new Labour government under Harold Wilson, which took office in October 1964 with a narrow majority of five seats in the House of Commons, turned the Rhodesian affair into a major political issue, and markedly stepped up its efforts to convince the reactionary Rhodesian Front, now with a strong political base under Ian Smith, to liberalize its rule and to thwart any move toward independence (Wilkinson 1976, 225). To this end, a Labour government memo of 27 October 1964 contained a thinly veiled reference to economic sanctions in the event of a move to assert Rhodesian independence (Windrich 1975, 208–9), the likelihood of which gradually increased during 1964–65. Then following the failure of talks between Wilson and Smith on 4–8 October, Smith issued a Unilateral Declaration of Independence (UDI) for Rhodesia on 11 November 1965.[1] Immediately after UDI the British government reversed its earlier position, and not only acknowledged the competence of the UN to deal with the issue, but even championed the application of limited UN sanctions in order to exert maximum pressure on the Salisbury government to submit to British jurisdiction. The UN embargo which followed was to a considerable extent a widened application of the measures applied unilaterally by Britain immediately following UDI.[2] Indeed, throughout the crisis, ultimate responsibility for the territory lay in British hands, not with the UN Security Council or General Assembly. The measures subsequently adopted by the Security Council were regarded as extensions of British actions, and most were instituted in direct response to renewed British appeals to increase the pressure on Smith, even though they generally represented compromises between the (extreme) African and (moderate) British points of view. Nonetheless, it was clear that the widespread international outrage expressed over UDI would have led to repeated, and probably irrepressible, demands for Security Council action (Kapungu 1973, 24). John Halderman has observed that the very fact that the UN took up the issue demonstrated the ambiguous nature of its authority; while it confirmed its potential power as a collective security organization by designating a mere colony as the target of sanctions, the uneven application of the measures called for demonstrated the UN's inherent limitations as an independent actor (1968, 672–73).

Aside from the patent illegality of the Rhodesian UDI, the policy of racial superiority upon which the Smith government was based greatly aggravated the political crisis. Indeed, the phenomenon of decolonization in Africa and Asia on the basis of self-rule, against which the Rhodesian UDI was clearly set, was closely related to the liberation of native peoples from white (European) colonial rule. In Rhodesia a small European minority of only 250,000 maintained political control over a disenfranchised African majority of some four million. Racial discrimination was a long-time feature of the Rhodesian political landscape, which the British had repeatedly criticized since the formation of the Federation in 1953 (leading to Harold Macmillan's "wind of change" speech in 1961), even while refusing to assent to UN discussion over sovereignty; however, the situation had become much more explosive by the early 1960s. There was no question as to whether this infringement of basic human rights was an issue for world concern, since maintaining fundamental principles of human rights is an essential purpose of the UN, repeatedly enshrined in the Charter as well as in the 1948 Universal Declaration of Human Rights (GA Resolution 217 [III]). In addition, it has been held that the suppression of human rights constitutes a threat to the established norms of international behavior, and hence a violation of principles which could be construed as customary international law (Higgins 1963, 87). The related cases of South Africa and Portuguese colonial rule in Africa had similarly been regarded within the new UN anticolonial orthodoxy as constituting a type of permanent aggression, warranting retaliatory action by the international body (James 1969, 404).

Within this general context, it was significant that neither of the initial Security Council resolutions on the Rhodesian problem (216 and 217 of 12 and 20 November respectively) classified the Rhodesian situation as a "threat to the peace," although the General Assembly earlier (5 November, but without proper authority) had made such a designation, through GA Resolution 2022 (XX) (*AJIL* 1966, 60:922). Resolution 216 recalled the valid Assembly recommendation for action in GA Resolution 2024,[3] condemned the UDI and called upon "all states not to recognize this illegal racist minority régime in Southern Rhodesia and to refrain from rendering any assistance to this illegal régime" (*YUN* 1965, 132). Eight days later, Resolution 217:

determine[d] that the situation resulting from the proclamation of independence by the illegal authorities in Southern Rhodesia is extremely grave, that the Government of the United Kingdom of Great Britain and Northern Ireland should put an end to it, and that its continuance in time constitutes a threat to international peace and security. (*YUN* 1965, 133)

Although by its wording Resolution 217 fell under Chapter VI of the Charter (specifically Art. 34) rather than under the collective security provisions of Chapter VII (leading to British Prime Minister Harold Wilson's curious reference to "Chapter VI 1/2" of the Charter), the Security Council proceeded to recommend certain specific punitive measures by member states, including general nonrecognition of the UDI (paragraph 6), and a call for an arms and oil embargo and a general severance of economic relations with the colony (paragraph 8). Even these limited measures were thought sufficient to bring about Rhodesia's submission to the rule of law, indeed in the prime minister's optimistic (and much maligned) prediction "within a matter of weeks, not months."

However in spring 1966 the situation was aggravated by the appearance of an oil tanker (the *Joanna V*) near Beira, a port in Portuguese Mozambique, with an oil cargo believed destined for Rhodesia in direct contravention of Resolution 217. The Security Council adhered to an urgent British request for international authority to stop delivery of the shipment (in an attempt to preempt those states desiring more stringent action), and passed Resolution 221 on 9 April 1966 (ten votes to none, with five abstentions), whereby it "determine[d] that the resulting situation constitutes a threat to the peace," and called on the British government to prevent, by force if necessary, the arrival of any vessels and to detain the *Joanna V* if it actually discharged oil there (*YUN* 1966, 112). This action succeeded in *Joanna V* (and a second tanker, the *Manuela*) from landing at Beira. Resolution 221 also called (paragraphs 2 and 3) on Portugal, the colonial authority in Mozambique, to prevent the discharge and transshipment of the oil through its territory to Rhodesia (which was sufficient to persuade the two ships to leave voluntarily) and called upon all other states (paragraph 4) to ensure the diversion of any of their vessels believed to be destined for Beira with oil for Rhodesia. Apart from upgrading the designation of the situation to a "threat," this development was significant insofar as it transformed a passive, partial embargo into an actual blockade, albeit one limited to a specific port (Beira), to only two oil tankers, and to a specific product (oil). For nine years following Resolution 221, a British aircraft carrier and (later) two British frigates with air support from Madagascar patrolled the coastal waters around the port in an expensive (and increasingly futile) effort to prevent the supply of oil to Rhodesia, by sea and thence pipeline.

Many legal experts doubted the validity of the Security Council's threat designation, particularly since Resolution 221 had been passed without the positive concurrence of all five permanent Council members.[4] The ruling was clearly the result of a highly subjective judgment by the powers, an act of political expediency in offering international support for a limited British venture to enforce Resolution 217, although this of course was within the Council's authority. John Howell argues that the usual procedure for international enforcement action was actually reversed: rather than first designating the situation as a threat to the peace and then taking steps to cope with it, the Council first assumed competence to deal with the issue (November 1965) and only later (April 1966) called it a threat (1969, 781). Doubtless this decision was facilitated, and criticism of it muted, by the near-universal condemnation of the white supremacist Ian Smith régime, a consensus made possible only because of what John Halderman considered "an exceptional confluence of divergent political forces" (1968, 703). Even so, differences of opinion arose over the main aim of the operation: whereas the UK viewed it as a means of bringing the Smith régime back into the fold, for a return to legality as a basis for further negotiations, the African "front-line" states in the OAU considered the immediate establishment of majority rule leading to an independent Zimbabwe to be the overriding objective. The Assembly repeatedly called for the immediate transfer of rule and even for the use of British force to bring down the rebellion, as in two strongly worded 1966 resolutions, 2138 and 2151 (*YUN* 1966, 114–16); and Julius Nyerere's government in Tanzania actually broke with Britain over the issue. From the other direction, the British Conservative Party under Edward Heath also split with the government over the unilateral oil embargo imposed in December 1965.

The Rhodesian situation deteriorated further during 1966, due partly to the inadequacy of the voluntary sanctions of Resolution 217, even though Rhodesia's level of trade with sanctioning countries had declined (*YUN* 1967, 99–103). In addition, an international network had arisen, linking South Africa, Portugal, and Rhodesia (each a case of white European minority rule over a disenfranchised black African majority) in the systematic evasion of the operation, which became a formidable impediment to its future effectiveness. Furthermore, contrary to expectation, the Rhodesian white community closed ranks behind the Rhodesian Front's intransigent attitude.

After the failure of the Smith-Wilson talks on the cruiser ship *Tiger* in early December 1966, the Security Council, on request from Britain's delegate Lord Caradon, passed Resolution 232 on 16 December, eleven votes to none with four abstentions. Resolution 232 reiterated the "threat to the peace" inherent in the Rhodesian situation, and decided that all states and their nationals should cease importing certain selected Rhodesian commodities (enumerated in operative paragraphs 2 and 5), including asbestos, iron ore, chrome, pig iron, sugar, tobacco, copper, meat and meat products, hides, skins, and leather. This import embargo was supplemented by a partial embargo on member states' exports to Rhodesia, including arms, ammunition, military aircraft, military vehicles, equipment and materials for the manufacture or maintenance of arms and ammunition, and all oil and oil products; even so, this prohibition was far from complete, covering only about 15 percent of Rhodesia's imports and two thirds of its exports (Renwick 1981, 31). Resolution 232 further called on all states to avoid rendering any financial or economic aid to the Smith régime. To underscore the obligatory nature of these measures, Resolution 232 reminded member states that nonadherence would constitute a violation of their obligations under Art. 25 of the Charter. It also called upon states (paragraph 8) to report to the secretary-general on their measures taken in accordance with paragraph 2 of Resolution 232, and requested the secretary-general to report on the progress of the embargo by 1 March 1967.

The failure of these limited measures to force a change in the attitude of the Smith government, and particularly the execution on 7 March 1968 of three Rhodesian blacks (despite a last-minute royal reprieve) under restrictive terrorist legislation implemented in Rhodesia in late 1967, led to further Council action in May 1968. Taking note of GA Resolution 2262 (XXII) of 3 November 1967, the Council imposed a much more comprehensive embargo through Resolution 253 of 29 May 1968, including a complete prohibition on the import and export of all goods to and from Rhodesia (excepting goods for humanitarian purposes), and all other activity designed to promote such commercial exchange. Resolution 253 also called for the prohibition of financial transactions, particularly the export of funds to Rhodesia for investment purposes, and any other payment of credit except pensions. It further prohibited all airline flights between member states and Rhodesia, and even called upon states to refuse entry into their territory of all Rhodesian citizens (again excepting humanitarian need). Finally, it requested states to withdraw all consular and trade representation in Southern Rhodesia. This was not, however, the mandatory and comprehensive embargo to which allusion is sometimes mistakenly made; for example, neither transportation nor communication links with Rhodesia were severed. On the other hand, the Security Council left further measures open to individual states, inviting them (through paragraph 9) "to take all possible further action under Article 41 of the Charter to deal with the situation in Southern Rhodesia, not excluding any of the measures provided for in that Article"; and called upon states (through paragraph 18) to report their compliance by 1 August 1968 (*YUN* 1968:152–54).

Resolution 253 also established a special seven-member Sanctions Committee (expanded in 1970 to fifteen), charged with two tasks: (1) to examine member states' responses to the secretary-general made in compliance with paragraph 18; and (2) to seek additional information regarding implementation of the embargo, including the investigation of reports of circumvention or of outright noncompliance by states. The committee was also empowered to make specific recommendations to states on how to stop, or limit, such violations by private individuals or enterprises within their legislative domain. As such, the voluntary control system of Resolutions 217 and 232, dependent upon the word of individual governments, could now be monitored by an independent authority; prior to that time, the lack of an autonomous means for UN verification had left the numerous accounts of violations in the mass media largely unsubstantiated. The subsequent publication of potentially damning evidence against states and firms in suspected or actual violation of the embargo was an unprecedented means of pressuring governments to comply with the operation, utilizing the instruments of social opprobrium and political pressure. The committee was widely credited with having at least some deterrent effect in limiting blatant violations of the embargo, even though governments were often reluctant to pursue committee allegations (Doxey 1987, 45). In all, the committee investigated over 350 cases and published a total of thirteen reports on the crisis, showing increasingly sophisticated and detailed analysis of trade figures.

Following Resolution 253, the Security Council could take few additional substantive steps against the Smith régime, apart from incrementally tightening the nonmilitary embargo (military sanctions under Art. 42 were of course ruled out completely). This was unfortunate in light of the gaping hole in the embargo provided by South African and Portuguese trade, which enabled Rhodesian trade to recover to its pre-UDI levels by 1969 (Doxey 1980, 74–75), even in oil (as indicated in the Bingham report), and to expand substantially thereafter. Rhodesia's political self-confidence also grew discernibly during the late 1960s, due to its successful defiance of the embargo and its containment of the fledgling insurgency campaign. The intractability of the Smith government led to a complete breakdown of the *Fearless* negotiations in October 1968, and to the promulgation of a new and profoundly racist constitution in 1969, providing for separate homelands for blacks along the lines of South Africa's bantustan policy, and seemingly eliminating all possibility of a voluntary future transfer to majority rule.

The Council's next step was Resolution 277 of 18 March 1970 (*YUN* 1970, 81–83), which condemned the "Republic of Rhodesia," condemned all South

African and Portuguese collusion with Rhodesia (and demanded the withdrawal of all South African troops from the colony), and called upon states to take further steps to prevent the circumvention of the embargo by their nationals. Specifically it called upon all states to sever all transportation links with Southern Rhodesia (paragraph 3), and demanded the immediate severance of all diplomatic, consular, trade, military, and other official relations with the colony. The Council was successful in gaining the adherence of most of the twenty states which had maintained consulates in Salisbury at the time of the UDI (Galtung 1967, 380–81).

The Security Council was thereafter even more limited in its options; through Resolution 288 of late 1970, it merely "urge[d] all states to fully implement all past resolutions pertaining to Southern Rhodesia, in accordance with their obligations under Art. 25 of the Charter." Rhodesia's repudiation of all formal ties to the British Crown led to a third set of bilateral negotiations in 1971, now conducted by the Conservatives under Edward Heath, who backtracked further from Britain's earlier demands, and even accepted the 1969 constitution as the basis for future negotiations. However, the Pearce Commission, which conducted a six-month survey of Rhodesian attitudes toward the 1971 plans, found white acceptance but nearly total rejection by the black population, including even the avowedly nonviolent African National Council of Rhodesia under Bishop Abel Muzorewa.

In the early 1970s the trend for the Council was to emphasize mutual support schemes and to chastise uncooperative member governments. For example (and in accordance with Art. 50 of the Charter), Resolutions 326–29 (1973) called upon member states to take steps to aid Zambia, due to its intense difficulties in applying the full embargo, particularly following Rhodesia's unilateral closure of its border with Zambia in January 1973. Other resolutions, particularly 314 and 318 (1972) mildly reprimanded the United States for allowing the importation of Rhodesian chrome under the congressional Byrd amendment; and Resolution 320 specifically named the United States as a party to the violations. Through Resolution 333 (May 1973), the Security Council called on states to prevent insurance companies from insuring flights of people or cargo to Rhodesia, and to ensure that marine insurance contracts did not apply to goods shipped to or from Rhodesia (although the French, British, and United States all abstained). Through Resolution 388 (1976), the Council decided to prohibit the insuring of Rhodesian products, trade names, and franchises. Then through Resolution 409 (1977), the Council prohibited the use or transfer of funds in any state to the Rhodesian régime for any use other than pensions. However, the British government continually vetoed all attempts to impose a communications ban on Rhodesia; this was done for humanitarian reasons as well as to control the flow of information to and from the colony (Galtung 1967, 392).

During the 1970s the escalating guerrilla war, waged between ZAPU and ZANU supporters based in neighboring Zambia, Botswana, Angola, and

Mozambique, and the Rhodesian government (actively abetted by South African security forces) gradually superseded the sanctions operation as the principal vehicle for change in Rhodesia. Rhodesia's security position deteriorated further after the release in 1974 of many nationalists, including Joshua Nkomo of ZAPU and Ndabaningi Sithole of ZANU. The Lisbon coup of 25 April 1974, which ended the forty-year Salazar/Caetano dictatorship and led to the independence of Portugal's African colonies Mozambique, Angola, Guinea-Bissau, and the Cape Verde Islands, provided additional bases for guerrilla strikes into Rhodesian territory; and ZAPU and ZANU formally combined forces in 1975 into the Patriotic Front (PF), although disunity within the rival camps was a continual barrier to more effective resistance.

By 1976 Ian Smith was forced by Rhodesia's deteriorating military situation and pressured by Britain, South Africa Premier John Vorster, and Henry Kissinger to accept the principle of majority rule for Rhodesia, which led to the first all-party conference on Zimbabwe/Rhodesia in Geneva in October 1976. Further posturing by Smith, leading to the controversial "internal settlement" of 1978, led to additional tightening of sanctions (through SC Resolution 409) and to U.S. revocation, under the Carter administration, of the controversial Byrd amendment. The increasingly successful insurgency campaign by the Patriotic Front, and the PF's boycott of the elections of April 1979 (together with international condemnation of the vote through SC Resolution 445), forced Smith back into another round of negotiations. The Commonwealth Heads of Government Meeting at Lusaka (August 1979) and subsequently the Lancaster House agreement, negotiated principally by Lord Carrington, led to a settlement on majority rule and sovereignty for Zimbabwe, preceded by a temporary and transitional British administration under Lord Soames. As such, the renunciation of UDI on 17 December 1979 led to the end of sanctions and a dissolution of the UN Sanctions Committee, through Security Council Resolution 460 (21 December), and ultimately to the election of Robert Mugabe as prime minister in February 1980, and to an independent Zimbabwe the following April.

ASPECTS OF THE DISPUTE PERTAINING TO NEUTRALITY

An analysis of Swedish and Swiss attitudes toward the Rhodesian question must first consider the major features of the crisis as it pertained to the overall problem of neutrality within the UN system. In so doing it is necessary to recall some of the major features of the Italo-Abyssinian crisis (which preceded the Rhodesian affair by almost exactly three decades) in order to better establish the sequential development of neutrality vis-à-vis systems for collective security. There are, of course, many parallels between the two crises, not least because they were the initial instances of mandatory sanctions levied by the two organizations and as such were considered to be trials or tests, and potential precedents for future international enforcement action. They also arose at critical times for each organization: the ability of the League to ensure peace was being openly questioned by the early and mid-1930s, while the UN was just emerging from a serious financial crisis stemming from its extensive operations in the Congo, and had seen its first member (Indonesia) withdraw, temporarily, from membership in January 1965.

Nonetheless, the differences between the two cases are nearly as striking as their similarities. As illustrated above, the circumstances of the Rhodesia crisis hardly conformed to the classic sanctions scenario, whereby an act of aggression is countered by an internationally coordinated punitive sanctions operation (as with the Italian case). It was only due to the flexibility of the Security Council's authority and means of operating that the Rhodesian crisis could be brought up at all, and thereafter (at least until May 1968) addressed without the positive support of two of its five permanent members (France and the USSR).

In the present context, the Rhodesian affair differed from the Italian crisis primarily insofar as a position of neutrality was largely inapplicable. In the earlier case, a sharp distinction existed between the Italo-Abyssinian dispute, which erupted into a full-fledged war between two sovereign states, and resulted in the League's sanctions operation against one of the belligerents (Italy), thus raising a number of sensitive issues for some neutrals. However, in the Rhodesian case, the sanctions operation was not wholly separable from the Anglo-Rhodesian dispute over sovereignty; indeed the UN's actions were largely extensions of, and coterminous with, Britain's own unilateral pressure against Rhodesia, though broadened and backed by the authority (both legal and moral) of the UN. Thus the two strands of the general crisis—the Anglo-Rhodesian dispute and the sanctions operation—largely coincided. A policy of neutrality was a practicable option in neither of these two aspects.

In the first instance, there was no feasible opportunity to mete out equal treatment to the two sides in the conflict, comparable to the option (adopted in 1935 by the Swiss and Luxembourg governments) of the dual arms embargo, since Rhodesia was merely a rebelling colony rather than a sovereign state. Indeed such equality of treatment would have been patently illegal, insofar as it would imply recognition of the Rhodesian régime in defiance of every Security Council resolution on the situation, and would be regarded by international lawyers as aiding and abetting a colonial rebellion from its recognized municipal power. Quite understandably, the British government was adamant in its rejection of all notions of neutrality in the affair; Harold Wilson told the General Assembly in December 1965, "This is a moral issue. More than two years ago, when Leader of the Opposition...I said that this Rhodesian issue was one in which there could be no neutrals. There is no neutrality here in this Assembly" (quoted in Windrich 1975, Doc. 24, 240). Surely the fact that even South Africa and Portugal refrained from de jure recognition of the Rhodesian régime shows that it was unfeasible for any state to attempt to maintain official equidistance between the two antagonists, Britain and its colony.

Another point of contrast with 1935–36 was that the Rhodesian situation involved a civil dispute rather than armed conflict. From the beginning the British government categorically ruled out all use of military force against Smith, despite being continually pressured to use force by the black African states of the Commonwealth and OAU, through repeated Assembly and committee resolutions. Later, of course, violence erupted between the Zimbabwean nationalist insurgents, operating from bases in neighboring states, and Rhodesian and South African security forces, which intensified in the 1970s. The question of determining the international legal status of the insurgents was first raised at the May 1968 Teheran Conference on Human Rights, which in fact recognized the legitimacy of the struggle of the African liberation groups, and held that captured insurgents were to be treated as prisoners of war under the 1949 Geneva Conventions (*YUN* 1968, 151–52, 538–48, 557). This was also accepted by the General Assembly in Resolution 2383 (XXIII). Still, from the position of third states, the traditional laws of war and neutrality scarcely applied to the guerrilla campaign.

Another difference with the Italian case was the unlikelihood, indeed the virtual impossibility, of a general war breaking out as a result of the sanctions operation. In the League crisis, there was a widely perceived danger of war erupting as a direct or indirect consequence of the international sanctions operation, despite the prevailing (British) attitude of "all sanctions short of war"; and many member states' enthusiasm for the operation was tempered due to fears of Italian military retaliation, which had been actively threatened against participating states. In sharp contrast, the Rhodesian sanctions operation offered little scope for a wider international conflict. Even those (African) states demanding military intervention to put down the rebellion directed these demands toward the use of British, and not concerted UN, intervention, thereby ruling out a coordinated African (OAU) campaign. For its part, Rhodesia was unable to wage a sustained, even limited, war effort to counter the embargo, apart from limited incursions into neighboring territories to strike at guerrilla bases. Even Zambia, the state most exposed to Rhodesian counterattack, was an especially strong advocate of stiffer sanctions, again unlike the timidity of Italy's immediate neighbors in 1935–36. Furthermore, the insurgency campaign of the 1960s and 1970s was largely a separate development from the sanctions operation, rather than complementary to it, and represented a distinctly new phase of the crisis.

Still another difference between the two events lay in the balance of forces at work. Both crises were superficially similar in that it was scarcely realistic to attempt to treat the sanctioned state and the rest of the international community as equal parties. Nonetheless, the UN operation against Rhodesia was considerably more one-sided than the League's embargo had been. Although in the earlier case some fifty states originally concurred in the blockade, Britain gave clear lead to the operation. Since both Britain and Italy had been major powers, a position of equidistance was not entirely unrealistic, and a policy of quasi-neutrality or nonintervention was adopted by several League members as well as nonmembers. However, the degree of mismatch in 1965 was much more conspicuous. Any and all attempts to maintain equidistance between nearly the entire international community, on the one hand, and on the other a small landlocked colony in central Africa, ruled by a minority of just a quarter-million settlers, was unrealistic to the point of absurdity. In addition, the UN's rapid development toward universality by the early 1960s sharply limited the scope for legally circumventing the embargo by way of nonmembership. This quasi-universality also tended to dissipate any controversy surrounding the original imposition, and later the extension, of the international embargo, a problem which had plagued the earlier operation. In addition, the UN's overall objective was much more circumscribed—to bring about the submission of the Rhodesian régime to the rule of British law as a step toward majority rule and independence of the colony—than had been the League's, which punished Italy even while keeping Germany in the background as a potential future target for a similar operation. It is true that many considered the Rhodesian embargo as a possible prelude to similar measures against South Africa; even so, they were never thought to be a step toward UN military sanctions or to outright armed conflict.

These circumstances thus sharply limited the right of states to declare and maintain a neutral position in the Rhodesian crisis, as opposed to the Italian dispute. In 1935 neutrality had been a possible, if limited, option; while legally possible, it was also considered morally inadmissible, particularly for League members. On the other hand, in 1965 the UN's approach to universal membership, the manifestly one-sided nature of the situation, and the circumscribed collective security powers of the UN, all meant that neutrality was legally inapplicable, as well as inadmissable as a moral stance. Moreover, Portugal's assertions of "neutrality" in the affair (coupled with demands for financial restitution due to damage to its African colonies accruing from the embargo, as a thinly disguised means of abetting the white Rhodesian régime) did little to bolster the image of neutrality vis-à-vis a UN-sponsored sanctions operation. The Rhodesian operation did not call into question the compatibility of neutrality and UN obligations, and thus posed no imminent or prospective danger for neutral states. Due to these factors, the arguments calling for neutrals' participation in the operation were more compelling—and the excuses for abstention on the basis of neutrality less tenable—than in the earlier crisis.

NOTES

1. For the complete text of the UDI, see *International Legal Materials*, vol. 5, no. 2 (March 1966), pp. 230–31.

2. Through the "Enabling Act" of 11 November 1965 (later called the "Southern Rhodesia Act"), Britain refused recognition of Rhodesian passports issued after 11

November 1965; placed an embargo on the import of Rhodesian tobacco and sugar; and excluded Rhodesia from the Sterling Area and from all Commonwealth Preferences. See *International Legal Materials*, vol. 5, no. 2 (March 1966), pp. 232–34.

3. Through Resolution 2024 (XX), adopted on 11 November immediately after UDI, the Assembly: (1) condemned UDI; (2) invited Great Britain to implement all Assembly resolutions designed to put an end to the Rhodesian revolt; and (3) recommended that the Security Council consider the situation in Rhodesia as a "matter of urgency" (*YUN* 1965, 124).

4. See Kapungu, 1973, p. 26; Howell, 1969, p. 773; Fenwick, 1967, pp. 753–55; and the views of many U.S. Congressmen, summarized in McDougall and Reisman, 1968, pp. 5–6, nn. 21–3.

7

Sweden and the Rhodesian Operation

From the outset, the Swedish government was a keen participant in the UN's Rhodesian operation. Such was its response that a former Swedish foreign minister has suggested that Sweden's official policy in the affair had no pretensions of neutrality whatsoever (Blix 1970, 24); and indeed neutrality was never cited as a hindrance to Sweden's full concurrence with the Security Council during the Rhodesian crisis, even by the political opposition. Kapungu notes that Sweden was among a handful of states (along with Tanzania and Zambia) which responded enthusiastically to the sanctions operation (1973, 86).

The development of Sweden's official attitude toward the crisis can be subdivided broadly into two periods. The first phase covers the period from UDI in November 1965 until the Security Council's decision to impose relatively comprehensive sanctions (Resolution 253) in May 1968; the second phase covers the period following this widening of the embargo. This temporal division is not merely a convenient breaking point in the analysis: the period 1967–68 also ushered in a number of significant changes in both the conduct and content of Swedish policy, whereby its initial caution and pragmatism gave way to much more vocal expressions of active support for the "moral" issues of decolonization and antiracialism, and the rights of small states in the international system. During this period Sweden also adopted far-reaching, permanent sanctions legislation. This trend toward international activism or "active neutrality" on Sweden's part (in what is sometimes referred to as the "radicalization" of Swedish foreign policy [Barnes 1980]), was particularly relevant within the UN context, for each of the two main developments in Swedish policy marked an increasingly symbiotic linkage with the UNO: international activism with the General Assembly, sanctions legislation with the Security Council. A central task of this chapter is therefore to demonstrate that the theme of gradual but consistent development in Sweden's increasingly favorable attitude toward international sanctions during the League and UN periods reached a culmination during the Rhodesian dispute, in spite of the seeming disjunction suggested by Sweden's adoption of a much more activist international posture.

THE GOVERNMENT'S INITIAL STEPS

On the day of the Rhodesian UDI (11 November), the Swedish government issued a communiqué stating that it "has consistently maintained in the United Nations that an independent Rhodesia must have a régime that gives reasonable guarantees for the political, economic, and social rights of all its inhabitants. The Government has therefore no intention of recognizing the new Rhodesian régime" (*DSFP* 1965, 128). The statement also declared that the Swedish consul in Salisbury would be recalled immediately and that the government was actively considering what further steps could be taken in line with subsequent Security Council resolutions. It was notable that both these actions were taken even before the Security Council had called upon states not to recognize the Ian Smith régime, which came the following day through Resolution 216.

After the passage of Resolution 217 on 20 November, which again condemned the racial policy of Southern Rhodesia, called upon all states not to recognize the régime and recommended a trade embargo, Sweden's Prime Minister Tage Erlander underscored (22 November) his government's full compliance with the aims of the resolution and urged others to do the same: "It is the self-evident duty of all states to defend the United Nations and the principles of the UN Charter" (*DSFP* 1965, 120). The following day (November 23), the government announced that the Swedish consulate in Salisbury had been shut down. To provide protection for the 145 Swedes remaining in Rhodesia (mainly missionaries and their families), the former consul was personally watching for their safety, and the overall situation was being monitored by the Swedish legation in Pretoria, South Africa (*DSFP* 1965, 66–67).

In further compliance with the SC Resolution 217, Sweden's UN ambassador also announced, through a letter to the secretary-general, that his government had placed all trade between Sweden and Rhodesia under licensing control by the Swedish Board of Commerce.[1] This restriction also applied to credits opened on or before 11 November, and to all goods exported prior to 1 January 1966. A supplemental decree (11 February 1966) stipulated that all goods sent to or from Rhodesia after 14 February required special clearance for transit through Sweden (*SOU*, 1970, 19:27–28). At the time of UDI, Swedish-Rhodesian trade was not at a particularly high level, with imports from the colony amounting to 10.1m kronor (or slightly under $2m, as shown in

TABLE 7-1
Sweden's Annual Trade with Rhodesia, 1965-78
(in thousands of U.S. dollars)

Year	Imports from Rhodesia (1)	Exports to Rhodesia (2)
1965	1,960	3,413
1966	182	51
1967	0	1
1968	0	0
1969	0	2
1970	0	0
1971	0	0
1972	1	0
1973	0	3
1974	0	0
1975	0	1
1976	0	0
1977	0	0
1978	0	0

Source: UN Doc. S/10852/Rev. 1, pp. 111-12, 119-20; UN Doc. S/11927/Rev. 1, Vol. II, Appendices I and II, pp. 125-28 (for figures 1975-74) and UN Doc. S/13000, SS no. 2, Appendix, Table 1, p. 17 (for figures 1975-78).

table 7-1, col. 1), up 10 percent from the SwKr 9.0m recorded in 1964. Swedish exports to Rhodesia had risen from SEK 13.3m in 1964 to 17.7m in 1965 (*SOS* 1965:93; 1966:91).

The legal basis for these initial steps was a body of existing legislation, specifically two earlier "preparedness laws" of 1939 and 1940.[2] Nonetheless the government lacked authorization to seize Swedish shipping except during wartime, and thus it could not lawfully interfere with Swedish ships believed to be illegally destined for Rhodesia. Accordingly, after SC Resolution 221 was passed, the government undertook (13 May 1966) to widen this existing legislation, to allow itself greater navigational authority to seize illegal goods in peacetime, if this were recommended by the UN Security Council (*SFS* 1966, 1:158). The relevant provisions were automatically applicable if the Riksdag did not object to them within one month of the relevant Security Council resolutions, or if, within two months of its coming into effect, the Riksdag failed to give its formal approval. Nonetheless, this extension of power remained both provisional and temporary, being subject to alteration and valid only until the end of June 1968, although it was later extended to December 1971 (*SFS* 1970, 1:107).

This 1966 law was in fact formulated in anticipation of more permanent and comprehensive sanctions legislation, which however was only completed in 1971; thus the only legal authorization for the Swedish government to implement Security Council decisions on sanctions (other than the initial licensing of trade) during a full five-year period in the late 1960s was through the temporary law of 13 May 1966 (*SOU* 1970, 19:35–36). Later the government applied this law to all goods designated in SC Resolution 232 of December 1966 (*SFS* 1966, 2:766). Subsequently the government undertook, in accordance with paragraph 8 of Resolution 232, to report all these measures to the UN Secretariat (UN Doc. S/7781, Annex II, 1967, 57–58).

Two features distinguished the government's attitude during the Rhodesian crisis. One was the completely loyal manner in which Sweden, in close cooperation with Denmark and Norway, strove to fulfill its obligations under the Charter, with no reservations on account of its policy of neutrality. The second feature (foreshadowing a trend in its African policies) was Sweden's strong unilateral concern with the case. This was indicated by Foreign Minister Törsten Nilsson's initial statement on the crisis to the Riksdag, in which he vigorously criticized "the ruling minority [which] is barricading itself with all available means behind its white palisade" (*RP*, AK 1965, 40:6).

Swedish policy in fact went considerably beyond the call of duty for member states outlined in Arts. 25 and 49 of the Charter and stipulated through relevant Council resolutions. Each of its initial measures against Rhodesia was implemented unilaterally, prior to formal UN recommendation. First, the decision to close down the Swedish consulate at Salisbury was taken on 11 November, the day of the UDI and the day before Resolution 216 was passed; this break was significant partly because of its contrast with Denmark and Norway, both of which retained their Rhodesian consulates until 1970 (UN Docs. S/7005 and S/7008, 1965). Second, during the week prior to Resolution 217 (20 November) the government prepared decrees pertaining to Rhodesian trade, in anticipation of a resolution requesting states to sever trade with Rhodesia; then immediately after Resolution 217 the government could announce the implementation of its own complete trade embargo (*DSFP* 1965:67). Third, these unilateral measures were taken in the absence of a mandatory Council decision to do so under Chapter VII of the Charter, since the sanctions were merely advisory during the thirteen months from UDI until Resolution 232 in December 1966. In addition, Sweden had taken steps (again more rapidly than Denmark or Norway) to prevent even Swedish citizens living abroad from violating the embargo (*RP*, FK 1967, 12:38; Myrdal). Hence the Swedish government not only applied the embargo well before most other member states; its actions even preceded the relevant Security Council resolutions themselves.

The government preempted the Security Council in a fourth and still more important manner. As early as his 9 December statement, Nilsson had "expressed the opinion that the present situation in Southern Rhodesia does in fact constitute a threat to peace and [that] in this case the Security Council would have grounds for a mandatory decision relating in the first place to economic sanctions" (*RP*, AK 1965, 40:6). That same day the Swedish representative to the Fourth (Colonial) Committee of the General Assembly supported a draft resolution which noted with deep concern the serious threat to international peace and security in southern Africa, aggravated by the Rhodesian rebellion (Kay 1970, appendix E, 218–19). This opinion was also reiterated on several other occasions during the following year (*DSFP* 1965, 130; 1966, 43).

One of the main reasons for Sweden's insistence on an early extension of sanctions was its concern that non-obligatory measures would soon prove inadequate, with a consequent loss of credibility for the UNO:

The prestige of the United Nations—one of its greatest assets—is at stake.... As recommendations only are in question, there is a risk that states ... may feel themselves free to maintain normal economic relations with the régime in Southern Rhodesia. In this way the effectiveness of the sanctions would be drastically diminished and the ability of the Smith régime to defy world opinion would correspondingly increase. (*RP*, AK 1965, 40:7)

Even the British government, which had initiated Security Council action, pointedly criticized the early Swedish insistence on the imposition of mandatory sanctions, apparently fearing that this forceful Swedish stance could jeopardize the pending bilateral Anglo-Rhodesian talks aboard HMS *Tiger* in December 1966; the Swedish government had in fact repudiated such negotiations throughout the previous year (*RP*, AK 1966, 12:30, 60; Nilsson). Accordingly, Sweden regarded the extension of the embargo through Resolution 232 more as a matter of course than a significant new development. Immediately following the decision the government even lamented the fact that "much valuable time has been wasted before the UN got the opportunity to take a more direct responsibility for the settlement of the conflict" (*DSFP* 1966:49).

Later, a similar pattern emerged in its efforts (through repeated representations to the Fourth Committee, the Committee of Twenty-Four and the Assembly itself) to widen Resolution 232 to include a complete embargo. Nilsson stated in early 1968 that "sanctions against Rhodesia should ... be total.... We have done everything we could in order to ensure that the implementation of sanctions should become more effective than what it has been up to now" (*RP*, AK 1968, 13:5, 17). The government's attitude was also strongly affected by a sharp rise in political repression in southern Africa in early 1968. The execution of three Rhodesian blacks in March 1968 (soon after the sentencing to death of 36 Namibians in Pretoria) was harshly denounced by Nilsson in the Riksdag (*RP*, AK 1968, 13:3). The executions led directly to full Swedish support for an Algerian draft in the Security Council for the imposition against Rhodesia of the full range of nonmilitary sanctions listed in Art. 41, and even induced Swedish support for voluntary economic sanctions against South Africa (*DSFP* 1968:111–12). The government's efforts to impose measures "as comprehensive as possible" against Rhodesia caused it to "greet with great satisfaction the adoption of Resolution 253" (UN Doc. S/ 8786, Annex II, 83).

On one interpretation, this attitude would seem to contradict Sweden's continual insistence that only the Security Council was authorized to determine whether a threat to the peace existed. However, a distinction must be made between expressions of governmental opinion, and policy, on an issue; the difference lay in Sweden's insistence that the official, legal determination as to the existence of a threat remained the sole prerogative of the Security Council (*RP*, AK 1966, 12:31; Nilsson). This view was based on two factors. One was its long-standing insistence on a proper implementation of the UN Charter, in both letter and spirit. Sweden's loyalty to the UN was based largely on the important assumption that the collective security mechanism would be implemented properly and in accordance with the Charter, that is by the Security Council rather than the General Assembly (*DSFP* 1965:123); Sweden accordingly regarded as unconstitutional any Assembly call for sanctions and/or the use of force against Rhodesia (*RP*, AK 1966, 12:31; Nilsson). In addition, the government argued that specific General Assembly action under the 1950 Uniting for Peace Resolution (which allowed for Assembly discussion and recommendation on issues pertaining to international peace and security in case of Security Council deadlock) was out of order in this particular crisis, since the Council had already initiated action. This legalistic approach, with its emphasis on the authority of the rule of law both within Sweden and in the international system, also reflected the views of longtime Foreign Minister (and formerly, professor of civil law) Östen Undén. The force of Swedish tradition on this issue was strong: Undén's successor, Törsten Nilsson, asserted that "for a country with Sweden's traditions, it is self-evidently impossible to give support to violent solutions, no matter how strongly we sympathize with the oppressed population" (*RP*, AK 1966, 37:85).

The second reason for Sweden's insistence that the Security Council must initiate any UN action was more pragmatic. The government argued that sanctions must be carefully formulated, relatively circumscribed in content, and orchestrated on a universal scale to achieve the desired aim, namely the submission of the Smith régime to British constitutional authority. Even though it shared the widespread hostility toward Rhodesia, the Swedish government feared that empty, overanxious expressions of militancy on the part of the black African states, particularly in their calls for the use of force by Britain and/or the UN, were not only unrealistic, but threatened to split the existing near-consensus in the UN in favor of pressuring Salisbury as well as the associated governments in Pretoria and Lisbon. For these reasons Nilsson judiciously cautioned the Assembly majority to avoid "exaggerated resolution-making which could exacerbate the tendencies, not least among the larger member states, towards a certain indifference to the resolutions of the Assembly" (*RP*, AK 1966, 12:31; Nilsson).

On this basis, Sweden established the early precedent of supporting all generally worded Assembly resolutions condemning the régime, yet abstaining on all resolutions specifically advocating the use of force by Britain to put down the rebellion (*RP*, AK 1966, 37:85). Thus Sweden was able to support GA Resolution 2024 (XX, of 12 November 1965) condemning the UDI and urging nonrecognition of any minority Rhodesian régime, but refraining from calling for any specific punitive measures. On the other hand, it abstained on both (far-reaching) Assembly resolutions on the crisis passed during its 21st session in late 1966, Resolution 2138 (22 October) and particularly Resolution 2151 (17 November). In the government's view, this line of policy was fully consistent with its expressed opinion that the Council's most effective action would be additional mandatory sanctions.

Sweden also demonstrated its support for UN actions through its forceful advocacy of provisions for mutual support for third states affected adversely by the embargo. This decision was a clear step toward full acquiescence in economic sanctions obligations under the UN Charter, particularly in light of its decision not to adopt specific measures of mutual support for third states in 1935–36. As early as 1966 the government proposed a special UN study of the problem of "equitable sharing of the economic burdens resulting from sanctions and falling heavily on certain countries" (*DSFP* 1966:43). Sweden's UN Ambassador, Sverker Åström, first raised the question of burden-sharing within the UN before the Special Committee on 12 December 1966 (*RP*, AK 1967, 12:34). These calls initially referred to Zambia, which depended heavily on Rhodesian electricity, from the Kariba Dam on the River Zambezi which separates the two countries, to operate its essential copper mining industry. Here again Sweden preempted the Security Council, which did not call for mutual support actively until Zambia unilaterally closed its border with Rhodesia in 1973 to halt anti-guerrilla incursions (e.g., SC Resolutions 326 and 327, 1973). Later, the UN requested support for Mozambique as well, through SC Resolution 386 (1976), which was in fact cosponsored by Sweden, in its capacity as a nonpermanent Security Council member during 1975–76.

One means of engendering support for UN activities in southern Africa was through a common Nordic approach, mainly including Denmark and Norway, as a means of forging a more limited consensus and a western bridge to the more activist "front-line" states. This process began in 1963 with a Scandinavian initiative to establish an international expert group to examine the situation in South Africa. During 1966 a second Nordic initiative was launched through two separate agreements (Stockholm in April, Aalborg in August) at the foreign ministry level, through which each government stressed its unequivocal support for UN sanctions, including support for complete mandatory sanctions at the earliest possible date, and their rejection of violence as a means of ending the rebellion (*DSFP* 1966:54). This bridge-building initiative produced more than a modicum of success in later years, particularly as the focus extended to the North-South dialogue, beginning at the First UN

Conference on Trade and Development (UNCTAD) in 1964 and at UNCTAD II in 1968 at New Delhi. Such cooperation expanded further during the 1970s, culminating in the unofficial group of "like-minded" states. This development provided certain reminders of the old "ex-neutral" group within the League of Nations, held together at least partly on Swedish impetus; now it offered a means of promoting greater small state collaboration within the UN system.

On the other hand, Denmark had stirred dissension within the Nordic group by unilaterally advocating (in 1963 and 1965) draft resolutions within the UN's Special Political Committee to induce a Security Council decision to apply sanctions against South Africa.[3] Sweden did maintain a direct interest in UN consideration of this issue, particularly since its minister without portfolio, Alva Myrdal, had chaired the first UN Committee of Experts on South Africa, which in 1964 had suggested many potential hazards in a sanctions operation and recommended further study of "the economic and strategic aspects of sanctions" (UN Doc. S/5658, 20 April 1964, paragraph 110). However, Sweden demurred on the question of sanctioning either Portugal or South Africa: the former due to their common membership and growing trade links within EFTA, and the latter partly because of the substantial, and rapidly increasing, level of Swedish investments in South Africa.[4] The government argued that "We must therefore beware of the illusion that this weapon [sanctions] ought to be used more frequently" (*DSFP* 1969:50–51). Its attitude was clearly tempered by the ICJ's important 1966 ruling on the South-West Africa case, whereby the Court refused to uphold the legal validity of the moral arguments against apartheid as a reason for revoking South Africa's earlier (1923) League mandate over South-West Africa (Falk 1970, 126–33, 378–402). Swedish officials expressed disappointment with this ruling (*DSFP* 1966:31).

THE RIKSDAG'S RESPONSE

The government's initial position on the Rhodesian crisis engendered widespread, even enthusiastic, acceptance within the Riksdag, including support for the government's early call for mandatory sanctions. The significance of Sweden's strong unilateral stance was acknowledged throughout the political spectrum, from parties as diverse as the Conservatives and the Communists. For example, Liberal leader Bertil Ohlin urged the government to continue its "pressure to get the Security Council to include a binding decision on economic sanctions from the members of the UN" (*RP, AK* 1966, 12:40; esp. Wedén, 64). The Liberals' position was in fact even more uncompromising than was the SAP government's view, particularly as it called strongly for UN sanctions against both South Africa and Portugal;[5] the government, however, rejected this option, particularly as against Portugal, through EFTA.[6] Though somewhat less forthright on the issue, the Center Party also appeared to concur with the view that binding sanctions were necessary, and its leader, Gunnar Hedlund, considered it "distressing" that some states had been nonchalant toward the recommendations in Resolutions 216 and 217 (RP, AK 1966, 12:49). The small Left-Wing Socialist Party was, of course, adamant that the government and the Security Council should widen the embargo against Rhodesia, as was the Communist Party (*RP*, AK 1966, 12:70, 79).

Only the Conservatives appeared rather more skeptical than the government on the possibility of concrete results through sanctions, saying that "there will be much to explain if the effect is not that which is anticipated, something which naturally would not strengthen the prestige of the UN, either now or later" (*RP*, AK 1966, 12:53; Bohman). The Conservative leader also queried whether the Swedish reaction had not been excessively harsh, although his attitude was based partly on the mistaken assumption that even the export of medical supplies to the colony would be severed. Yet even the Conservatives did not propose a declaration of Swedish neutrality relative to the sanctions operation. Of all the speakers in the spring 1966 *remiss* debate, only one—the Social Democratic Foreign Minister, Törsten Nilsson—even mentioned neutrality, and that merely to reiterate that neutrality could play no role in such a crisis (*RP*, AK 1966, 12:59). Indeed in 1969 the government explicitly ruled out all possibility of playing a mediating role in southern Africa (*DSFP* 1969:50). This tendency to avoid all mention of neutrality in the UN operation clearly indicated that the government regarded sanctions as compatible with its neutrality; this was also significant in contrast with the two other major foreign policy issues under discussion in Sweden during the same period, the Vietnam War and EEC membership, both of which raised important issues bearing on Sweden's neutrality.

Some dissension did however arise on a related issue, whether the government should allow a Swedish industrial firm, ASEA, to participate in the Cabora Bassa power project in Portuguese Mozambique along the River Zambezi. The case directly concerned the Rhodesian embargo because electricity from the completed project would be sold to Rhodesia. The issue also became a major focus of Riksdag debate in March 1969 (*RP*, AK 1969, 13 and 28) and in fact it produced an apparent reversal of political roles. The Liberal Party, supported by the far left, called strongly for governmental intervention to prevent ASEA's involvement in the project, whereas the SAP government, in apparent if tactical agreement with the Conservative Party, again adopted the line of relative caution and refused to forcibly prohibit ASEA's participation.[7] However, the government did state that if and when electricity was actually delivered to Rhodesia (not expected until 1978) it would step in and halt any further Swedish participation (*RP*, AK 1969, 13 and 37; Nilsson). More notable than these differences of political opinion was ASEA's unilateral decision to withdraw from the project, pressured to do so by Swedish public opinion; this pressure was a striking indication of the degree of public interest which the Rhodesian situation had engendered in Sweden by the late 1960s, particularly as ASEA was the only participating firm to withdraw unilaterally. A very similar situation developed a year later (1970), when ASEA was compelled through public pressure to withdraw from its planned participation in constructing the Kariba North power station on the Zambian-Rhodesian border, even though such participation would not breach either the Swedish legal code or the UN embargo (*DSFP* 1969:105–6).

SWEDEN'S PRE-1965 UN SANCTIONS POLICY AS A FACTOR

Sweden's advocacy of sanctions against Rhodesia, and the political unanimity behind this decision, was largely attributable to the evolution of Sweden's position within the UN prior to 1965. From the outset, Sweden's enthusiasm for the UN was tempered by the unfortunate League experience and particularly by its narrow escape from World War II with its neutrality intact (unlike all its immediate neighbors). In 1945 Sweden's geopolitical situation was acutely exposed, adjacent to a much stronger and victorious Soviet Union and without the traditionally countervailing influence of German power in the Baltic region.

In 1945 there was virtual unanimity in Sweden as to the usefulness of postwar international political cooperation. Nonetheless there was some difference of opinion concerning the degree to which its neutrality should be altered or "relaxed" as a UN member; this debate centered mainly on the positions of the wartime and postwar foreign ministers, respectively Christian Günther and Östen Undén, the latter being considerably more flexible on the issue (Andrén 1967, 36–39). Indeed it was striking that Undén from the start placed so little emphasis on neutrality as the cornerstone for Sweden's postwar policy, particularly after its wartime success, although he did agree that neutrality should remain an important fall-back position in case of a great power conflict. Moreover, in one of the few academic contributions to the debate, Prof. Nils Herlitz, examining the coercive mechanism, even advocated a sanctions system operable against the great powers.[8]

The government set out its position regarding the nascent UN Organization in October 1945, in the first postwar session of the Riksdag (*RP*, FK 1945, 32; AK 34). In identical statements to the Upper and Lower Chambers, Prime Minister Per Albin Hansson and Undén stressed that postwar Swedish policy would be based upon participation in the UN, coupled with an avoidance of great power blocs:

We are willing to join a common security organization and in case of a future conflict to relinquish our neutrality to the extent demanded by the statutes of the Organization. But if, contrary to expectation, a tendency should develop within the Organization toward a division of the great powers into dual camps, our policy must be not to let ourselves be forced into any such grouping or bloc. (*RP*, FK 1945, 32:3)

These views were also expressed in the government's official proposition (no. 196) to the Riksdag in 1946 concerning UN accession, through which it accepted the veto right as an inevitable "consequence of the fact that a system of security under the conditions now obtaining in the world stands or falls in accordance with the unanimity and solidarity of the Great Powers on vital subjects on which war and peace are dependent" (Proposition 196, 1946, 14). This acceptance of the great power veto was crucial to Sweden's unequivocal acceptance of UN sanctions, both military and nonmilitary. This again represented a realistic interpretation of the Charter, since all UN military obligations, including rights of passage, presupposed a prior agreement between the Swedish government and the UN Security Council. In addition, the government acknowledged that economic sanctions could never be imposed against any of the five major powers. For these reasons even the Swedish military, which in 1920 had strongly opposed League membership, asserted that "positive Swedish collaboration within the UN is thus desirable" (Proposition 196, 12).

The lack of political opposition to the UN reduced the debates of June 1946 to little more than a formality that did not even require a vote (*RP* 1946, 28:11–30; AK, 29:3–21); "the opinion was expressed in all quarters that Sweden ought to cooperate actively, positively, loyally and in every way toward the successful achievement of international peace according to the means outlined in the Charter" (Håstad 1956, 41). Only one deputy (a Conservative, Fahlman) opposed Sweden's membership, on the somewhat vague grounds that the UN was an insufficient guarantor for Sweden's security (*RP*, AK 1946, 29:21). The rest of both Riksdag chambers fully supported the UN, but without undue expectations; or as Sandler, the former foreign minister, asserted, "without lamentations, without illusions, and without hesitation" (*RP*, FK 28:22–24).

Perhaps the most striking feature of the debate was the across-the-board acceptance that UN membership would inevitably derogate Sweden's neutrality; Undén even held that "in case of war which is caused by a decision on sanctions by the Security Council, there is no right for member states to carry forth a neutral policy. Sweden also accepts this consequence through its accession" (*RP*, FK 1946, 28:12). He again underscored this position in his first speech to the General Assembly, during its second session in October 1946:

By entering the United Nations, Sweden is accepting important restrictions on her liberty of action in cases where collective steps may be taken to prevent threats to peace. In the Swedish Parliament there was no difference of opinion when it came to accepting these international obligations. We undertook them with a full realization of their implications. (*AKU* 1946:9)

Nonetheless Sweden tended to shun a leading UN role after accession, largely due to its relative lack of maneuverability during the Cold War. The government generally downplayed the utility of the coercive mechanism in favor of strengthening the system for peacefully resolving disputes (Chapter VI of the Charter), leading to occasional descriptions of a "legalistic" Swedish UN policy (Eek 1955, 35). In terms of the sanctions problem, however, Sweden did support the first (halting) UN attempts to bring pressure on régimes of which it disapproved, including diplomatic protests against Spain (1946) and Albania and Bulgaria (1948).[9] However, during the Korean War Sweden's policy was sharply (and, arguably, unjustly) criticized in the West for vacillation after it initially supported the Western condemnation of North Korea as the aggressor, but thereafter abstained on the question of similarly condemning China, due to the fear that the war could escalate into a great power confrontation (Holmström 1972).

Sweden gradually assumed a more active posture within the UN during the 1950s. The election of a Swedish economist and foreign ministry official, Dag Hammarskjöld, to the office of UN secretary-general was unquestionably an important factor, as was his frequent use of Swedes, particularly Ambassadors Gunnar Jarring and Baron Beck-Friis, as UN mediators. Accordingly, Sweden began to participate in UN peacekeeping actions, beginning with the United Nations Emergency Force (UNEF) in the Suez in 1956 (*DSFP* 1956:100), and continuing in the Gaza, Congo, Kashmir, Cyprus, and Lebanon operations. In another important step, the three Scandinavian governments in 1963 became the first to designate special troop contingents for exclusive use in international peacekeeping operations, with each state bearing the cost of their maintenance (Haekkerup 1964, 675–81); this step was also important insofar as it showed that neutrals and allied states (both Norway and Denmark being NATO members) could cooperate even in security policy if related to the UNO. By this time the Swedish government considered the UN to be "a natural framework for the pursuit of an active foreign policy by a neutral nation" (*DSFP* 1963:14–15). Sweden's increasing level of international activity was also demonstrated through its two-year term as a nonpermanent Security Council member during 1957–58, during which time it played a useful intermediary role in two important crises, Kashmir and Lebanon (Eek 1959).

The gradual decline of the Cold War and the "melting" of the hitherto monolithic power blocs in Europe by the early 1960s also contributed to Sweden's increasingly activist role. The new topics of UN debate, particularly decolonization, shifted the focus of world conflict away from Europe, where Sweden's influence was limited by its position as the hinge of the Nordic balance of power, to outlying areas of Africa and Asia. Sweden's status as a small power with no inhibiting colonial past, and as a successful modern society stressing social welfare and the elimination of poverty yet retaining the essential elements of a free market economy, indeed led many Swedes to regard the "Swedish way" as a natural model and bridge to the developing states, stressing their common nonaligned posture and potential as trading partners. Sweden's racial homogeneity also arguably contributed to its increasing "international consciousness" (Board 1970, 196), a sense of identification with the growing movement in favor of national self-determination for areas in black Africa still under European colonial domination; it was an opportunity to identify more closely with what Edward Rowe (1964) called the "emerging anti-colonial consensus" in the UN. Here also, the Swedish government showed responsiveness to significant new international developments: changing priorities within UN debate, particularly decolonization, were coupled with an increasing degree of public awareness, concern, and involvement within Sweden to influence official action on these issues (Tarschys 1977, 139).

EXTENDING THE EMBARGO

The Security Council's extension of the embargo through Resolutions 232 and 253 led to further efforts by the Erlander government to tighten the restrictions on intercourse between Sweden and Rhodesia. This effort not only showed Sweden's continuing loyalty to the UN; moreover it seemed, according to the official trade figures, altogether superfluous. The total volume of commodity trade between Sweden and Rhodesia had been drastically curtailed, in both directions, already by 1966 (to SEK 0.9m and 0.3m for imports and exports respectively) due to the import and export restrictions imposed in November 1965; and by 1967 this trade had been all but eliminated (for dollar figures, see table 7-1). Thereafter virtually the only commercial relations between Sweden and Rhodesia involved medicinal goods and, in 1967, sculpture sent to nonprofit Rhodesian organizations (a permitted exception to the embargo). In 1969, only SEK 1,000 worth of electrical relays were sent (due to a small loophole in paragraph 3 of Resolution 253); and thereafter only small amounts of exports were reported in intermittent years, mainly in the form of humanitarian aid. In light of this success, Sweden's minister of commerce told the Social Democrats' annual party conference in 1969 that "in regard to Rhodesia it can be said without exaggeration that no nation has applied that decision [regarding sanctions] more strictly than Sweden" (*DSFP* 1969:57).

Despite this explicit confirmation of full Swedish compliance with the sanctions, and on the basis of the Council's Resolution 253, the government decreed on 28 June 1968 a further application against Rhodesia of operative paragraph 2 of the (1940) trade restriction law, applicable to both direct and indirect supply of goods to and from Rhodesia. The only exceptions were medicinal and educational supplies, news materials, and food aid (*SFS* 1968, 2[449]:1263–64). The decree also stipulated that (1) no one holding a Rhodesian passport would be allowed in Sweden, except on humanitarian grounds, under paragraph 5(b) of Resolution 253; and (2) all applications for flights to Rhodesia, in contravention of Resolution 253, would be refused. In line with these measures, the Scandinavian Airlines System (SAS) was one of the first international carriers to cancel its previously existing interairline agreement with Air Rhodesia (UN Doc. S/11927/Rev. I, Vol. I, Annex III, 215). The government also affirmed that no Swedish air carrier shipped any products to Rhodesia against Resolution 253; and it pledged to commission a special committee to examine the necessity for further legislation to remove any remaining constitutional barriers, which was in fact done in Sweden (see below) (UN Doc. S/8786, Annex II, 82–83).

THE ESTABLISHMENT OF PERMANENT UN LEGISLATION IN SWEDEN

The government's efforts to strengthen its legal authority to implement UN sanctions were rooted in its early difficulty in applying sanctions fully against Rhodesia on the basis of previous legislation. This problem had been only partially rectified through the temporary sanctions law of May 1966. By the late 1960s its efforts to enact general sanctions legislation reached fruition through the passage into law of two separate bills. The first of these was a temporary UN law concerning sanctions against Rhodesia (covering Resolution 253), passed in 1969; the second, utilizing this act as a springboard, was more far-reaching, permanent UN legislation, completed in 1971.

The 1969 Law Concerning Sanctions Against Rhodesia

The initial groundwork for this widening of executive authority was laid by a three-member UN Legal Committee of the Riksdag's first chamber, directed by Eskil Hellner and including Allan Hernelius and Yngve Möller. First constituted in February 1966 and officially decreed the following May, its main objective was to set forth guidelines for future Swedish sanctions legislation, by examining the probable long-term effects of a UN sanctions operation on the Swedish domestic legal code. These preparatory stages were completed during the period 1966–68. The government's preparations for the new law began in earnest in August 1968, following its implementation of Resolution 253, and continued until March 1969, when the bill (Proposition 78) was presented to the Riksdag's lower house.[10]

The bill envisioned an extension of the government's authority to take any additional measures not covered by existing legislation that would maximize the effectiveness of the embargo against Rhodesia. Specifically, it would authorize the government to enforce the embargo outside Swedish territory, by ordering a temporary stop on any activity (commercial or other) between Swedes and Rhodesians; any such injunction would be submitted later to the Riksdag for examination. It was clear that the Erlander government desired greater centralized control within Sweden over the implementation of Security Council resolutions, particularly with an eye toward reducing the time involved in effecting any future Security Council resolutions pertaining to the Rhodesian crisis. In doing so, the government cited the far-reaching unity within parliament and in public opinion, as evidence of widespread confidence in its Rhodesia policy; and it asserted that the Riksdag need not fear encroachments on its ability to debate such issues. Despite these claims, a number of outside experts questioned the need for this proposed legislation, the most prominent of which was, significantly, the Swedish legal society (*advokatsamfundet*).

Given the fact that the SAP had been returned to office in 1968 with an absolute majority of 50.1 percent (its first in the postwar period), passage of the bill was virtually assured beforehand. Nonetheless, in order to stem controversy over the proposal, the government stressed its limited applicability, particularly its relevance only to the Rhodesian case. For example, the proposal sharply distinguished between Security Council and General Assembly resolutions, and asserted that any proposals to extend the Assembly's authority to decree coercive sanctions would be rejected, partly on account of Sweden's neutrality policy:

Only the Security Council has competence to take a decision on compulsory measures. Strict observance of this rule is of vital importance for a neutral state's membership in the UN. We have as a UN member given up our neutrality only in the very limited extent which follows the voting regulations in the Security Council. To widen our duties to partake in compulsory measures is not compatible with the spirit of the Charter. (*RP*, AK 1969, 13:39; Nilsson)

On this basis the foreign minister also repudiated demands for closer Swedish identification with the Uniting for Peace Resolution, although he did not entirely rule out association with (non-binding) Assembly resolutions (*RP*, AK 1969, 13:39). His clear implication was that the proposed law would not widen Sweden's obligations to the UN, but would merely increase its capability of fulfilling its existing duties under the Charter. In addition, Trade Minister Lange opposed any extension of the law to cover Portugal, as contrary to GATT regulations. Even so, there was some difference of opinion, even within the SAP, over the actual intent (and extent of applicability) of the proposed law (*RP*, AK 1969, 28:39; Bergquist).

The government's relative caution on the issue, which was designed to appease the non-Socialist parties, paradoxically drew criticism from the Liberals, Center Party and Left-Party Communists, who argued: (1) that the scope of the law should be widened to cover illegal transactions by other states, and should even allow for unilateral Swedish measures against South Africa and Portugal; and (2) that Sweden should associate itself more closely with General Assembly resolutions.[11] On the other hand, Gösta Bohman, leader of the Conservatives (from 1969 called *Moderaterna samlingspartiet*, or the "Moderate Unity Party") argued that the law would hinder the formation of a national consensus on foreign policy issues (*RP*, AK 1969, 13:78–79). The Conservatives also proposed that the new law provide the possibility of compensation for Swedish firms sustaining losses as a result of an implementation of the law (*RP*, AK, 28:51–54; Kristensson). In response to these arguments, the government held that the proposed law would be only temporary, and would be superseded eventually by permanent UN legislation (contemplated for presentation to the 1970–71 Riksdag).

On this basis the bill was passed on 29 May 1969. The new Act Concerning Certain Sanctions Against Rhodesia[12] prohibited a wide range of transactions with the colony, including all activity promoting Rhodesian-Swedish trade and the granting of credits. In addition, it extended the government's authority to implement the trade restrictions even outside Swedish territory. The law was originally set to expire at the end of 1970, although it was later extended for one year (Proposition 202 år 1970; *SFS* 1970:750). It was also supplemented by two further measures. One was a rewording of the earlier (1954) Aliens Law, to prohibit the entry of any foreigner into the Nordic region (Sweden, Denmark, Norway, Iceland, and Finland) who had violated UN sanctions against any state (though with clear reference to the Rhodesian embargo). The new law also revoked the 28 June 1968 decree which had prohibited trade with Rhodesia in Swedish vessels, but which was rendered obsolete by this more inclusive legislation (*SFS* 1969, 1[233]:511–12; [234]:513–14).

The 1971 Permanent Law Concerning UN Sanctions

The government's efforts to achieve "full-power" authorization to implement UN sanctions were conducted on two levels: domestically through the Hellner (UN Legal) Committee, and internationally through official and semi-official representations to the Nordic Council. As early as 1966 (repeated in Oslo in January 1967) the Swedish government had proposed to the Council that each of the Nordic governments should conclude similar legislation pertaining to the UN Security Council decisions on sanctions. This initial effort had met with some success; by 1969 the other Nordic states (Norway, Denmark, and Finland—Iceland did not participate in the process) had enacted special laws regarding UN sanctions, indeed even prior to Sweden. Then in March 1968 the Swedish government formally tabled a proposal for common Nordic legislation which would enable the four governments to implement Security Council recommendations, as well as binding decisions, automatically, since, it argued, the UN Charter "presupposes that internal laws [on sanctions] ought to be brought into harmony."[13]

The Danish, Norwegian, and Finnish foreign ministers all opposed the Swedish initiative,[14] although the Danes appeared somewhat more receptive than the others to its aims. This negative response was significant in light of the continual effort between the governments in Oslo, Copenhagen, Helsinki, and Stockholm to coordinate UN policy. The main reasons given by all three states' representatives were twofold: first, that identical, permanent Nordic legislation concerning sanctions was unnecessary since each state individually had enacted similar, if separate, sanctions laws by mid-1968, and that such a measure would require them to alter those laws significantly. More importantly, they argued that a law applicable to mere Security Council recommendations would hinder their future freedom of action to choose whether, or the degree to which, they should adhere to the Council's request.

The Finns also added the argument that such a measure "can considerably reduce private trade activity and restrict the affairs of citizens" (Proposition A/196E, 944). Notably, neither Finland's negative response nor its permanent UN law of 29 December 1967 was grounded in its policy of neutrality—a seeming indication that neutrality was becoming a less substantive excuse for abstaining from UN operations. The attitude of all three governments was also negatively influenced by two other extenuating factors: pique at Sweden's decision in early 1969 to recognize the North Vietnamese régime (without prior Nordic consultation); and their common disinclination to accept any further limitations on their freedom of action which could jeopardize their on-going, sensitive trade negotiations with the EEC.

Despite these individually negative responses by the respective governments, the chairman of Sweden's Legal Committee, Eskil Hellner, thereafter (20 June 1968) appealed to the Economic Committee of the Nordic Council to recommend such a coordination in the UN legislation of the four countries (Proposition 196/E 1969, 947–49). This effort was supported by both the Swedish-UN Association and the Swedish Peace and Arbitration Society (Proposition 196/E 1969, 950, 951). After two separate discussions on the issue (in Oslo on 21 October 1968, and in Stockholm immediately prior to the decision, the Committee rejected the Swedish proposal on 31 January 1969.[15] It held that legislation on implementing Security Council recommendations was unnecessary, since their respective UN laws did not preclude such adherence. The Committee also turned down the more general Swedish appeal for common Nordic legislation pertaining to UN activity, since their individual laws "do not constitute a hindrance for a similar Nordic UN policy concerning such a decision" (NR, 17e sessionen, mars 1969, bil. 2, 953).

Despite this failure, the government was able to build on its provisional law of May 1969 by formulating such comprehensive UN legislation within Sweden itself. Its views were contained in the final report of the Hellner Committee, submitted in April 1970; in its official proposal to parliament (77, 1971); and in its arguments to the Riksdag in the debate of 18 May 1971.

The government's arguments in favor of Proposition 77 were basically threefold. One was that the UN Charter failed to specify the duties of member states to comply with Security Council recommendations; Sweden thereby needed relevant domestic legislation in order to redress this structural deficiency in the Charter by establishing a preset formula (Proposition 77, 1971, 15). Thus the government seemed to consider the general, good faith obligations of UN membership, derived from Arts. 2(5), 25, and 49 of the Charter, to be equally pertinent for legally binding and nonbinding measures (the distinction between which would be soon clarified, through SC Resolution 278 after the 1971 ICJ Advisory Opinion on the South-West Africa case). Although the provisory law of May 1966 had also referred to UN recommendations, since it was implemented before the sanctions against Rhodesia had been made mandatory, the 1971 proposed law undoubtedly was a new step, since it, in contrast to the May 1966 and May 1969 laws, would be permanent, with no set date of expiration.

A second major concern of the government was the "need for an instrument which can guarantee such implementation (of sanctions) without delay" (*SOU* 1970, 19:66). This concern undoubtedly stemmed from the year-long (June 1968–May 1969) period before the government could fully implement all the provisions of Resolution 253. The Legal Committee considered the need for rapid action on UN decisions to be sufficiently strong to override any possible adverse consequences arising due to automatic participation in a contentious enforcement operation; it specifically cited the Suez crisis (when UN Secretary-General Dag Hammarskjöld formulated UNEF, with Swedish participation, in only a few days' time) as recent proof of this requirement.

A third, and more contentious, reason given for proposing such a law was the need to extend Swedish executive power, to give it full-power authority on UN issues (*SOU* 1970, 19:50). The countereffect of such an extension, however, would be a decline in Riksdag influence, since it would eliminate the necessity of holding parliamentary debate over sanctions questions prior to governmental action. Any such consultation with Parliament would take place only after the fact, within a "reasonable period of time" (*SOU* 1970, 19:9). The Legal Committee was, however, alive to the possibility of political controversy arising as a result of this provision, so it estimated a waiting period of not more than one month, or if the Riksdag were in recess, within a month of being reconvened (*SOU* 1970, 19:68). In addition, the Committee assumed that the Advisory Council on Foreign Affairs would be consulted by the government beforehand, although such consultation was not stipulated in the proposed law.

In an attempt to mute criticism of the proposal, the government tended to downplay the more far-reaching elements of the bill. Although this attempt was partly tactical, it also attested to important elements of continuity in Sweden's sanctions policy. First, it held that the law could not be implemented unilaterally, but was contingent upon a prior Security Council resolution "requesting" or "calling upon" member states (the usual distinction between what are considered nonbinding and obligatory sanctions) to apply nonmilitary sanctions (Proposition 77, 16). It also emphasized that the law would apply only to Security Council, and not Assembly, resolutions, and did not thereby qualitatively alter its standing duties under the Charter. In addition, it saw no danger in extending its authority in the area of UN sanctions, since this would not increase the danger of Swedish involvement in a potential great power conflict. (Here it seemed clearly to rule out the likelihood of a repeat of the Korean conflict of 1950, when Sweden suffered loss of face as a result of its withdrawal of support for the Western position after China had been deemed an aggressor.)

Despite the government's attempts to downplay its overall significance, the proposal engendered considerable opposition, both within the Riksdag Foreign Affairs Committee and in the subsequent Riksdag debate of 18 May (*RP* 1971, 89 and 90:101–26). Although the Committee as a whole approved the bill, seven of its sixteen members lodged official reservations, including representatives from all three of the bourgeois (*borgerlig*) opposition parties (*RP*, UU 11, år 1971; *RP* 1971, 89:101–2). Generally there were two major strands of argument against the bill, on which all three non-Socialist parties were agreed. One argument, voiced mainly by the Liberals, was for the retention of the parliamentary principle on sanctions issues, by giving the Riksdag ultimate authority to decide whether UN recommendations should be followed.[16] In response, the government held that the Advisory Council would be advised of any measure beforehand, but that full debate would delay, and perhaps damage, the effect of the bill (Proposition 77, 33–37; 64–68). The government also noted that several other countries (e.g., Belgium, France, Italy) had already passed similar legislation valid also for Security Council recommendations (*RP* 1971, 90:110). The opposition's second point was that some general right to compensation for firms suffering financial losses should be included in the law (*RP* 1971, 89:104–5, 116–17; Hernelius). Although the government rejected this motion as impracticable, it conceded that special hardship cases would be examined individually (Proposition 77, 29–32; 62–64; *RP* 1971:90, 111). Both of these opposing points were related insofar as they betrayed concern that the government was willfully sacrificing the interests of Swedish individuals, firms, and political institutions in further, and needless, demonstration of international solidarity. They also argued that a complete severance of all postal and telegraphic links with Rhodesia (in line with a possible communications ban) provided for under Art. 41, and thus foreseeable under the new law, would be a "cruel act" against the people of Rhodesia, and would also harm innocent foreigners resident there (for example, Swedish missionaries). Another deputy (a Liberal, Dahlén) suggested that the law would be altogether superfluous, since a united Security Council normally would not stop at recommendations, but eventually would take binding decisions on sanctions anyway.

Significantly, the opposition raised few objections to Sweden's expressions of solidarity and its increasingly high international profile in the operation. Even the Conservative on the UN Legal Committee (Allen Hernelius) did not oppose the bill on the basis of Sweden's neutrality policy, although he was mildly critical of what he called the government's "certain perfectionism" in implementing the Rhodesian embargo even more resolutely than had Britain (*RP* 1971, 89:106). The hand of the opposition parties was also strengthened by the increasing precariousness of the Social Democrats' hold on power.[17] Still another factor, though difficult to measure, was the occasionally contentious personal style of the Prime Minister, Olof Palme, who was widely perceived by the opposition as preferring confrontation to the strategy of dialogue and compromise preferred by Tage Erlander, his mentor and predecessor in office, and his propensity for advocating greater centralized control over the state apparatus. These underlying factors fed suspicions that the government, in its push for this new authorization, actually aimed to extend party-political (SAP) control over the nation's foreign policymaking machinery. Thus the other parties opposed the measure on domestic as much as on foreign policy grounds.

Due to this combined non-Socialist opposition to the bill, it passed the vote (27 May 1971) by only a small majority: 152 to 144, with six (presumably Left-Wing Socialist) abstentions (*RP* 1971, 89:126). The new permanent UN law[18] thus permitted the government to implement both Security Council decisions and recommendations on sanctions without prior Riksdag approval. On the basis of this general measure, the government simultaneously enacted a decree implementing certain sanctions against Southern Rhodesia (*SFS* 1971, 1[176]:223–25), taking into account Security Council Resolution 277 (March 1970), which called on states to sever all transportation links with the colony. Subsequently (in December 1972) both the law and its accompanying decree were tightened to add that Swedish citizens, even those residing outside the country, found in breach of the UN legislation could be tried and convicted in a Swedish court, as well as foreigners using Swedish-owned vessels or airplanes (*SFS* 1972, 3[815]:2127–28; and [817]:2129, both of 28 December 1972) . With these minor alterations, the permanent UN law of 1971 remains the final source of governmental authority in the Swedish legal code regarding UN sanctions.

The dearth of subsequent confirmed reports of Swedish violations of the embargo well indicated the stringency of these measures, which were unquestionably as severe as those imposed in any other democratic country. One case in point was the government's swift handling of a reported violation of the embargo by a Swedish ship, the *M. Citadel*, registered at Landskrona in Sweden, shipping Toyota cars through Mozambique to a Rhodesian company. When notified, the Swedish government immediately "transferred the matter to the Chief Public Prosecutor for appropriate legal action" (UN Doc. S/11594/Rev. 1, 183). The occasional, though extremely limited, exchanges of products between Sweden and Rhodesia after 1971 (in no case rising above $3,000 worth; see table 7-1) were mainly the result of differences of opinion between Sweden and the UN over the definition of humanitarian goods which were allowed exceptions to Resolution 253 (paragraph 3[d]). For example, intermittent Swedish shipments of medical equipment and used clothes (which the government considered to fall within this category) after 1968 caused the Sanctions Committee to temporarily reopen these two earlier cases for investigation, as indicated in the committee's 9th Report (UN Doc. S/11265, Vol. 1, 23); however, the committee subsequently accepted the Swedish position that the shipments did not contravene the letter or spirit of Resolution 253, which effectively closed the case (UN Doc. S/12265; SS 2, Vol. 2, case no. 133, 256–57).

SWEDISH POLICY TOWARD RHODESIA IN THE 1970s

The second phase of Sweden's policy in the Rhodesian crisis (after 1968) was also marked by increasing efforts to channel moral and material support to African liberation movements, including those in Zimbabwe-Rhodesia. This changing aid strategy became a key element in Sweden's developing international activism, and reflected a tangible shift toward the views of the Afro-Asian majority in the General Assembly. Under the unfolding anticolonialist banner, Sweden's earlier condemnations of white minority rule, and its support for coordinated sanctions, were transformed into aid programs for movements struggling to effect change from within those territories, as part of a consciously adopted dual approach to the Rhodesian sanctions operation (*DSFP* 1969:122–23). Such aid was described as "a moral and material expression of our sense of solidarity with those who are leading the fight for material liberation, the right of self-determination, human rights and a reasonable material and cultural standard of living" (*DSFP* 1970, 181).

One of the most striking elements of this decision was the rapidity and conclusiveness with which it became assimilated as a cornerstone of Swedish foreign policy, particularly in light of the government's consistent opposition to granting liberation aid through 1967. Despite official claims to the contrary, the government's overall emphasis on the politics of decolonization was a recent element of Sweden's foreign policy (Huldt 1974, 31–33). At first Sweden's liberation aid was channeled solely through multilateral (UN) channels, particularly the specialized agencies, due to repeated Assembly resolutions calling for such aid (beginning with GA Resolution 2151 in November 1966). However, its direct bilateral aid thereafter increased as an integral component of the simultaneous, rapid expansion of its overall foreign aid program (*u-hjälp-sprogramme*), with the official adoption in 1968 of the much-discussed *en-procent mål* (one-percent goal) of aid as a percentage of total GNP,[19] which was finally achieved (after some delay, due to the 1973 oil crisis and the ensuing recession) in fiscal 1977–78. At first Sweden's liberation aid was concentrated on groups operating within the Portuguese territories (particularly FRELIMO in Mozambique and the MPLA in Angola); but by the mid-1970s, particularly after the Lisbon coup of 25 April 1974, aid was channeled mainly to ZAPU and ZANU in Rhodesia, especially after their loose association in 1975 within the Patriotic Front (PF).[20] This aid, however, remained entirely humanitarian in nature, since arms sales to these groups were ruled out from the start; indeed Sweden felt compelled to abstain on the question, first raised at the Teheran Conference in 1968, of applying the Geneva and Hague Conventions to the liberation groups in southern Africa, due to the unorthodox nature of the insurgency campaigns (*DSFP* 1968:112).

In keeping with this increasing liberation aid, the Swedish government exerted pressure periodically on the Security Council for a further widening of the Rhodesian embargo during the 1970s. Sweden's hostility toward the Smith régime intensified following the interim agreement between the Heath government and Smith in 1971, which bestowed some respectability on the latter; Swedish officials called it a "heavy blow" to the forces working for equality between the races (*DSFP* 1971, 162); and it was at this point (1971) when Sweden unequivocally accepted the principle of "no independence before [black] majority rule" (NIBMAR), even though it had to abstain on the first Assembly resolution calling for it (GA Resolution 2877 [XXVI]; *YUN* 1971, 112). The government also expressed regret over the invitation of Rhodesian athletes to the 1972 Olympiad in Munich (*DSFP* 1971, 156).

Swedish officials also responded positively to the report of Britain's Pearce Commission, set up to examine Rhodesian attitudes toward Heath's "Salisbury proposals" of 1971; the Commission concluded that most whites accepted the proposals but that the vast majority of blacks rejected them, due to its inadequate timetable for a transfer to majority rule. On this issue Sweden generally adopted a middle line between several Western countries, which supported the Salisbury proposals, and the African "front-line" states, which condemned them even before they were published and before black attitudes had been surveyed. Sweden, however, refrained from rejecting the agreement in advance, and generally opposed the advance repudiation of any negotiated settlement which provided for popular consultation and which promoted the principle of national self-determination. Following the report, the government reiterated its view that "in the meantime the UN must not remain passive. The mandatory sanctions must be retained and tightened up, if this is possible, to increase the isolation which we all know is becoming an increasing burden to the white minority" (*DSFP* 1972, 176).

Two years later, the government asserted even more strongly that "the Smith régime must be entirely cut off from contact with the international community" (*DSFP* 1974, 179). Then, following the collapse of the 1975 talks at Victoria Falls between Rhodesian officials and ZANU and ZAPU representatives, Sweden flatly rejected Smith's proposed "internal solution" as a "trick," and held that "no settlement which excludes the Patriotic Front and its guerrilla armies can have any possibility of success" (Karin Söder, 1977 UN Speech, 14). In this regard the government also emphasized statements made by former Portuguese officials after the fall of the Caetano dictatorship in 1974, who acknowledged that continual international moral and political pressure (even in the absence of an economic embargo) had had significantly negative psychological effects, even if it caused no visible or immediate changes in Portugal's colonial policies.

Sweden utilized its second term as a nonpermanent Security Council member in 1975–76 to push harder for a solution to the seemingly intractable Rhodesian problem. For example, in July 1975 the Swedish representative advocated sanctions in the field of civil aviation to prevent all landing rights to planes stopping over in Rhodesia.[21] In Council debate, following the Sanctions Committee's recommendations on widening the embargo (of 15 December 1975; see UN Doc. S/11913), Sweden, Britain, Guyana, and Tanzania together formulated a draft resolution which was passed as SC Resolution 388 (1976), prohibiting the insuring of commodities, franchises, and trade names in Southern Rhodesia (*Sverige i FNs Säkerhetsråd* 1975–76, 94–96). At that time Sweden's Ambassador Kaj Sundberg held that "economic sanctions are one of the most important means which the Charter puts at the disposal of the Security Council for the preservation of international peace and security," and declared that all possible means must be used to bring maximum pressure on Smith. Sweden in fact pushed for more comprehensive sanctions than the Council actually adopted, including a severance of postal and telegraphic communications, which would have exhausted the range of nonmilitary sanctions possible under Art. 41 of the Charter.[22] Also at this stage, Sweden's Prime Minister, Palme, forwarded a number of concrete proposals designed to support liberation groups (specifically the Zimbabwean Patriotic Front and SWAPO in Namibia), and to further isolate the South African and Rhodesian régimes (*DSFP* 1976, 63–64).

The high degree of political unity in Sweden on the sanctions question was illustrated by the unbroken continuity in policy following the historic displacement of the Social Democrats, after forty consecutive years in office, by a three-party bourgeois coalition under Thorbjörn Fälldin of the Center Party. Although Fälldin had promised during the campaign to "rid Sweden of socialism," this principle apparently did not apply to Sweden's foreign policy line; one of his first statements after assuming office was that "our acceptance of the ideas behind a new international economic order is an expression of our solidarity with poor and oppressed peoples. The government intends to give increased support to the struggle for liberation in southern Africa" (*DSFP* 1976, 64–65), a pledge which was amply fulfilled through actual Swedish aid. In 1977 the new foreign minister, Karin Söder, told the General Assembly, in terms at least as strong as those employed by Palme, that "Every form of black African protest in South Africa, Namibia, and Rhodesia has been brutally crushed. The majority of people is denied every possibility of political expression and participation. It is understandable that the liberation movements of southern Africa, in their despair, finally have seen no alternative to armed struggle."[23]

The government accordingly maintained its tight control over banned transactions with Rhodesia, although it made no effort to take relatively unenforceable unilateral measures, such as imposing a communications ban between Swedish citizens and Rhodesia. The government also told the Sanctions Committee in February 1978 that in accordance with Resolution 253, currency remittances from Sweden to Rhodesia were prohibited, but not remittances from Rhodesia to Sweden (UN Doc. S/13000, SS no. 2, Vol. 1, 191–92). The new Swedish coalition in fact took two further steps beyond the 1976 Palme proposals, mainly by pushing, successfully, for a UN declaration that South Africa's policies represented a threat to the peace, and for a mandatory arms embargo against it (this was imposed through SC Resolution 418 of 4 November 1977). In addition, in 1976 and 1979 the Riksdag passed laws restricting new Swedish investments in South Africa and Namibia, which became common Nordic policy in 1980; and in February 1985 the Riksdag passed controversial new legislation preventing the leasing of new plant, equipment, and vehicles from Swedish firms to their South African subsidiaries without special dispensation, and prohibiting all loans to the South African state.[24]

As a logical extension of its support for the liberation movements, Sweden maintained its high levels of aid to Zimbabwe after independence in April 1980, helping to keep its economy afloat during the difficult transitional phase. The new prime minister, Robert Mugabe, acknowledged that Zimbabwe's balance of payments deficit in 1979–80 would have been double the actual figure ($230m) had it not been for substantial foreign aid, "notably from Sweden" (Smith and Simpson 1981, 166). After an initial outlay of SEK 10m in April 1980, Swedish and Zimbabwean officials concluded an agreement in 1981 providing for SEK 100m in aid for fiscal 1982, of which only $20m was tied to purchasing Swedish goods and services; this figure was increased by 10 percent the following year.[25] Even so, there have been difficulties for Sweden resulting from its uncompromising anticolonial posture of the 1960s and 1970s, and Swedish aid policy has not been free from all controversy. For example, after the Mugabe government's crackdown on dissident ZAPU supporters of Joshua Nkomo, leading to reports of mass killings in Matabeleland in early 1983, the Swedish International Development Authority (SIDA) decided to freeze temporarily its plans for a new assistance program, until the internal situation within Zimbabwe became more settled.

NOTES

1. UN Doc. S/7010; *SCOR*, 20th Year (Supplement for October–December 1965), pp. 491–92.

2. From *SFS* 1939, vol. 1, no. 299; and *SFS* 1940: vol. 1, no. 176; both enacted during the early stages of World War II.

3. Denmark had first advocated sanctions in 1963, within the Special Committee on Apartheid (UN Doc. *GAOR*, 18th session, A/SPC/Sr. 380, pp. 15–16). Then on 3 December 1965 Denmark, through an important unilateral initiative (UN Doc. *GAOR*, 20th session, SPC, 476th Meeting, pp. 2–3), supported a draft SPC resolution (UN Doc. A/SPC/L. 118/Rev. 1) which would empower the Assembly, under the Uniting for Peace Resolution, to designate South Africa a threat to the peace and to request Security Council sanctions under Chapter VII of the Charter; see also Kay, 1970, Appendix E, issue no. 11, pp. 217–19. However, both Sweden and Norway abstained on this vote (UN Doc. *GAOR*, 20th Session, SPC, 481st meeting, p. 6).

4. By 1948 South Africa had become Sweden's third largest non-European trading partner, after the United States and Argentina. Their trade links expanded greatly dur-

ing the mid-1960s: Sweden's imports from South Africa rose from SEK 27m in 1964 to SEK 40m in 1965, while Swedish exports to South Africa rose from 118m to 147m during the same year (cited in *RP*, AK 1965, 40:37). By 1968 these figures had reached respectively 60m and 225m (Huldt 1974, p. 30).

5. For Liberal views on sanctioning South Africa, see *RP*, AK, 1965, no. 40, p. 17 (Ohlin); *RP*, AK, 1969, no. 13, pp. 20–23 (Wedén). On sanctioning Portugal, see *RP*, AK, 1966, no. 12, p. 40 (Ohlin); pp. 64–68 (Wedén); and especially *RP*, AK, 1967, no. 12, pp. 72–82. This strong Liberal stance even warranted mention in Sweden's official documents (*DSFP*, 1967, p. 120).

6. The government repudiated these arguments for pressuring Portugal through EFTA (*RP*, AK, 1967, no. 12, pp. 6–12, 16–17; also *RP*, FK, 1967, no. 12, p. 13 (Myrdal Committee report); *RP*, AK, 1967, no. 12, p. 10 (Nilsson); *RP*, AK, 1969, no. 11, pp. 187–206, esp. pp. 187–88; Lange.

7. *RP*, AK, 1969, no. 13, pp. 49, 56–58; Holmberg (Conservative), on the grounds of freedom for businesses; and Nilsson (SAP). Trade Minister Lange held that forcible prevention of ASEA's participation would contravene Sweden's free trade policy within GATT and EFTA, by politicizing what was wholly an economic agreement (*RP*, AK, 1969, no. 14, pp. 60–61; DSFP, 1969, p. 59).

8. See "Peace and Security after the Second World War: A Swedish Contribution," pp. 84–101; also "Kungl. Maj:ts. Prop. 196, 1946," p. 37.

9. On Spain, see Goodrich et al., 1969, p. 296; also *DSFP*, 1950–51, pp. 37–38; on the Greek question, *Svensk FN-lag*, SOU 1970, 19, p. 23.

10. "Kungl. Maj:ts Prop. no. 78 år 1969," BRP, Första Saml., pp. 1–94. A lengthy debate followed; *RP*, AK, 1969, no. 13, pp. 9–121; *RP*, AK, 1969, no. 28; pp. 37–54.

11. For their arguments see *RP*, AK, 1969, no. 13, pp. 20–23 (Ahlmark, Wedén); *RP*, AK, 1969, no. 14, pp. 16–17 (Hedlund, Centerpartiet); and no. 28, pp. 41, 45, Hermansson, VPK; p. 42, Wedén, Folkpartiet).

12. *SFS* 1969, vol. 1, no. 232, pp. 507–10, of 29 May 1969; entering into force on 10 June. Also UN Doc. S/8786, Add. II, Suppl. for July–September 1969, pp. 98–99 (English translation).

13. "Medlemförslag om nordiskt samarbete för genomförande av FN–lagstiftning," *NR*, 17e sessionen, 1969 (Prop. A 196/E), pp. 939–40.

14. See *NR*, 1969, Prop. A 196/E, p. 942 (Denmark); p. 944 (Finland); pp. 946–47 (Norway).

15. "Betankande av Nordiska rådets ekonomiska utskott över medlemsförslaget," *NR*, 17e sessionen, 1969, Bilaga 2, pp. 951–54.

16. For Liberal views on the question of prior parliamentary notification, see Motion år 1971, p. 1432, and *RP*, 1971, no. 89, p. 107 (Dahlén and Wirmark). See also Björk (Centerpartiet), *RP*, 1971, no. 89, pp. 108–9.

17. The SAP's share of the vote fell from its absolute majority of 50.1 percent in 1968 (Erlander's last election as PM) to 45.3 percent in 1970, under Palme and for the newly unicameral Riksdag; by 1973 it had fallen to just 43.6 percent, leading to the famous "hung parliament" between 1973 and 1976, with each bloc holding 175 seats (Särlvik, 1977, table 3-1, p. 74).

18. "Lag om vissa internationella sanktioner," *SFS* 1971, vol. 176, pp. 220–23, of 27 May 1971; entering into force on 1 July.

19. *RP*, AK, 1967, no. 12, p. 12; "Kungl. Maj:ts Prop. no. 101 år 1968;" *RP*, AK, 1968, no. 13, pp. 14–15.

20. This aid, most of which was channeled through the Office of the UN High Commissioner for Refugees, increased rapidly, from SEK 20m in 1977 to over SEK 81m in 1979; see *DSFP*, 1977, pp. 336–37; *Sveriges Budgetredovisning för budgetåret 1978–79*, p. 36.

21. UN Doc., *SCOR*, 30th Year, Supplement for October–December 1975, Doc. S/11963, para. 7, p. 67.

22. A communications shutdown had been in fact urged upon the UN by Sweden's Ambassador Sverker Åström as early as 13 October 1970. See also "Anförande av ambassador Kaj Sundberg den 6 april 1976," *Sverige i Förenta Nationernas Säkerhetsråd 1975–76*, Bilaga 52, p. 239. Also *DSFP*, 1976, pp. 190–91.

23. Speech by Söder to the UN General Assembly, 29 September 1977; mimeographed by the Swedish Foreign Ministry, 1978, p. 2.

24. See *New York Times*, 14 October 1976, p. 2:3; BRP, UU utlåtande no. 9, 1975, p. 195; *New York Times*, 22 August 1976, p. 21:1; *DSFP*, 1976, p. 196; *Financial Times*, 21 February 1985, p. 2:1.

25. "Zimbabwe," *Svenskt u-samarbete* (Stockholm: SIDAs informationsbyrå, 1982); "Bistånd 82–83," *Svenskt u-arbete* (Stockholm: SIDAs informationsbyrå, 1982), p. 8.

8

Switzerland and the Rhodesian Operation

The Security Council's imposition of mandatory economic sanctions against Rhodesia concerned the Swiss authorities, due to its apparent threat to each of the two "strands" identifying Switzerland's particular situation: its permanent neutrality and its nonmembership in the UN. First, it provided an opportunity to test the Federal Council's view since 1945 that Swiss neutrality was ipso facto incompatible with participation in even a limited UN sanctions operation. Second, the case coincided in time with Switzerland's grand debate over the broader question of UN accession, and the embargo thus affected Switzerland also in its capacity as a nonmember. These factors complicated the government's difficulties in simultaneously pursuing a policy of accommodation with, and independence from, the UN organization.

NEUTRALITY VERSUS NONMEMBERSHIP

During the early stages of the crisis, the Federal Council spent much time and energy in an attempt to establish Switzerland's legal position, in relation both to the UN embargo and to the rebelling colony itself, which provided the justification for the measures it later adopted. Indeed from the outset the government considered the Rhodesian crisis a "test of principle [which] must be given priority over other considerations" (Boczek 1969, 94). The Federal Council's initial reaction to Resolutions 216 and 217, through a press release of 17 December 1965 (Bindschedler 1968, 13), was that Switzerland, for "reasons of principle" stemming from its neutral status, was not legally bound to participate in the UN embargo. It also held that "a permanently neutral state such as Switzerland should be anxious, not merely in wartime but also in time of peace, and particularly in a period of international tension, to pursue a policy which would not work contrary to its traditional neutrality."

This argument was reiterated in February 1967, soon after the embargo had been made compulsory: "Switzerland as a neutral state in principle cannot be considered bound to obligatory sanctions under the UN" (Bindschedler 1968, 14). However, the government also held that neutrality would not be interpreted as complete disinterestedness, which would "create adverse risks" [sic]; for example, such an attitude might enable Switzerland to bypass the embargo by allowing violations to occur, "which equally, would favor Rhodesia. This is also to be avoided" (13). The government interpreted this incompatibility between neutrality and sanctions very broadly: Rudolf Bindschedler (then legal advisor to the Swiss Political Department) asserted in connection with the Rhodesian crisis that:

the principle of collective security—a basic principle of the United Nations—and the obligation, which arises therefrom, to participate in compulsory measures proclaimed against a State breaching the peace, are, however, incompatible with this position [of neutrality]. This is true regarding participation not only in military sanctions, but also in compulsory political, economic, or financial measures. (Bindschedler 1968, 15)

Notwithstanding the apparent clarity of this statement, it was inconsistent with the initial Swiss position in the League of Nations, which was that military, but not economic, sanctions were incompatible with neutrality.

These statements indicate that the Swiss government clearly rejected participation in the sanctions operation on the basis of its policy of neutrality rather than its nonmembership in the UN (Boczek 1969, 86, 88). For this reason, it was claimed, "the Federal Government of Switzerland was legally justified in refraining in the case from either, on the one hand, participating in the imposed sanctions or, on the other hand, aiding the object of sanctions, the Government of Rhodesia" (Bindschedler 1968, 13). Due to this emphasis on neutrality, the government at the outset regarded as "irrelevant" the question of whether the operation had binding legal force, and also whether the Rhodesian affair fell under domestic (British) or international jursidiction (Bindschedler 1968, 15).

These assertions of neutrality relative to the crisis were, however, based on tenuous legal and political grounds. And indeed, despite this stated position, the Federal Council thereafter proceeded to acknowledge both the political realities of the affair and the absence of many of the basic preconditions for classical neutrality in the sense of the Hague Conventions, discussed in chapter 6 (1981 UN Message, 49). One factor was Rhodesia's colonial, nonsovereign status. The rights and duties accruing to neutral states only enter into force during a conflict between two sovereign states, or in a civil dispute when the rebel insurgents have been recognized internationally as a belligerent party; neither case applied to the Rhodesian affair. Even in its initial statement

(17 December 1965) the Federal Council agreed that the dispute was "not a war in the meaning of international law. The various states participating in the sanctions therefore considered themselves not bound to the laws of war" (Bindschedler 1968, 13). The Swiss even expressed doubt over the existence of an international conflict at all, since neither the Rhodesian rebellion nor the resulting sanctions operation involved the use of armed force. Thus the Swiss position betrayed a latent paradox: whereas it refused sanctions due to neutrality, it simultaneously viewed the Rhodesian problem as a domestic British affair, outside the UN's aegis, and one which did not threaten the peace[1]—all of which would eliminate the need to declare neutrality. The Swiss first proclaimed their classical posture of neutrality, then proceeded to deny its basic presuppositions in the actual case.

On the other hand, the government presupposed that a qualitative distinction could be made between ordinary neutrality in the sense of the Hague Conventions, which was (and was recognized by the Swiss as being) inapplicable to the crisis; and Switzerland's own permanent neutrality, which, as an integral component of Swiss foreign policy, features in Switzerland's response to every international crisis. This emphasis on its own special position was induced by two factors. One was its difficult situation during the League's embargo of Italy in 1935–36; the other was the International Law Commission's recent (1964, reiterated in 1966) opinion that Swiss neutrality had attained the status of customary international law.[2] This opinion, though nonbinding legally, conferred additional sanctity upon Swiss neutrality, and moreover suggested that this policy could not be abrogated by a Security Council decision pertaining to the application of sanctions (Wildhaber 1970, 159; 1969 UN Report, 103). Thus its neutrality was continually cited in the case, particularly during the early stages; not as Swiss policy per se, but rather only as a general and long-standing principle. The measures subsequently adopted by the government were taken in the name of Switzerland, a state which happened to be also a traditional neutral; but they were not regarded as components of a specifically neutral policy, due to the various circumstances of the conflict.

Indeed the Federal Council professed full awareness of the inevitable political difficulties awaiting any country which refused outright to cooperate with the UN's operation, particularly on such an issue in which the great bulk of world opinion was ranged against an illegal régime. Conversely, the nature of the operation itself ensured that Switzerland was not free, in political terms, simply to "go its own way" (J. Freymond 1976, 299). Revealingly, the Swiss foreign minister from January 1966, Willy Spühler, told the Swiss *Nationalrat* that "politically, although not legally, Switzerland faces the same problems in the Rhodesian situation as a neutral state that is a member of the United Nations" (Boczek 1969, 88). Thus the government's refusal to participate was in fact "purely political since there is no doubt that Switzerland could have joined in the sanctions without thereby violating any rule of international law or her obligations as a neutralized [sic] country" (Boczek 1969, 93–94).

On the other hand, the Swiss had a much stronger case for nonparticipation based on its status as a nonmember of the organization. For example, under the *pacta sunt servanda* principle of international law Switzerland could not be bound to UN actions, notwithstanding the possible effects of Charter Art. 2(6) pertaining to nonmembers. The Federal Council emphasized this point: "According to the prevailing doctrine on treaties of international law, this provision entails no legal obligation for non-member states" (1969 UN Report, 13), concerning either recommendations or binding UN actions. In this respect the government adopted, unsurprisingly, a very restrictive interpretation of the legal applicability of the UN Charter (1969 UN Report, 76); and the Federal Council's position that nonmembership could not entail UN obligations was later (1971) upheld by the International Court of Justice in its important advisory opinion on the South-West Africa case (YUN 1971, 585). Nonetheless the Swiss had a clear obligation in customary international law not to aid a rebelling territory (Rhodesia) against its metropolitan power (Britain).

These problems of interpretation led to a gradual but clear alteration in the government's assessment of the situation. For example, on 10 February 1967 the Federal Council held that "for reasons of principle, Switzerland, as a neutral state, cannot submit to the mandatory sanctions of the United Nations" (UN Doc. S/7781, Annex 2, 58). In contrast, a May 1974 reply to the UN secretary-general recalled that "In its statement of 10 February 1967 ... the Federal Council pointed out that, for reasons of principle, Switzerland was unable to consider itself bound" (UN Doc. S/11594/Rev. 1, SS no. 2, 155). The relative vagueness of the latter statement seemed to indicate that neutrality was no longer Switzerland's key consideration in the crisis. At the same juncture (1974), the government clearly emphasized Switzerland's nonmembership; it told the secretary-general, in response to a reported violation of the embargo, that "Switzerland, as a state not a member of the United Nations, has taken independent measures designed to prevent Swiss territory from being used for commercial transactions falling within the scope of the sanctions policy" (UN Doc. S/11594/Rev. 1, SS no. 2, 235). This trend reached its apotheosis after the conclusion of the crisis (1981), when the government (significantly, as part of its official message formally proposing Swiss accession to the UN), stated that:

The sanctions ... did not pass without incidence in Switzerland, since our country, which was not a member of the UNO, was not legally bound to apply the decisions of the Security Council. In the case of Rhodesia, which was then a colony, it was doubtful that it was an international conflict in the sense of international law, and that of the law of neutrality.... The principle of parity of treatment, which thereby inspires all viable policies of neutrality, appears hardly applicable in a conflict between two unequal parties, with one party having violated the law and the other, the entire international community. (1981 UN Message, 49–50)

This shift in views from neutrality to nonmembership could have been attributable to differences between the Federal Council's original perception of the

Rhodesian dispute and its later assessment of the affair with the benefit of hindsight. Whatever the cause, this important shift in rationale behind its position was never acknowledged in official Swiss statements.

Another factor behind Switzerland's changing perspective was the manner in which it was treated by the Security Council and Secretariat. The initial Council resolutions on the Rhodesian affair (216, 217, and 221) were directed toward "all states" without discriminating between UN members and nonmembers; and the British government and the Security Council officially informed the Swiss Federal Council of these measures. Starting with Resolution 232 (paragraph 7) of December 1966, Security Council resolutions began to "urge, having regard to the principles stated in Art. 2 of the Charter, States not members of the United Nations to act in accordance with the provisions of paragraph 2 of the resolution" (UN Doc. S/7781, 2). In addition, paragraph 8 called upon "all States Members of the United Nations or of the specialized agencies to report to the secretary-general the measures they had taken in accordance with the provisions of paragraph 2 of the resolution." This request applied to Switzerland due to its postwar membership in virtually all the specialized agencies but not in the core UN organs, and it was reiterated in each of the Rhodesian resolutions subsequent to 232; and all resolutions and (later) reports by the Sanctions Committee were duly communicated to all nonmember governments as well as to member states.

This trend indicated clearly that the UN Organization itself intended equal treatment for all states and opposed exempting any state from participation, even though it retained that right under Art. 48(1). And as Switzerland by the early 1970s was one of but a handful of nonmember states (particularly after the accession of the two Germanies in 1973), these requests for nonmember compliance were increasingly directed specifically toward the Swiss government. Moreover in 1974 the Legal Council of the UN disagreed with Switzerland's general view that it was not obligated under Charter Art. 25 to implement the embargo (UN Doc. S/11594/Rev. 1, SS no. 2, 156). The Security Council's refusal to treat Switzerland any differently from member states also held broader implications for Switzerland's eventual decision to apply for membership, since the government had long assumed that Swiss accession hinged upon special (UN) recognition of its neutrality, as in the League era. In fact a notable trend in the government's campaign for Switzerland's UN membership in the 1970s was its increasingly open acknowledgment that demands for a special UN exemption from military sanctions would be unrealistic and even counterproductive (1977 UN Report, 134).

SWITZERLAND'S PRE-1965 UN POLICY AS A FACTOR

These problems in maintaining a consistent rationale toward the Rhodesian operation also found precedent in Switzerland's continuing difficulty in reaching a viable modus vivendi with the UNO during the previous two decades. Although from the start Switzerland acknowledged the necessity of cooperating with the postwar international organization, its attitude in 1945 was tempered by two factors which also predominated in the earlier debate over League accession: (1) the widespread fear that the UN would continue to maintain the character of the wartime "victors' league"; and (2) the possibility that Swiss neutrality could again be called into serious question should it bind itself to apply coercive sanctions against an aggressor (Qurasi 1978–79, 97–99). Both these elements were of course closely related to its unfortunate League experience; and the government's resolve to preserve its integral neutrality in all circumstances was reinforced by its success in avoiding direct involvement in World War II through armed, insular neutrality.

Based on its League precedent, the Swiss clearly expected to receive a special exemption from all military sanctions obligations under the Charter, analogous to the 1920 Declaration of London. Indeed it assumed that such special recognition was a necessary precondition for Swiss membership, even though the powers at Potsdam had accepted the principle of neutral and even enemy state membership, in fact offering the neutrals what Bernard Dutoit called "very lenient" terms (1962, 38). However, there was also a marked discrepancy between the tendency for many Swiss to criticize the Charter's veto provision as a derogation from the principle of sovereign equality of all states, while simultaneously asserting that "without a doubt, the situation in which Switzerland finds herself, by her statute of neutrality, is unique and constitutes a privilege" (Petitpierre 1980, 99).

On the other hand, circumstances in 1945 militated against such UN recognition. At the UN Conference at San Francisco the relevant subcommittee tacitly accepted a French motion that permanent neutrality should be considered incompatible with UN membership (UNCIO, Vol. 6, Doc. 944, 459–60). The first UN secretary-general, Trygve Lie, compounded these doubts when he stated, during a visit to the Swiss capital of Bern in summer 1946, that "the notions of the international body and neutrality lie at totally different levels; contact between them is impossible" (quoted in Belin 1956, 79). A number of Swiss officials and academics were very critical of the UN's contradictory signals concerning the position of neutral states,[3] which tended to reinforce Switzerland's natural tendency to remain aloof from the new organization. In addition, the strong extra-European element of the UN was scarcely conducive to a general understanding of, or sympathy for, the peculiar historical basis of Swiss neutrality (Lalive 1947, 88). Thus compared to the situation in 1919–20, the Swiss position and that of the organization were more divergent: whereas the Federal Council was even more intent on gaining special international recognition for its position than in 1918, the organization was much less disposed to grant such recognition.

This problem indeed posed an insuperable barrier to the Swiss government, which in late 1945 decided not to apply for UN membership, fully realizing that a proposal to accede to the Charter without a special dispensation from the UN would never be approved in the necessary referendum (Siegfried 1950,

183). The government adopted a unanimous report by a special consultative commission which met in Bern in November 1945, whose experts considered that UN membership would fundamentally undermine the basic premises of Swiss neutrality.[4] Even so, however, the commission provided little commentary on the numerous other features of the Charter (such as the unanimity principle) which opened clear possibilities for a viable neutral policy even within the UN. The Swiss foreign minister, Max Petitpierre, himself was strikingly inconsistent on the importance of this veto stipulation for neutrality: whereas in 1946 he told the Swiss *Nationalrat* that the veto provision constituted "an element of uncertainty and insecurity," he seemed to reverse this view the very next year in claiming that "the incompatibility [between neutrality and collective security] is more apparent than real...the usage of the right of veto . . . permits each of the other members to proclaim their neutrality" (Petitpierre 1980, 210). Curiously, the government also made no distinction between economic and military sanctions (Comm. Cons. Suisse 1945, Vol. II, 119), although the two were at least as separable under the Charter as under the League Covenant; and subsequently it indicated—with specific reference to Art. 41 of the Charter—that it considered all types of sanctions, both economic and military, as incompatible with neutrality,[5] a view which represented a major change from its attitude in 1918–19. These inconsistent views appeared to indicate that the Swiss government continued to base its arguments on its attachment to traditional neutrality, rather than on a rational understanding of the Charter provisions themselves, thereby suggesting that neutrality remained an impediment to the adoption of a long-term, consistent strategy toward sanctions; this attitude contrasted sharply with the more logical Swedish view of the Charter, which recognized the ultimate right of neutrality as a fall-back position even while admitting of sanctions obligations. Moreover, it gave no indication as to what the Swiss response might be in the event of a limited UN economic embargo against an aggressor. In the Swiss Assembly, Petitpierre reiterated this perception of a basic dichotomy between neutrality and sanctions by stating that Switzerland "is convinced . . . that . . . in maintaining her neutrality she will be rendering a greater service than in affording assistance to the imposition of sanctions against other countries" (Petitpierre 1980, 198–99).

After 1945 Swiss policy was based on a careful distinction between what the government considered "political" and "nonpolitical" international cooperation. On the one hand, Switzerland's abstention from the "political" UN has limited it to mere observer status in five of the six core UN organs, despite its agreement to host the UN's European offices in the old Palais des Nations complex in Geneva. The only exception has been its 1948 adherence to the Statute of the International Court of Justice (ICJ) at The Hague, which was open also to nonmembers through Art. 93(2) of the Charter. Significantly, the Swiss government gave its approval to the Statute with no neutrality reservations, despite a possible conflict with neutrality arising from the acceptance (on one interpretation of the Statute) of an advance obligation, under Art. 36(2), to undertake coercive action against a state defaulting on a Court judgment, if called for by the Security Council (F. Pictet 1975b, 544). The Federal Council argued on the other hand that action against a defaulting state (Art. 94) and coercive measures under Art. 25 and Chapter VII were separate from one another, a view accepted also by some international lawyers;[6] however, other authorities (including the Security Council's own Committee of Experts) have held that Arts. 25 and 103 form "complementary obligations" for nonmembers (see UN Doc. S/191, 1946), thereby suggesting that the government was not entirely candid as to its obligations in its 1947 Message on ICJ accession (Bindschedler 1963, 370, n. 74).

On the other hand, Switzerland has participated in a wide range of activity under the broader aegis of the UN system, including those activities it considers technical, scientific, cultural, humanitarian, or economic in nature. This has included most of the subsidiary organs, created by and answerable to the UN General Assembly under Arts. 7(2) and 22; and autonomous specialized agencies attached to the UN through agreements with the Economic and Social Council (Art. 63) but which retain their own legal personality (Arts. 57–59). Switzerland has in fact joined virtually all of the latter, save for the Bretton Woods financial institutions created in 1944, and even that exception has been due to financial rather than political (i.e., neutrality-related) considerations (Burgenmeier 1981, 240).

This sharp distinction between "political" and "nonpolitical" activity (formally expressed through an Opinion in [Swiss] Administrative Law in 1954)[7] however seemed to betray an even more conservative, insular view of neutrality than it held during the League era; it indicated a qualitatively *new* tendency to shun international political cooperation altogether, a point illustrated by its long delay before joining even the Council of Europe in 1962 (*FF* 1962, 2:1080). This attitude was also somewhat ironic insofar as Switzerland was cited frequently as a potential or actual model for a European or world political and economic organization based on a federative structure.[8] However, again on this point the government's view was inconsistent, when in 1969 it "explicitly reject[ed] . . . the allegation that Switzerland's neutrality policy asks for nonparticipation in any political organization . . . such a principle in no way forms a classic element of the Swiss policy of neutrality" (1969 UN Report, 117; Keller 1976, 30–31).

Switzerland's situation was also affected by changes in its international environment, which gradually eroded many of the foundations of its postwar policy. One key point is that Swiss neutrality since 1945, for the first time in its history, has ceased to be a direct function of the balance of power between its neighboring states, leading Bohn to assert that "one of the primary justifications for its neutrality has disappeared" (Bohn 1977, 343–44). Particularly the development of close economic and political linkages between most of its immediate neighbors, first through the OEEC and OECD and later within the

EEC, wholly altered the European political and economic environment in which Swiss neutrality operates; these steps toward integration have even partially incorporated Switzerland itself (Weber 1963, 136). Even the legal underpinnings of Swiss neutrality have been called into question, since neither of the postwar superpowers, the USSR and the United States, were formal adherents to the earlier agreements of 1815, 1919, and 1920 pertaining to Swiss neutrality (Dutoit 1962, 54). In addition, UN practice itself, particularly its developing universality, the active role played by other neutral countries, and the increasingly symbiotic connection between the specialized agencies (to which Switzerland adhered) and the UN General Assembly (to which it had not) tended to erode its traditional attitude that its interests were best protected outside the UNO, even though this attitude continued to be expressed through 1965.[9] Thus by the mid-1960s Switzerland's increasing need to adapt to its changing international environment became, in itself, a catalyst for the government's changing views toward the UN system.

PARTIAL SWISS RESTRICTIONS AGAINST RHODESIA

Based on its twofold attitude of refusing full participation in the operation while also acknowledging the prevailing political realities, the Swiss government announced its implementation of a series of measures indicating partial cooperation with the Security Council. The outgoing foreign minister, F. T. Wahlen, announced that Switzerland could not remain indifferent to the situation and that it refused to recognize the Smith government, which accorded with Resolutions 216 and 217. Switzerland did however (along with many other European states) maintain its consulate in Salisbury. Second, the Federal Council invoked Art. 41 of the Swiss constitution through which the manufacture, purchase, and sale of arms were made subject to governmental licensing arrangement, which effectively severed the supply of all arms to Rhodesia (Boczek 1969, 84, n. 10). (Switzerland had similarly complied with Security Council Resolutions 180 and 181 in late 1963, which had recommended an arms embargo against Portugal and South Africa respectively.)

Third, the government blocked the assets of the Reserve Bank of Rhodesia on deposit with the Swiss National Bank, after receiving contradictory requests on them from both Britain and Rhodesia. This was a significant gesture of support, due to the international connections of the Swiss banking system; indeed only South Africa, Britain and Switzerland held sizable Rhodesian official assets (despite Wahlen's claim that the amount in Switzerland was small), although the total sum involved was never publicly divulged. The government froze these assets just two weeks after a similar move by the Bank of England; one source called it "a declaration of support for the Bank of England in its refusal to recognize the Reserve Bank of Rhodesia in Salisbury as a legal institution" (*New York Times*, 18 December 1965, 10: 3, 4). Notably, that same week the Rhodesian Bank stopped publishing its weekly statement of assets and liabilities. On the other hand, this act did not affect the private Swiss bank accounts held by numerous individual Rhodesians throughout the crisis, a factor which later assumed added significance due to Switzerland's refusal to prevent the entry of persons carrying Rhodesian passports.

The government's fourth and most important step was its imposition of certain restrictions on bilateral Swiss-Rhodesian trade. One of its primary aims was to prevent Swiss territory from being used as a reloading or rerouting station (*Umschlaplatz*) for other states or private businesses to evade the UN embargo: "The Federal Council will see to it that Rhodesian trade is given no opportunity to avoid the United Nations sanctions policy through Swiss territory. . . . It decided . . . to make imports from Rhodesia subject to mandatory authorization and to take the necessary measures to prevent any increase in Swiss imports from that territory" (UN Doc. S/7781, Annex 2, 58). The government proceeded to establish a ceiling on Swiss imports from Rhodesia, on 17 December 1965.[10] This doctrine, the *courant normale*, was also applied against Italy in 1935; it aims to stabilize the total volume of imports from the designated state to the average level of the period of reference, normally the three years immediately preceding the adoption of sanctions (although in this case the limitation was based on the two-year period 1964–65, since Southern Rhodesia had been part of a federation through 1963). All Rhodesian imports were thereby subjected to licensing control in order to keep the total volume steady; however, Swiss exports to Rhodesia (other than arms) were not so restricted. This policy was designed both "to stabilize the economic relations so as not to harm the efficacy of the sanctions; [but also] according to the nature of the measures decreed by the UNO, it could not constitute a means sufficient to be associated with them" (1981 UN Message, 50). By now the government had come to regard the *courant normale* as a sacrosanct principle of Swiss neutrality (Bindschedler 1968, 14); others, however, have disputed the necessity of applying the *courant normale* as part and parcel of neutral policy (e.g. Verdross 1967, 16), particularly when it is applied against only one party to a conflict rather than against both antagonists (as occurred in both the Italian and Rhodesian cases).

The government implemented these four initial measures without referring directly to the Security Council's recommendations in Resolution 217, despite the obvious linkage between the two developments. It thereafter repeatedly emphasized the autonomous nature of its actions, which were implemented "independently and without recognizing any legal obligation to do so" (UN Doc. S/7781, Annex 2, 58). The Swiss seemed to fear that specific acknowledgment of the UN embargo as a catalyst for their actions would suggest that the government was following the Security Council's lead rather than acting independently as a neutral nonmember state. The Federal Council was, understandably, intent on avoiding the setting of a precedent in customary international law binding nonmembers to UN sanctions, which would thereby (falsely) indicate Swiss acknowledgment of any obligation to the UNO under Art. 2(6). Thus Arnold and Baldwin's assertion that Switzerland as a nonmember state accepted sanctions in principle (in Windrich 1975, Doc. 50, 273) is clearly contradicted by these official statements.

Although Switzerland's response was accompanied by repeated references to the "permanence" of its neutral principles, one of the main rationales behind its policy was virtually the opposite from that put forth in 1935–36. In the earlier crisis the policy (*courant normale*) was the same, yet the government's primary justification for it was reversed: in 1965 the government refused to cut all trade with Rhodesia because of its insignificance. Swiss-Rhodesian bilateral trade was in fact at a very low level, the continuance of which could scarcely jeopardize the overall effectiveness of the operation. As table 8-1, col. 1, shows, at the time of the UDI Switzerland's share of Rhodesia's exports (totaling $640m in 1965) was only $5,678,000, or slightly under 1 percent. Swiss exports to Rhodesia, meanwhile, totaled only $1,641,000 out of Rhodesia's total imports of $334m or just .7 percent.[11] The government thus argued that maintaining this trade with Rhodesia would not subvert the overall effect of the embargo, yet would have an important symbolic value, as a means of underscoring Switzerland's nonobligation to the UN. On the other hand, it was arguable that this low level of trade was a poor case for nonparticipation, since its severance would represent a relatively painless demonstration of international solidarity—particularly given the Swiss government's penchant for stressing "solidarity" as an integral component of Swiss foreign policy.

SWITZERLAND'S ATTITUDE FOLLOWING MANDATORY SANCTIONS

The Swiss government's basic position in the crisis remained largely unchanged following Resolution 232 in December 1966. In response to Resolution 232 (but as before, not in direct reply to the Security Council's inquiries) the Federal Council, in a statement of 10 February 1967, spelled out its opposition to participation in a mandatory sanctions operation (UN Doc. S/7781, Annex 2, 58). While it again stressed that the overall level of Swiss-Rhodesian trade was a negligible factor in the effectiveness of the embargo, it nonetheless announced a number of measures designed to tighten the restrictions already in place.

The main change was its modification of the formula for computing the Rhodesian *courant normale,* whereby it granted authorizations on the basis of the volume of imports during the three-year period 1964–66; this was done through a decree of 10 February 1967.[12] This decision was based on the reduction in Swiss imports from the colony during the latter year (1966), both in quantity of goods and in total value (as shown in table 8-1, col. 2), which thereby reduced the average for the three-year period. Hence by effectively lowering the ceiling against which the *courant normale* was measured, Switzerland's total level of imports from the colony would be further reduced (Boczek 1969, 85, n. 36). This system allowed Swiss importers the right to choose freely the period of measuring their imports, which according to the govern-

TABLE 8-1

Switzerland's Annual Trade with Rhodesia, 1964-79

Year	Imports from Rhodesia in thousands of:		Exports to Rhodesia in thousands of:	
	US Dollars (1)	Swiss Francs (2)	US Dollars (3)	Swiss Francs[1] (4)
1964	2,489	10,494	1,500	6,500
1965	5,678	24,568	1,641	7,100
1966	4,155	17,975[3]	1,890	8,200
1967	3,925	16,986	1,939	8,400
1968	3,483	15,039	2,513	10,900
1969	3,625	15,629	1,540	6,600
1970	4,296	18,491	1,969	8,500
1971	4,511	18,541	2,851	11,700
1972	4,582	17,496	3,230	12,300
1973	7,749	24,389	3,834	12,100
1974	7,352	21,869	4,546	13,400
1975	7,298	18,810	2,763	7,100
1976	7,644	19,149	2,001	5,000
1977	8,518	20,384	1,929	4,600
1978	10,998	19,544	1,900	3,300
1979[2]	6,400	11,400	2,000	3,600

Source: *Annuaire Statistique de la Suisse,* 1968, 1975, 1980 (for SwFr export
figures and all 1979 figures); UN Docs. S/11927/Rev. 1, SCOR, 31st
year, SS no. 2, Vo. II, Appendices I, II, pp. 125-128, (for US dollar
figures 1965-74); S/13000, SCOR, 34th year, SS no. 2, Vol III, Appendix, p. 17 (for US dollar figures 1975-77); and Doc. S/13750,
35th year, SS no. 2, Vol. II, pp. 146-47 (for all 1978 figures, and all
SwFr import figures).

[1] Swiss exports to Rhodesia in SwFr are rounded to the nearest third digit,
as given in the Swiss Annual Statistics.

[2] All 1979 figures are rounded to the nearest third digit, as given in the
Swiss Annual Statistics.

[3] The Swiss *courant normale* for 1964-66 was SwFr 17,679,000, or
$4,087,000.

ment might lead to "fluctuations . . . between the years," since import licenses
within the quota generally had a three-month duration.[13] This situation actually led to a temporary excess of imports, but the situation was corrected to
the equilibrium by the end of 1967 (*RCF* 1967, 37). On the basis of this new
limitation in Swiss-Rhodesian trade, the government declared that "the import restrictions are thus strengthened. Any possibility of increasing these imports is excluded and the United Nations sanctions policy cannot be contravened" (Bindschedler 1968, Anhang 2, 14–15). Even so, these additional
import restrictions still did not apply the other way, to the level of Swiss ex-

ports to the colony; this distinction was also corroborated by UN figures, which showed that the value of Swiss imports from Rhodesia declined from 1965 to 1967, whereas its exports to the colony increased slightly during the same period (table 8-1). At that time (10 February 1967) the government also noted that it was maintaining the ban on export of war matériel to Rhodesia, and the blockage of the Rhodesian Reserve Bank's funds in Switzerland. However, no further measures were deemed necessary since the remainder of the measures in Resolution 232 were inapplicable to Switzerland, which exported no oil, motor vehicles, aircraft, or spare parts to Rhodesia.

The secretary-general's first report to the Security Council concerning states' compliance with the operation (February 1967) indicated the Swiss refusal to participate fully. Of the seventy-five states responding to his questionnaire, all but three (Portugal, Malawi, and Switzerland) had reported full application of the embargo (*New York Times*, 25 February 1967, 6). On the other hand, some forty-seven states did not reply, which indicated that Switzerland was considerably more open with its trade statistics than were many member states. As in 1935–36, Swiss policy could not simply be equated with those states which purposefully subverted the embargo (in this case, primarily Portugal and South Africa).

Given the Federal Council's overriding concern with establishing its legal nonobligation to the UN, the Federal Council provided precious little commentary on the important political and moral issues inherent in the Rhodesian situation. In one sense, this reluctance to speak out on the issues was consistent with Switzerland's traditional low-key posture in international affairs. Even so, it failed to corroborate Switzerland's long-held view that its permanent neutrality presupposed support for basic principles of international law, which presumably included (as in this case) opposition to the systematic suppression of human rights and national self-determination, and the illegal assumption of independence.

Switzerland's reticence was also clearly inconsistent with its outspoken criticism of the Soviet invasion of Hungary in 1956; and the Czech crisis in spring 1968, which coincided with the debate over the widening of the Rhodesian embargo leading up to Resolution 253, elicited very forceful Swiss denunciations of the Soviet Union from across the political spectrum, which illustrated vividly the strong anticommunist strain in Swiss political opinion (*BS, CN* 1968, 483–518). At the same time the government studiously avoided taking a stand on the Vietnam War, citing its uncertain juridical status, while canceling, in 1966, a scheduled conference of the World Peace Council, due to its antiwar posture. The vast differences between this position and the simultaneous, vocal Swedish denunciations of American involvement in Southeast Asia also provide an enlightening indication of the widening parameters of permissible neutral activity in the postwar period.

There were in fact indications of a lenient Swiss attitude toward the policy of apartheid in southern Africa, including official restrictions on anti-apartheid speeches by foreign nationals in Switzerland (Rist 1968, 11, n. 13). Its attitude was no doubt affected by the significant financial stake of the major Swiss banks in the South African economy. This view extended to the Portuguese dictatorship as well, when—again in vivid contrast to Sweden, which was openly aiding Socialist leader Mario Soares—Switzerland gave temporary asylum to the former Portuguese president, Antonio de Spinola, after the collapse of the dictatorship in Lisbon in 1974 (*New York Times*, 12 April 1976, 12). Thus it was a major divergence from Switzerland's usual diplomatic discretion on African issues when its delegate to the 1968 Teheran Conference on Human Rights, M. A. Lindt (a former UN High Commissioner for Refugees) openly condemned South Africa's apartheid policy (Rist 1968, 9, n. 4). As late as 1973, the Federal Council made only passing reference to the "preoccupations of many in the Swiss public on racial discrimination in South Africa" (*RCF* 1973, 20). Public pressure groups in fact played an important role in the Swiss debate, led by the *Campagne contra les relations bancaires Suisse/Afrique du Sud* and, from an early date, a group called Interform, set up to press for greater Swiss compliance in the Rhodesian operation, although the government denied its existence (*The Times*, 20 December 1966, 6e). However, by the late 1970s there appeared to be growing concern among Swiss officials that the government's reluctance to condemn apartheid was having a detrimental effect on Switzerland's foreign relations (1977 UN Report, 7, 119-121).

Switzerland's position on the Rhodesian affair also reportedly provoked dissension within the Swiss foreign office by some who wanted the government to couple its restrictions on Swiss-Rhodesian trade with a declaration of willingness, alongside the neutral UN member states, to accept the principle of mandatory sanctions. Some of them cited the Swedish example, apparently convinced of the reasonableness of the Swedish view that neutrality was a barrier to neither UN membership nor to participation in a mandatory sanctions operation (*New York Times*, 14 February 1967, 3). In fact, during the ensuing decade a growing consensus held that Switzerland should assume a more active world role, and eventually this became an element of the government's own campaign to secure Swiss membership in the UN. As early as March 1966 the new Swiss foreign minister, Willy Spühler (the first in a line of Socialists holding the position), created a minor sensation when he told a conference at the University of Lausanne that the primary aims of Swiss neutrality and of the UNO coincided, and that Swiss adherence would affect neither its democratic institutions nor the federal structure of the Swiss state (*BS*, CN 1969, 734). This view was gradually adopted by the entire Federal Council (which from 1959 encompassed all four major parties in a permanent grand coalition, the so-called *Zauberformel*, or "magic formula") in an important series of three reports and one official message from 1969–81, increasingly advocating UN membership for Switzerland.[14]

Simultaneously, however, public hostility toward the UN arose in Switzerland, at least partly due to the Security Council's repeated requests for Swiss participation in the Rhodesian operation. This development caused some delegates in the specialized agencies (presumably after informal contact with the Swiss UN Observer from 1966, Bernard Turrettini) to speculate that the imposition of mandatory sanctions in December 1966 had dealt a serious blow to prospects for eventual Swiss accession to the UN (*New York Times*, 14 February 1967, 3: 4). Indeed later the increasingly prominent Swiss antiforeignization movements, including both national groups (the Republicans and National Action) and the local faction in Geneva called "Vigilance," succeeded in forcing through important constitutional limitations on the government's authority to involve Switzerland more deeply in international affairs (Malinverni 1978). These opposing viewpoints considerably complicated (and lengthened) the growing debate over UN membership in Switzerland by the late 1960s, and illustrated the divisions within the Swiss political community which arose along with the Rhodesian operation (*BS*, CN 1968, 235ff).

The decision by the UN Security Council to impose a full trade and financial embargo against the Salisbury régime in May 1968 produced no basic changes in the Federal Council's position, since this decision expanded rather than qualitatively altered the nature of the operation. The government did, however, appear to be somewhat more cooperative with the UN's efforts. Shortly before Resolution 253 (5 May 1968) it restated the earlier view that "reasons of principle do not permit of Switzerland, as a neutral state, giving support to the mandatory sanctions of the United Nations" (1969 UN Report, 68); and this general attitude was again expressed (though without direct reference to neutrality) in another "autonomous statement" of 4 September. However, the latter statement actually referred to the UN measures directly, and even assured the UN that the government would take action if necessary to prevent Swiss circumvention of the blockade: "With reference to the latest resolution of the Security Council, it (Switzerland) will attempt, independently and always in the context of the Swiss legal order, to see that Rhodesian trade cannot avoid the Security Council sanctions through Swiss territory."[15] It also pledged not to grant any export risk guarantees to firms selling products to Rhodesia, in order to prevent profiteering by private Swiss businesses at the expense of participating UN member states (*RCF* 1968, 18). Despite these reassurances, Switzerland continued to refuse to apply the full embargo and maintained its trade with the colony (UN Doc. S/9252/Add. 1, Annex III, 7).

Switzerland's decision to retain consular representation in Rhodesia, along with other (primarily European) states in disregard of Resolution 253, elicited further correspondence from the UN secretary-general. Following a UN note of 7 January 1969 concerning the Swiss consulate in Salisbury, the Federal Council replied with a direct, and rather conciliatory, letter (21 January) to Secretary-General U Thant. It held that "this operative paragraph [concerning consular relations] is only optional in character. Moreover, the main reason why the Federal Authorities have decided to maintain a Consulate at Salisbury is to protect the interests of some four hundred Swiss citizens resident in Rhodesia. The Consulate is confining its activities to the settlement of current matters." The note also stated that the Swiss consul in Salisbury had been transferred to another post and that "the consulate was under the responsibility of a manager" (UN Doc. S/9252/Add. 1, Annex VIII, 7–8).

The situation deteriorated further when the Smith régime promulgated the "Republic of Rhodesia" on 2 March 1970, which led to further pressure for the universal severance of all official relations with the territory. The Swiss response to this development was somewhat vacillatory: the following week the Federal Council stated that it planned to keep the consulate (but without an accredited consul) open for the time being (*New York Times*, 11 March 1970, 12:1). However on 17 March, following a special cabinet meeting, the Swiss government announced the immediate removal of the consulate (*New York Times*, 18 March 1970, 7:1). Switzerland was one of the last states to take this action, leaving only South Africa, Portugal, and the Greek dictatorship with consular relations with Rhodesia. Rhodesian officials also expressed their surprise at the Swiss decision, which preceded by just two days a Security Council call for all remaining states to remove their consular representatives from Rhodesia (Resolution 277). After that time, Swiss interests in the territory were handled from the Swiss consulate-general in Johannesburg (*RCF* 1970, 16).

In comparative terms, the Swiss government's attitude toward the UN's operation was also noteworthy insofar as it appeared far less cooperative than not only Sweden, but also its two German-speaking neighbors, Austria and West Germany. These two states warrant mention in connection with Switzerland since their positions corresponded with each of the two "strands" inherent in Switzerland's peculiar international situation, Austria as a permanent neutral, and West Germany as another nonmember of the UNO. Both also bore similarity to Switzerland due to their developed industrialized economies in central Europe, which enabled them to serve as outlets or middlemen in triangular transactions for the purpose of evading the Rhodesian operation; and both states allegedly played a leading role in violations of the embargo (Kapungu 1973, 92).

The Austrian example held important implications for Swiss policy because of two factors. One was the fact that the establishment of Austrian neutrality, formally established through its Constitutional Act (*Verfassungsgesetz*) of 26 October 1955, had explicitly cited Swiss neutrality as a model for Austria, thereby reiterating the bilateral (Austro-Soviet) "Moscow Memorandum" of 15 April 1955. The second factor was the subsequent, collective great-power recognition of Austria's permanent neutral status, coupled with their unqualified support for Austria's membership in the UN, which was accomplished in December 1955. Given this recognition, many Swiss officials have argued that the powers thereby bound themselves to exempt Austria from any obligations inconsistent with its permanent neutrality.[16] Austria's active cooperation with UN security preparations, including peacekeeping activity and assuming a nonpermanent seat on the Security Council, also provide a relevant parallel.

It was therefore significant for Switzerland that Austria considered neutrality, both in its occasional and permanent variations, to be no hindrance to the application of sanctions against Rhodesia (Zemanek 1968, 32). The Austrian government implemented the embargo fully, including even the nonobligatory measures listed in Resolution 217 (for example, it immediately severed its imports of Rhodesian tobacco). These measures resulted in a relatively rapid reduction in Austro-Rhodesian trade, which was entirely severed, in both directions, by 1970 (UN Doc. S/13000, SS no. 2, Vol. III, App. I, 16). On the other hand, the government limited its response to "this particular case and under the given circumstances" and did not admit to the compatibility of neutrality and collective enforcement operations as a general principle; here it was clearly resisting the setting of a precedent which could bind Austria fully to all UN sanctions operations in the future (Zemanek 1968, 32). In this respect, the Austrian case did register similarities with Swiss policy.

In some ways West Germany's nonmember status (prior to September 1973) more closely approximated that of Switzerland, since both states were incorporated to a very similar degree in the overall UN system through membership in numerous subsidiary organs and specialized agencies. In addition, the Bonn government agreed with the Swiss Federal Council that Art. 2(6) of the Charter did not legally bind it to apply sanctions decided upon by the Security Council (Kapungu 1973, 91–92). Even so, unlike Switzerland the Federal Republic expressed full compliance with mandatory sanctions; soon after Resolution 232 it stated that "by identifying itself with the decisions of the United Nations," it had both implemented and enforced the Rhodesian embargo; and this view was reiterated following Resolution 253 in May 1968.[17] There was, however, some gap between word and deed in the West German case: although its overall level of trade with Rhodesia fell considerably, and its imports from it were markedly reduced from 1965 to 1968, they were never fully severed; and its exports to the colony showed a gradual increase during the 1970s (UN Doc. S/11594/Rev. 1, App. I, 128).

VIOLATIONS IMPLICATING SWISS FIRMS

Although Swiss policy toward the Rhodesian operation appeared to be more conciliatory by 1968–69, reports of violations of the embargo by firms registered in Switzerland, and possibly across Swiss territory, began to circulate during the same period. If confirmed, such activity would be in direct contravention of Security Council policy. Exposure of possible violations typically consisted of an initial report by Britain (the unofficial monitor of the embargo) through its diplomatic or intelligence services or the media, which was then submitted to the Sanctions Committee for substantiation or refutation.

The problems in determining the extent to which the Swiss government was obligated, and empowered, to prevent such activity were not easily resolved, and it took nearly a decade before proper measures could be agreed upon.

The Federal Council's declared intention to prevent violations from occurring across Switzerland's physical territory placed it in an awkward position. Quite apart from the problems raised by the anomalous combination of its nonmembership and permanent neutrality, Switzerland's relatively unrestricted liberal market economy presupposes a free hand for private firms to conduct interstate trade with minimal state interference, in what has been termed an "ideology of free trade" (*Maldeveloppement Suisse-Monde* 1975, 18). The Security Council's request that states ensure that their nationals comply with the embargo also raised difficulties for federal states such as Switzerland, which lacked sufficient executive competence to regulate the activities of its nationals, particularly outside its physical territory (Renwick 1981, 78). This factor was closely related to the peculiar nature of Switzerland's business legislation, which is often loosely enforced (or even unenforceable), due to the pervasive influence of Swiss-based multinationals, and since enforcement often devolves upon cantonal rather than federal authorities. The relatively relaxed transshipment laws under the Swiss legal code enabled a number of enterprises (both real and fictional) to circumvent the UN embargo: occasionally as an outpost for the shipment of goods to and from Rhodesia utilizing transit zones in Switzerland's international airports (particularly Cointrin in Geneva and Kloten in Zürich), or, far more commonly, in arranging and/or financing such trade without the goods themselves even entering Swiss territory.

In addition, Switzerland's accessible private banking system provided the rebels with ample opportunity to arrange anonymous financial transfers, and many individual Rhodesians maintained Swiss bank accounts throughout the crisis (Arnold and Baldwin 1975, 273), even while the Rhodesian government's funds in Switzerland remained blocked. The frequency of reported (and often substantiated) violations of the embargo, often with direct Swiss collaboration, gave Switzerland an increasing amount of unwanted international notoriety, particularly after the Security Council through Resolution 277 (1970) specifically requested states to enforce the embargo outside their territory.

Generally, two types of violations occurred: (1) those involving direct Swiss importation of Rhodesian goods, in violation of Resolutions 232 and 253 but in accordance with the *courant normale;* and (2) those involving the collusion of Swiss firms in triangular operations designed to promote the sale of illicit goods to or from Rhodesia. One of the first reports of imported Rhodesian tobacco was a contract by J. Heisler and Co. to buy 2,000–3,000 tons. The government stated that an inquiry was underway, and if the place of origin were indeterminate, it pledged to treat it as Rhodesian and to apply the total against the 1969 quota, which remained based on the average for 1964–66 (UN Doc. S/9252, Annex XI, 40–42). Similar violations were reported in shipments of beef from Rhodesia, which the Federal Council made no attempt to hide.[18] Beef and tobacco were in fact the two main Swiss imports from Rhodesia, after 1965 accounting for nearly the entire total of imports from the colony (see table 8-2, cols. 5 and 6). However, many other cases of suspected imports were also reported in various commodities, including chrome, corn, and sugar (UN Doc. S/19852/Rev. 1, 89).

Under the second category of violations, numerous cases arose in many commodity areas. One example was the export of Rhodesian chrome and ferro-chrome, through the South African company UNIVEX, which used the Zürich-registered company Handelsgesellschaft to coordinate the sale of the chrome throughout Western Europe (UN Doc. S/9252, Annex XI, 15). Activity by UNIVEX was also reported in the sale of fertilizer back to Rhodesia, through NITREX AG of Switzerland, to enable greater agricultural self-sufficiency for Rhodesia during the embargo (UN Doc. 9252, Annex XI, 30–31). In the latter case, the Swiss government supplied a typical response: the fertilizers in question were not manufactured in Switzerland nor had they entered the Swiss customs area, so that "this is therefore a typical case of triangular trade, in which the role of NITREX is simply that of a middleman. Since the goods in question did not pass through Swiss customs inspection, the federal authorities have no way in law, or even in practice, of proceedings against NITREX AG" (UN Doc. S/9252, Annex XI, 34–36). As a result of this UN investigation, the government did, however, issue a warning to Swiss ship-owners that they must not carry any goods bound for or originating from Rhodesia as a consequence of UN resolutions.

A third case, the reported sale by a Swiss company of three Boeing 707 aircraft to Air Rhodesia via Portugal, was a prime example of the use of false-end contracts. Despite abundant evidence implicating companies in both Switzerland and Liechtenstein, the Federal Council never investigated the matter, accepting at face value the destination papers at hand which listed a Portuguese rather than a Rhodesian destination (UN Doc. S/11178/Add. 2, 4–6). Later, following reports of Swiss trade in ammonia with Rhodesia, the government even declared that an extraterritorial enforcement by Swiss authorities "would contravene international positive law" (UN Doc. S/10852/Rev. 1, 104). Although this view was consistent with the traditional legal separation of state and individual activity, it clearly did not accord with the UN's specific (and equally valid) call on states to impose an extraterritorial implementation of the embargo.

By far the most serious single violation of the Rhodesian embargo involved direct Swiss participation in plans, drawn up in 1972, for the Rhodesian Iron and Steel Company Ltd. (RISCO) at Que-Que to double its production capacity to one million tons yearly. This expansion would be financed mainly by three Swiss companies, Handelsgesellschaft (HGZ) AG, Femetco AG, and Getraco-Finmetal SA. Furthermore, according to the UN Sanctions Committee, "to satisfy the Swiss authorities, it has been necessary to interpose a South

TABLE 8-2
Swiss Imports of Major Rhodesian Commodities, 1964-1978

Year	MEAT AND EDIBLE MEAT OFFAL Quantity(Kgs) (1)	Value(1000SwFrs) (2)	UNMANUFACTURED TOBACCO Quantity(Kgs) (3)	Value(1000 SwFrs) (4)	TOTAL OF COLS (2) & (4) (5)	OTHER COMMODITIES Value (6)	QUANTUM (index 1964-66=100) (7)
(1964	1,471)	5,701)	593)	2,503)	8,204	2,290)	Courant Normale 100
(1965	2,427)2,084	10,438)9,451	1,088)886	4,709)3,933	15,147	9,420[1])	
(1966	2,354)	12,215)	977)	4,587)	16,802	1,173)	
1967	2,221	11,466	972	4,701	16,167	819	107.50
1968	1,510	10,142	959	4,489	14,631	407	83.07
1969	1,492	10,908	961	4,534	15,442	187	82.55
1970	2,099	13,369	964	4,484	18,253	238	103.13
1971	2,060	13,272	961	5,024	18,296	245	101.69
1972	1,531	12,634	968	4,815	17,449	47	84.08
1973	2,238	19,074	956	5,087	24,161	228	107.57
1974	1,565	17,276	958	4,578	21,854	15	84.91
1975	1,347	12,723	960	6,027	18,750	60	77.60
1976	1,443	13,543	953	5,580	19,123	26	80.60
1977	1,737	15,294	948	5,071	20,365	19	90.37
1978	1,807	13,959	960	5,488	19,447	96	93.11

Source: UN Doc. SCOR, 34th Year, S/13750, SS no. 2, Vol. II, p. 147 (Twelfth Report of the Sanctions Committee, 1979).

[1] The 1965 figure includes SwFr 8,298,581 of imports of precious and semi-precious stones, unworked, cut or otherwise worked, but not mounted, set, or strung.

African company to borrow the funds from Femetco AG and lend them on to RISCO" (UN Doc. S/11597, SS no. 2, 3–4). For this purpose, a dummy company, the South African Steel Corporation (Pty) Ltd. was created and registered, through which the money (some $19.3m) could be channeled to Rhodesia. The creation of a fictitious South African firm "to satisfy the Swiss authorities" was potentially a very serious development, for as the committee itself asserted, "the inference might be drawn from this statement that the Federal Authorities themselves were in some way implicated in the affair" (UN Doc. S/11597, SS no. 2, 71–72). These developments were given the highest priority by the Sanctions Committee, which sent special requests for information to the Swiss, Austrian, and West German governments.

However, the Swiss reply (as opposed to the other two) was received "with disappointment" by the Committee, since the government held that "neither the documents provided nor the information received from the Swiss companies concerned led the Federal Authorities to conclude that the companies in question were indeed involved" (UN Doc. S/11597, SS no. 2, 70–71), although it did leave open the possibility for a reconsideration of the case. Even so, the Federal Council was most anxious to avoid giving the impression that it was in any way a party to the scheme, and on the basis of the committee's second inquiry, it reopened its investigations, and on 7 April 1975 even provided the committee with evidence of illicit dealings by the implicated Swiss firms (UN Doc. S/11927/Rev. 1, 198–99). On the basis of these findings, the government asserted that it "cannot be suspected of having lent any aid whatsoever in such transactions as the committee assumes took place" (UN Doc. S/11597/Rev. 1, 198–99), and it reiterated this assertion the following year (UN Doc. S/11265, SS no. 2, Vol. I, 177). However, when actual shipments of steel billets (presumably from RISCO) began to be reported through Lorenço Marques, the government merely reiterated its inability to stop triangular operations involving goods which did not cross Swiss territory (UN Doc. S/12265, SS no. 2, Vol. 1, 177).

Another embarrassing case for Swiss officials was a reported large-scale trading ring in motor vehicles involving Anacardia SA of Lugano with Rhodesian companies, possibly even for police or army use (UN Doc. S/11594/Rev. 1, SS no. 2, case no. 197, 185). Although the Swiss government (after three successive UN requests for additional information) held that the results of its own investigations "do not confirm the allegations" of the UN, the Committee (31 October 1975) requested additional assurances that a sufficiently thorough Swiss investigation into the activities of Anacardia and its director, a Dr. Morgash, had been conducted (UN Doc. S/11927/Rev. 1, 135–37). A similar case at that time was a reported promise of a $6m loan from Industrie-Maschinen of Zürich (directed by Rolf Egli of RISCO) to the Rhodesian railway system, in direct contravention of Resolution 288 calling for a ban on transportation to the colony (S/11594/ Rev. 1, 212). Again the Swiss government replied only that Egli had given his formal assurances that no loan had been made in violation of Swiss laws, indicating that it had simply taken Egli's word at face value (UN Doc. S/11265, SS no. 2, Vol. I, 167). Such instances cast further doubt on the veracity of the government's stated claim to be investigating reported violations informally (UN Doc. S/11594/Rev. 1, paragraph 68, 21).

Yet another problem arose in connection with the Swiss policy of allowing individuals holding Rhodesian passports into Switzerland, in contravention of Resolution 253 (paragraph 5), due to its practice of accepting the validity of documents issued by proper authorities, even if the state or territory was not recognized officially by Switzerland. However, the government also made the curious observation that the admission of holders of Rhodesian passports "implies no recognition of nationality, since passports are considered simply as travel papers." The UN Legal Council considered this statement "irrelevant," and said that Swiss policy "manifestly violates the spirit and intent of the resolution" (UN Doc. S/12265, SS no. 2, Vol. I, 215–19). However, in response the Federal Council claimed that it was under no obligation, and had undertaken no unilateral commitment, to comply with said paragraph 5, and that "Switzerland cannot be required to strengthen the measures already adopted" (UN Doc. S/13750, SS no. 2, Vol. I, 116–17).

Switzerland's political difficulties caused by these ongoing cases were complicated further by the Sanctions Committee's decision in October 1975 to make a comprehensive investigation of all reported violations involving Switzerland, which led to a detailed UN compilation of information on all aspects of Swiss-Rhodesian trade. This decision in turn led to a distinctly more accommodating Swiss tone toward the UN, concerning both its regular trade and the reports of violations. The government had already decided, for example, to terminate inter-air agreements between Swissair and the Central African Airways and Air Rhodesia, on 31 October and 30 November 1974 respectively (UN Doc. S/11927/ Rev. 1, Vol. II, 46).

Then in June 1976 the Swiss Permanent Observer to the UN notified the secretary-general of a press statement by two officials in the Federal Political Department. In an admission unthinkable a few years earlier, the Swiss observer said that his government was reviewing its external trade with Rhodesia in view of the adverse image suffered by Switzerland, particularly among the African countries (UN Doc. S/11265, SS no. 2, Vol. I, 21). Swiss cooperation was also forthcoming in another case, a reported deal by which a New Zealand firm would send fourteen air-trainer aircraft to Rhodesia via a dummy corporation in Switzerland. After the New Zealand government had denied the required export license to the company, the Swiss government independently notified the Sanctions Committee that it had taken measures to alert New Zealand authorities and to frustrate the efforts of the Swiss company to circumvent the embargo. In response, the committee "expressed its appreciation for the initiative shown by the Swiss authorities . . . and hopes that the authorities will continue to exert similar vigilance in the future against unlawful attempts by entities within Swiss jurisdiction to violate the Security Council sanctions against Southern Rhodesia" (UN Doc. S/11265, SS no. 2, Vol. I, 290). Other similar revelations also created embarrassment for individual Swiss firms (UN Doc. S/11529/Rev. 1, 152–53).

Notwithstanding this considerable international criticism, it remains arguable that the overall Swiss position was less detrimental to the embargo than the committee reports implied. First of all, the frequency of reported violations tended to produce a prior assumption of guilt even before refutation or confirmation, and some were ultimately discovered to be legal contracts with Portugal or South Africa. Second, in the absence of far-reaching legislation, the government was in fact largely powerless to prevent the use of Swiss banking and financial channels by firms acting as middlemen for various triangular operations, so long as such operations did not touch Swiss territory, which made it difficult to locate precisely the point at which the law had been breached. Third, a relatively small number of individual Swiss businessmen and firms were involved, and there was little indication that the Swiss government itself was a party to the violations. In addition, not all confirmed violations went unprosecuted by the Swiss authorities. At least one such case, a breach in the arms embargo against South Africa by Buehrle and Company, a major Swiss arms manufacturer, was handled swiftly and decisively by the government (*New York Times*, 28 November 1970, 6:4).

MODIFICATIONS OF SWISS POLICY IN THE 1970s

Apart from these difficulties over violations of the embargo, the continuation of Swiss-Rhodesian trade also elicited further UN attention during 1975–77, with direct effect on Swiss policy. The Sanctions Committee's sixth report (1973) indicated a marked increase in Swiss exports to Rhodesia after reaching a post-UDI nadir in 1969 (see table 8-1, cols. 3 and 4). Even more revealing were the figures on Swiss imports from Rhodesia, to which the *courant normale* principle applied. The first striking figure was the sharp increase in Swiss imports from Rhodesia from 1964 to 1965 in advance of the embargo, due partly to a suspiciously large shipment in 1965 of Rhodesian precious and semiprecious stones (table 8-2, n. 1 and col. 6). This increase may have been due to a normal expansion of trade with Rhodesia (along with Zambia and Malawi) after the breakup of the Federation in 1963; for example, Swedish-Rhodesian trade also increased, although to a much lesser extent, from 1964 to 1965. There is no indication as to whether Swiss importers deliberately expanded commercial contacts with Rhodesian firms in anticipation of a UN embargo (and the imposition in Switzerland of the *courant normale*). However, this seems a plausible explanation, due to the suspicious nature of this trade (precious stones) and particularly in light of the many violations later confirmed.

After a general decline in imports from Rhodesia from 1965 to 1968 (due to the imposition and tightening of the trade restrictions of 1965 and 1967), the import figures showed an increase in both dollar and Swiss franc terms (table 8-1, cols. 1 and 2). The year 1973 alone showed a particularly sharp increase in Swiss-Rhodesian trade, with imports from the colony (measured in both currencies) rising almost 40 percent; this was mainly due to an increase in Switzerland's importation of Rhodesian meat (table 8-2, cols. 1, 2, 5). This rise in Swiss trade tended to corroborate Renwick's assertion that "undertakings by countries not applying sanctions to hold trade to 'normal' levels have tended to prove of limited real affect and to be subject to very elastic interpretation" (1981, 79–80); it also followed the overall pattern of Rhodesian trade. These increases seemed clearly to contravene the *courant normale* principle, despite the government's explanation that "fluctuations between the years" were a natural consequence of its particular trade restrictions.

Switzerland's sensitive and difficult situation was also indicated by the Sanctions Committee's revelation in 1973 that, out of all reporting countries, Switzerland was the second largest overall exporter to Rhodesia. With total exports reaching some $4m, Switzerland was second only to Malawi ($6m), and it was ahead of the United States, Britain, and West Germany (although of course these figures excluded the South African Customs Union, which by that time exported an estimated $180m worth of goods annually to Rhodesia). Switzerland's notoriety particularly extended to tobacco trade, one of the main commodity areas for Swiss imports from Rhodesia (see table 8-2, cols. 3, 4); and by importing in 1973 around $1.6m dollars worth, Switzerland "appeared to be the only reporting country of significance" (UN Doc. S/11178, 103). By 1973, Switzerland's import of some $8m dollars' worth of Rhodesian goods was the fourth largest total, behind only the United States, Malawi, and Zambia (again excluding South Africa). The continuation of this trade led the Sanctions Committee to recommend to the Security Council as early as May 1971 to call upon the governments of Switzerland, Australia and West Germany to stop their illegal trade with Rhodesia (S/11178/Add. 2, SS no. 2, 265). On 23 August 1974 the UN secretary-general directly requested the Swiss government to tighten up its sanctions legislation (UN Doc. S/11594/Rev. 1, SS no. 2, 159). In a note of 28 July 1975 the UN again objected to the continuation of Swiss trade, particularly because the January–March 1975 figures—supplied, as always, by the Swiss government, in detailed form—showed a further increase.[19]

A sharp, unexplained rise in Switzerland's imports of Rhodesian beef in 1973 also led to a further tightening of the *courant normale* in 1974,[20] by which the majority of Rhodesian beef (70 percent) was limited to the average level of 1964–66; table 8-2, cols. 1 and 2, shows the immediate decline which this action brought about. The Security Council, in a note of 28 July 1975, considered this trade "particularly serious," and sought additional Swiss explanation. However, after sending reminders to the Federal Council on 8 October and 12 November, but without any reaction, the UN included Switzerland on its eighth quarterly list of nonrespondents (UN Doc. S/11927/Rev. 1,

SS no. 2, 35–39). A week later the Swiss government did respond, but said only that "it was hardly possible to draw conclusions from them [the first quarter's figures], for the entire year 1975" (39). In addition, the UN again complained that the Swiss had failed to restrict its level of exports to Rhodesia (UN Doc. S/12265, SS no. 2, Vol. I, Annex IV, 259).

In light of these continuing difficulties, and in an attempt to mollify the UN's concerns, the Swiss government in November 1976 undertook to clarify its position further. It was significant that, at this point and for the first time, the government attempted to answer the Sanctions Committee's complaints about the increasing levels of Swiss trade by pointing out that the *courant normale*, limiting Swiss imports from Rhodesia, had always been measured by volume of trade rather than monetary value, either in Swiss francs or US dollars (UN Doc. S/12265, Vol. II, Annex IV, 244). By this reckoning, the government had been measuring Swiss trade from a base level of 3,858 tons and not the figure of $4,087,000 (the average level of 1964–66). It therefore asserted that this "volume was not reached in any of the years between 1967 and 1975. On the contrary, the average for that period is 2,771 tons, and is therefore considerably lower than the normal flow." This assertion is also borne out by table 8-2, covering the two main commodity areas; the 1965 level of meat imports was never (and the 1964–66 average only rarely) reached in subsequent years, although the tobacco average of 1964–66 was slightly, but consistently, exceeded. In addition, the Swiss pointed out that the UN figures, always measured in U.S. dollars, were misleading, for two reasons: one was the general rise in prices over the period in question, due to increased worldwide inflation; the other was the depreciation of the dollar in the late 1960s (leading to the abolition of the Bretton Woods system of fixed exchange rates in 1971), and the simultaneous rapid appreciation of the Swiss franc.[21] This development inflated the figures originally computed in Swiss francs, according to which Swiss-Rhodesian trade had increased much more modestly, from an average of SwFr 17.7m in 1964–66 to a high of 24.4m in 1973, then down to 18.9m in 1975 (see table 8-1). These figures bolstered the Swiss contention that its trade with Rhodesia was not increasing as sharply as the UN claimed; and the Sanctions Committee's expert consultant subsequently verified the Swiss contention that its overall volume of trade had decreased from the levels of 1964–66 (UN Doc. S/13750, SS no. 2, Vol. I, 59; Vol. II, Annex III, 154–57). Even so, it remains unclear why the Swiss authorities waited nearly a decade to clarify this issue with UN officials. The answer most likely lies in the sudden increase in Rhodesian-Swiss trade (in dollar terms, but to a lesser extent in francs as well) during 1973 and 1974, which due to the usual delays in publishing finalized year-end figures, only elicited UN inquiries after mid-1975. In addition, this effort to clarify the issue came at a time when the government was also taking a more accommodating position on the question of outright violations of the embargo by individual Swiss firms, while also warming to the idea of Swiss accession to the UNO.

By 1977 both UN and Swiss authorities took a number of additional steps to resolve these continuing problems. The recurring reports of violations and increasing Swiss trade with Rhodesia led the acting chairman of the UN Sanctions Committee to request a private meeting with the Swiss Permanent Observer to discuss these matters (UN Doc. S/12529/Rev. 1, SS no. 2, Vol. 1, Annex 1, 73–74), which was held on 26 July 1977. As a direct result of this meeting, the Federal Council began preparations for a report on all commercial relations between Rhodesia and Switzerland, although it was also evident from the government's annual reports to parliament during the period 1973–77 that a gradual change of heart in favor of mollifying the UN's concerns was occurring.[22] After considering a preliminary draft report (3 October 1977), the government established working groups to reexamine certain aspects of bilateral commercial relations between Switzerland and Rhodesia. Then on 12 December the Federal Council approved a six-point ordinance, which for the first time prohibited persons domiciled or headquartered in Switzerland from concluding or executing actions connected with Rhodesian trade (UN Doc. S/12529/Rev. 1, SS no. 2, Vol. I, 33–35, 280–83). The decree prohibited the following: (1) the acquisition or sale of goods originating in, or destined for, Rhodesia which never touched Swiss territory; (2) the granting of credits or transfer of funds to persons domiciled or headquartered in Southern Rhodesia; (3) the provision of services relating to operations in (1) and (2) above. The only exception was for goods and funds for medical purposes or teaching, books and publications, and food for humanitarian purposes. This (nonretroactive) ordinance entered into force on 1 January 1978 (*RO* 1977:2180–81). Through an order of 25 January 1978, the Principality of Liechtenstein prohibited essentially the same transactions (UN Doc. S/13000, SS no. 2, Vol. I, 141–42).

This undertaking by the Swiss government represented a striking turnabout from its long-held view that it was powerless to prevent or curtail triangular transactions involving Swiss firms. It could also be interpreted as a significant, if tardy, step toward complying with the UN sanctions operation; it was not merely coincidental that the government's decree banning such transactions was enacted only a few months after the publication of its third special UN report, through which it first went on record as favoring Swiss accession, and recognizing UN membership as compatible with neutrality (1977 UN Report, 140). The ordinance also clearly accorded with Security Council Resolution 409 (27 May 1977) which prohibited the use or transfer of funds in any state to the Rhodesian régime, for purposes other than payment of pensions; as such, the Sanctions Committee "expressed its satisfaction at the measures promulgated by the Swiss authorities" (UN Doc. S/13000, SS no. 2, Vol. I, Annex IV, 236). It was odd that the government should consider that the ordinance, which represented a major shift from its previous position, had been "taken in accordance with the Federal Council's independently-determined policy regarding the sanctions established by the Security Council against Southern Rhodesia" (UN Doc. S/13750, SS no. 2, Vol. 1, 110), since clearly the many violations and particularly the special meeting between the Swiss Permanent Observer and the acting chairman of the Sanctions Committee had precipitated this decision.

Despite its late adoption, the new ordinance appeared to have an appreciable effect on Switzerland's position in the Rhodesian affair, particularly on Swiss-Rhodesian trade. Swiss exports to the colony (in francs) declined nearly 30 percent in 1978, but then rose again slightly during 1979. Meanwhile Swiss imports from Rhodesia remained almost unchanged in 1978, but then fell nearly 40 percent in 1979 (see table 8-1), although as the embargo was lifted at the end of that year, there was no further sanctioning year against which to compare the 1977–78 figures, to ascertain whether they revealed any discernible pattern. (The Swiss annual statistics showed a further decline in 1980, to SwFr 8.7m, which did suggest that it also affected the post-embargo trade pattern; *Annuaire Statistique* 1983, 210–11.) On the other hand, the ordinance did not always result in closer official investigation of reported violations, as its refusal to investigate further the case of a bank loan from Industrie-Maschinen to Rhodesian railways well illustrated (UN Doc. S/13000, SS no. 2, Annex IV, 189).

These developments in the Rhodesian embargo, and the related Security Council decision in late 1977 to impose a mandatory arms embargo against South Africa were also accompanied by a distinct stiffening of official Swiss rhetoric on the issues of apartheid and racialism in southern Africa. One precipitating factor was the arrest, trial, and detention of a Swiss missionary in Rhodesia in 1977 for alleged illicit activity (*RCF* 1977:16). Then after his unprecedented African tour in 1978 as the new Swiss foreign minister, Pierre Aubert condemned the system of apartheid before the *Nationalrat*, asserting that "it has been a long time since Swiss authorities have declared it morally unacceptable" (it had been in fact a decade, since Ambassador Lindt's 1968 statement in Teheran). As evidence that this was more than an isolated statement, Swiss Ambassador Bieler stated in Lagos in August 1977 (with prior Federal Council approval) that apartheid represented "a system contrary to the tradition and to the ideals of the Swiss people as well as to the principles recognized in the area of human rights by the international community" (*BS*, CN 1978, 227).

NOTES

1. See Bindschedler, 1968, pp. 10–11; Guggenheim in *NZZ*, 9 April 1967, p. 7; *NZZ* editorial, 24 December 1966, p. 1; Boczek, 1969, pp. 84–85, n. 33.

2. *Yearbook of the International Law Commission*, 1964, Vol. II, p. 184; also 1966, Vol. II, p. 231, which held that such an element of customary international law can also bind a third state not a party to the original treaty.

3. Robert, 1950, pp. 85–86; Belin, 1956, p. 79; Guggenheim, 1945, pp. 32, 38, 47; also Guggenheim in ILA, Report of the 41st Conference, 1947, pp. 48–49; and especially Rappard 1946a, pp. 11–12; and Rappard 1946b, pp. 1038–42.

4. "Commission Consultative Suisse," 1945, Vols. I and II. See Vol. II, p. 13 (Petitpierre); also individual experts' views: Vol. I (14 November 1945), pp. 13–14 (Rappard); pp. 89–90 (Godard); and especially pp. 52–53 (Schindler).

5. See e.g., *FF* 1947, Vol. 2, pp. 535–36; 1969 Swiss UN Report, pp. 21, 23, 102–5 *passim*, 121.

6. *FF* 1947, Vol. 2, p. 536; also *RO* 1948, p. 1033. See in support of this view Kelsen, 1950, p. 495, and Hudson, 1947, pp. 866–71.

7. "Beziehungen zum Ausland," Jurisprudence des autorités administratifs de la Confédération (1954), pp. 9–13; an English translation is provided in Hughes, 1962, Appendix I, pp. 167–71.

8. See on this point Edberg, 1951, p. 198; de Rougemont, 1953; Siegfried, 1950; and Muret, 1966, esp. p. 149.

9. See for example *BS*, CN, 1956, p. 759 (Petitpierre); *RCF*, 1960, p. 27; and as late as October 1965 Foreign Minister F. T. Wahlen told the National Council that "so far our country has suffered no injury from the fact that it is not a Member of the United Nations" (quoted in 1969 Swiss UN Report, p. 53).

10. Arrêté no. 1 du Conseil fédéral sur la limitation des importations (du 17 décembre 1965), *RO* 1965, pp. 1217–18; entering into force on 23 December.

11. Boczek, 1969, p. 83, n. 26; also "Issues Before the 23rd General Assembly," p. 74, Table 1; and Bindschedler, 1968, p. 14.

12. Arrêté no. 2 du Conseil fédéral sur la limitation des importations (du 10 février 1967), *RO* 1967, p. 209–10, entering into force on 21 Feb. 1967.

13. See the Sanctions Committee's eighth report; UN Doc. S/11927/Rev. I, Appendix I, p. 126, n. e.

14. *FF* 1969, Vol. 1, pp. 1457–1617, Federal Council Report to the Federal Assembly of 16 July 1969; *FF* 1972, Vol. 1, pp. 1–68, Report of 17 November 1971; *FF* 1977, Vol. 2, pp. 781–948, Report of 29 June 1977; and *FF* 1982, Vol. 1, pp. 505–702, Message of 21 December 1981. Hereinafter references to these documents refer to the separate mimeographed editions printed by the Swiss government's printing office, of which the first (1969) was also printed in an English edition.

15. UN Doc. S/10229, paragraph 52, p. 15 (fourth report of the Sanctions Committee). See also RCF, 1968, p. 17.

16. See among others, for Austria, Verdross, 1958, p. 417; Zemanek, 1968, p. 31; and for Switzerland, Dutoit, 1962, pp. 47–48; 1977 Swiss UN Report, p. 111; 1969 Swiss UN Report, p. 39; and Zemanek, 1961, p. 414.

17. UN Docs. S/7776, and S/9252, Annex III (second report of the Sanctions Committee). However, trade contracts signed prior to Res. 253 would be allowed to be fulfilled; UN Doc. S/7781, Add. 5, Annex C.

18. See for example UN Doc. S/11594/Rev. 1, SS no. 2, pp. 146–47; and in the *Polana* case, involving a shipment of beef to Switzerland, the government refused to supply the relevant bills of lading to the UN (UN Doc. S/10229, SS no. 2, pp. 11–12, 14–15, 197).

19. UN Doc. S/11927/Rev. 1, case no. 214, pp. 35–37 (eighth report of the Sanctions Committee). The Swiss government's computations of Swiss–Rhodesian trade varied slightly from the UN figures (in dollar terms) in the years 1964–69 and 1975–76. See also UN Doc. S/13750, SS no. 2, Vol. 2, case no. 214, pp. 146–47.

20. Arrêté du Conseil fédéral (no. 3) sur la limitation des importations, du 6 février 1974, *RO* 1974, pp. 486–87. The decree was retroactive to 1 January 1974.

21. Whereas the franc/dollar ratio was 4.33 to 1 in 1967, it fell to 2.58 in 1975; this corresponded to a decline in the conversion factor from 23.27 during the late 1960s (fixed rate up until 1971) to 38.9 in 1975. By 1978 the deterioration in the ratio was even more striking: the dollar had fallen below two Swiss francs, to a factor of 56.3 (UN Doc. S/13750, SS no. 2, Vol. II, Annex III, p. 146).

22. For indications of this trend toward a more conciliatory attitude, see *RCF*, 1973, p. 19; 1974, p. 21; 1975, p. 19; compared with 1976, p. 17, and especially 1977, p. 16, which admitted to the reported increases in illicit "triangular operations" involving Swiss firms.

Part IV

Conclusions

Part IV

9

Sweden, Switzerland, and the Sanctions Question

This final chapter will draw a number of conclusions based on the foregoing analysis. It will begin with a general summary of Swedish and Swiss policy in the two operations, in order to determine how each state has responded to calls for international sanctions. Second, it will suggest a specific set of factors accounting for those differences in Sweden's and Switzerland's policies, which could serve as generally operative factors, relating to how other states might be expected to respond to similar cases of sanctions. Finally, it will consider the extent to which the four case studies have demonstrated scope for compatibility between neutrality policies and collective security operations.

THE NEUTRALS' ATTITUDES TOWARD SANCTIONS

Sweden's Response to the Sanctions Operations

The Swedish government generally supported the calls for sanctions in both cases, in both word and policy. This support tended to reflect Sweden's positive attitude toward the overall aims of both organizations. In fact, Sweden was predisposed toward supporting the operations because of a fortuitous convergence of a number of different factors, relating to Sweden's relations both with the international organizations and with the target states. A particularly important general factor was the widespread perception in Sweden that its neutrality was not a major obstacle to full participation in either event.

Nonetheless, a number of differences also marked Sweden's policies in 1935–36 and 1965–79. In the earlier crisis, Sweden supported what could be called a "minimalist" application of sanctions, meaning that it applied only those measures strictly requested by the League. For example, in 1935–36 it chose not to adopt measures for mutual support (Proposal V), which were optional to member states, nor did it materially reduce its exports to Italy to complement the import embargo. Sweden did apply the partial export embargo in respect of the commodities on the League's list (mainly its relatively insignificant sales of iron ore and iron alloys), but the overall amount of Sweden's exports to Italy during the crisis showed only a slight reduction as compared with the pre-sanctions period. It continued to sell its major exports to Italy, particularly iron and steel products and paper pulp, and only in the categories of electrical machinery and pig iron were Sweden's exports substantially reduced (and that probably due to changes in Italy's own trade requirements). This result compared unfavorably with France and Great Britain, both of which cut their total exports to Italy to a much greater degree. Sweden was also unwilling to decree the severance of valid trade contracts on the private market, or to impound goods from Italy that had arrived in Sweden by 18 November 1935.

There was also a slight variance between Sweden's declared acceptance of the total import embargo (Proposal III) and its actual trade performance, whereby its imports from Italy, though sharply reduced, were never entirely cut off. This was due to the continued fulfillment of long-term contracts already paid for, and to the exemption of Italian goods arriving in Sweden before the 18 November deadline. This factor likewise prevented an immediate shutdown in trade with Rhodesia. During the Italian crisis, the time span was much shorter, and as noted in chapter 4, no participating state achieved an entire shutdown of imports from Italy, although Britain came very close to doing so. Thus this small, and declining, level of trade with Italy was not a serious matter.

However, during the Rhodesian crisis Sweden demonstrated a willingness to take measures above and beyond the minimum requirements of participation. The government's initial steps (including its immediate closure of the Swedish consulate at Salisbury; its early preparations for severing bilateral trade links; and particularly its preemptive call for the Security Council to designate the Rhodesian situation a threat to international peace, as a prelude to mandatory UN sanctions) all demonstrated its intention to apply unilateral pressure along with supporting the measures recommended by the UN. This attitude indicated a "maximalist" interpretation of its sanctions obligations. Another indication of this attitude was Sweden's early decision (1966) to support Zambia's calls for mutual support, years before the UN did so; still another was Sweden's decision, both concurrent with and related to the Rhodesian affair, to supply increasing levels of financial aid to the African liberation movements in Rhodesia, South Africa, and the Portuguese colonies. This was a key component of its dual approach to colonial issues in Africa, which was designed to induce political change from within the region while also applying external pressure in the form of multilateral sanctions.

Possibly the most significant indication of Sweden's increasing support for international sanctions as a basic component of its foreign policy was its passage of permanent sanctions legislation. As discussed in chapter 4, the first Swedish law pertaining to sanctions was enacted during the Italian crisis, so on this point we can see a clear trend in Swedish policy over a considerable period. The sanctions law of April 1936 authorized Swedish authorities to impose a credit stop in the event of financial sanctions requested by the League of Nations. However, its significance was limited by its temporary validity and by the fact that it applied only to one type of transaction (financial credits). Furthermore, several other states had applied similar and indeed more far-reaching sanctions legislation, which indicated that Sweden's act, while a positive step, was something rather less than an outstanding display of national loyalty to the League.

The government's authority to apply sanctions was expanded considerably through the Act Concerning Certain Sanctions against Rhodesia, passed in 1969, which enabled the full application of the comprehensive trade embargo of SC Resolution 253, and more widely through the Law on Certain International Sanctions of 1971. The latter act empowered the government to decree, without prior parliamentary approval, a severance of all financial and commercial activity between all Swedes (even those residing outside Sweden) and any state if requested to do so by the Security Council. Significantly, the law is equally valid for Security Council recommendations as well as its binding decisions concerning sanctions, and thus it has effectively drawn Swedish policy closer to the UN on the economic sanctions issue.

These developments indicate a general and consistent trend in Swedish policy: its earlier, ad hoc support for sanctions on a case-by-case basis has been gradually supplanted by continuous support for economic (but not military) sanctions as a general principle and basic component of its foreign policy. This interpretation is supported by an examination of Swedish policy on a historical continuum since 1918. Sweden had joined the League over strong, combined opposition from the Conservative Party, the Agrarian League, and the far left; and even the Social Democrats and Liberals, who favored membership, were determined to limit Sweden's sanctions obligations. After accession, the government's receptivity to sanctions consistently hinged on the success of its efforts to (1) water down the Covenant's sanctions obligations, by instituting a nonautomatic procedure and by allowing for the possibility of exemptions for endangered states; and (2) develop arbitration and disarmament together with sanctions in order to strengthen each strand of the "security triad." Once these developments began to take shape, the government's reluctance to accept sanctions obligations was gradually relaxed by the early 1930s, enabling its cooperation with the Italian operation. This increasingly favorable attitude toward economic sanctions was equally evident in the UN period, in light of Sweden's unopposed UN entry in 1946 and its full participation in the Rhodesian operation. This trend has been facilitated by Sweden's generally pragmatic and utilitarian view of its own neutrality, meaning that its neutrality is flexibly interpreted and has proven able to coexist with new international obligations.

Another crucial factor in this evolution was the rapid dissipation of political disagreement over Sweden's League policies after 1920, in spite of chronic governmental instability prior to 1932. This interparty support for Sweden's League (and later UN) membership, and to a large extent even for the details of official policy, has been instrumental in the government's ability to apply a coherent and consistent sanctions policy. This political unity was demonstrated by the high degree of continuity in Sweden's Rhodesian policy during the important political changeover from an absolute Social Democratic majority in 1968 to exact parity between the two political blocs (1973–76), and then to the displacement of the Social Democrats altogether in 1976 by a three-party bourgeois coalition. This development would appear to substantiate the hypothesis put forth in chapter 2, that the strong cultural basis of Swedish national unity could be translated into political consensus on foreign policy issues, fostering the development of a consistent policy toward sanctions. The degree to which this trend is applicable also to the broader issue of collective security will be addressed in the final section.

SWITZERLAND'S RESPONSE TO THE SANCTIONS OPERATIONS

The general scenario has been quite different in the Swiss case. Whereas Swedish support for sanctions was increasingly wholehearted, Switzerland's attitude was continually lukewarm and occasionally obstructive. Its relative lack of enthusiasm resulted from many different factors (see below), the first and perhaps most obvious of which is the fact that Switzerland, unlike Sweden, was not a fully obligated member of either the League's or the UN's security system. In fact the causal relationship between its limited international obligations, and its response to sanctions, has been occasionally misconstrued by the Swiss government. For instance, while the Federal Council has claimed that its reluctance to participate has been mainly the function of its lack of strict legal obligations to the two organizations, the reverse has been more true; it was Switzerland's clear and longstanding determination to avoid all obligations potentially threatening its neutrality (i.e., those which would involve it in others' disputes), which led initially to its "qualified" League membership, and later to its decision not to join the UNO.

In the earlier crisis, Switzerland's historically close cultural and political relations with Italy sharply tempered its attitude toward the League's embargo, and caused it to hesitate on the question of its own participation. This hesitancy produced a policy which suggested an attitude of actual obstructiveness to the League's aims. It is not entirely clear how far the government used Switzerland's very real problems in the crisis to cloak an attempt to thwart the sanctions themselves, and thus the extent to which it betrayed a more general rejection of sanctions obligations per se. The Swiss attitude toward, for example, the arms embargo against Italy (Proposal I), which the government applied against both belligerents equally, was one manifestation of a policy which, while seemingly inspired by the neutral duty of impartiality, in fact appeared to aid the Italian cause unilaterally, since Italy already held a decisive strategic advantage in the conflict, and because Switzerland's geographical position was conducive to the illegal flow of arms to Italy.

Another possible indication of Swiss obstructiveness is suggested (though not proven) by reports that political pressure from Mussolini led to Swiss efforts within the League's Committee of Eighteen to thwart the imposition of an oil embargo. Moreover, Switzerland's partial compliance with the economic embargo was designed to associate Switzerland with the League's general aims while limiting the damage to Italo-Swiss relations as much as possible. It bears repeating that this was an understandable aim, resulting from justified fears for its own economic and political well-being as a result of an international embargo against one of its closest and most powerful neighbors. This interpretation of Switzerland's complicated policies in 1935–36—that it partially complied with the operation—is rather more charitable than a number of other writers who have asserted the (mistaken) view that Switzerland refused sanctions altogether; others, even after acknowledging its partial acquiescence, have interpreted its actions wrongly.[1]

The Italian crisis also held long-term implications for Swiss foreign policy insofar as it induced a basic reconsideration of the very premises of its previous policy of cooperation with the League as a collective security organization. The government considered its shift from "integral" to "differential" neutrality within League membership (formalized through the February 1920 Declaration of London) to be a major change in its traditional foreign policy strategy; and the first major test case for the League proved to be a telling and even precipitous turning point for this hitherto untested policy of association with a sanctions system. A particularly important background factor was the Swiss fear that even limited economic sanctions against Italy could lead to war: either by escalation to League military action, or by provoking Italian counterstrikes. Such a war would almost certainly embroil Switzerland, given its close proximity to Italy and the presence of the League's headquarters on its own territory. Due to these perceived dangers, the Swiss became rapidly convinced that differential neutrality, which assumed that a feasible distinction could be made between economic and military sanctions, was at best a meaningless formula, and at worst a dangerous illusion.

Perhaps inevitably, Switzerland's difficulties in this case resulted in a far-reaching retrenchment in its overall outlook toward collective security. In contrast with the retrospective Swedish view of the crisis, which was the tentative conclusion that sanctions did not work in this case but were not by definition ill-conceived, the Swiss conclusion was that sanctions *in principle* were dangerous to their neutrality and security, and thereafter must be avoided so far as possible. The widespread Swiss belief that sanctions are inherently incompatible with their security interests was thus largely the product of the Italian operation; and it continued to govern Switzerland's attitude toward the sanctions issue for decades into the postwar period.

The Swiss government's problems in the Rhodesian dispute were very different from those in the earlier crisis, even though the government employed several of the same arguments and policies as in 1935–36. Its initial attitude was twofold: first, it asserted its independence from the UN by refusing to adhere to the operation and by applying its own measures; and second, it aimed to avoid helping the object of the embargo (Rhodesia), primarily by limiting its trade to the pre-sanctions level.

However, Switzerland's real difficulty in the crisis lay in inconsistencies in its stated rationale behind this policy. The Federal Council's position, particularly when seen over the longer term, provided a good example of how a state may rationalize its policies by utilizing outmoded arguments, only to quietly abandon this position once its irrelevance becomes apparent. Initially, it cited Switzerland's traditional neutrality as the main reason for its nonparticipation, even though the dispute clearly did not endanger, or even involve, the main principles of neutrality; and indeed the Swiss government itself thereafter acknowledged the nonapplicability of the Hague rules of neutrality to the crisis. A logical disjunction in the Swiss attitude was thereby exposed: the Swiss cited a particular policy (neutrality), then proceeded to deny its basic premises in the actual case. Thus an important consideration in Switzerland's later policy in the affair was its gradual acceptance of this fact. Quietly but clearly the Federal Council began to alter its argument for nonparticipation, away from neutrality to the (more logical) view that its nonmembership in the UN, and hence its lack of a legal obligation to the organization, was the main reason for its abstention.

Switzerland's actual policies during the crisis showed mixed results, and there appeared to be some discrepancy between even the government's stated aims and actual developments. For example, in both cases Switzerland's imports were limited by decree to the level attained prior to sanctions (the *courant normale*). However, whereas Swiss imports from Italy in 1935–36 fell considerably during the sanctioning period, Swiss policy in the Rhodesian affair was strongly criticized because of sharp increases in the value (though not volume, which was the actual criterion used) of its imports from Rhodesia. Moreover, Swiss exports were not subject to a similar restriction in either event: as against Italy because no total export embargo was requested by the League, and in the latter case because (it was argued) it would be impossible to monitor accurately.

In both crises Switzerland was subjected to international pressure and criticism due to its refusal to cooperate fully with the embargoes. In 1935–36 other states' delegates voiced criticism in subcommittee debate; in the Rhodesian dispute, the UN's special Sanctions Committee applied pressure, through direct representations to the Swiss government and through its publication of verified evidence of violations by Swiss firms. Indeed in both crises Swiss policy attained considerable notoriety: in the earlier case because the government initially professed "tacit support" for the aims of the League, only to refuse to implement several of the actual measures recommended; and in the Rhodesian case due to increases in the value of Swiss-Rhodesian trade after 1965, which exposed Switzerland as one of a handful of states refusing to participate in the operation. Moreover in both crises this international criticism forced the government to modify its policy, though it was reluctant to admit as much. For example, in the Italian crisis, the government agreed to consider modifying its controversial dual arms embargo by allowing some future arms sales to Abyssinia (though this never materialized); similarly, it backtracked from its controversial requests for mutual support.

In the Rhodesian crisis the government denied that its measures were in any way influenced by the UN's operation, and insisted that they had been applied autonomously. Nonetheless, international pressure over a period of years appeared to influence Swiss policy, specifically by inducing the Federal Council to impose additional restrictions in 1974 and 1977. Probably the clearest connection was Switzerland's comprehensive review of its trade policy with Rhodesia in 1977, immediately following the private (and unprecedented) meeting between the Swiss Permanent UN Observer and the acting chairman of the Sanctions Committee.

It is tempting to categorize Switzerland's attitude toward international sanctions, insofar as it was demonstrated in these two crises, as one of opposition to sanctions in principle. One of the recurring themes in the Swiss debate has been the instinctive, at times almost verging on the irrational, defense of neutrality whenever sanctions have been mentioned. It is argued that the government's automatic, defensive reaction has prevented it from adopting a more rational, coherent, and long-term position on the sanctions issue. Switzerland's response to the very differing circumstances of the two crises also seems to support this assertion, for its opposition to sanctions due to neutrality was seemingly as strong at the outset of the Rhodesian affair, when its neutrality was not under threat, as in the Italian crisis, when it was directly threatened. Strong attachment to its permanent neutrality appears to have been a primary cause of the inconsistency which has marked Switzerland's overall attitude toward the sanctions question since the outset of the League era. Switzerland's relative inconsistency on this issue, particularly in light of its continual insistence on the permanence and invariability of its neutral principles, has been in fact one of the most surprising findings of this study.

This long-term inconsistency can be more accurately gauged in light of the overall schematic development of Switzerland's attitude toward sanctions since 1918. In the initial Swiss debates over League membership, the government accepted the compatibility of economic sanctions obligations and neutrality; this view represented an even more liberal acceptance of League duties than did Sweden's initial policy. However, in the Italian crisis the government gave a much more attenuated interpretation of its obligations, insofar as it considered the economic embargo against Italy to be unacceptable and a threat to Swiss neutrality. Thus the Swiss parliamentary commission's claim in 1935, that Swiss policy was "exactly that which it declared as its duty in 1919 and 1920" (*BS*, CN 1936, 610) was spurious, since the Federal Council did not fully apply the measures requested by the League.

This stricter interpretation of neutrality was maintained during the debate over UN membership in 1945. The Swiss Consultative Commission held unanimously that the obligations of UN membership, including economic sanctions, were de facto incompatible with neutrality. There were, again, valid reasons for Switzerland's abstention, not least of which was the continued possibility of being asked to sanction an important neighbor such as Italy or Germany, since neither was a permanent Security Council member nor a World War II allied state. Even so, the arguments expressed in the 1945 debate failed to acknowledge important features of the UN Charter which allowed for neutrality in some cases, such as the Security Council's (seeming) inability to sanction any of its permanent members and their allies, or to obligate any state to apply military sanctions without its prior consent. This lack of commentary became more striking in retrospect, since the Swiss government later admitted that these mitigating factors were significant in the context of UN membership. Another possible difficulty lay in the government's distinction between UN sanctions and other measures taken by the Security Council under Art. 94 of the Charter to enforce an ICJ decision (to which, on one interpretation of the Statute, Switzerland was bound to comply; Hudson 1947, 866–71).

Again in 1965, Switzerland held that its neutrality prevented it from participating in sanctions, but as we have seen, this view was again gradually abandoned. By the 1970s it appeared that the government's views of sanctions were coming in a sense full circle, approaching its attitude of 1919–20, that neutrality was not an absolute barrier to participation in a sanctions operation. This changing attitude was in fact central to the government's ongoing (but ultimately abortive) campaign to secure Swiss membership in the UN.

Another continuing problem for Switzerland in its attempt to resolve the sanctions problem has been the government's inability to obtain, and maintain, a popular mandate for a foreign policy based on international cooperation. The case studies have supported the hypothesis put forth in chapter 2, that Switzerland's strong subcultural segmentation, and lack of a distinct foreign policy élite, have been important factors inhibiting the development of a clear and consistent sanctions policy. As early as 1920, the government's seemingly clear and rational view of sanctions, and its remarkable success in obtaining League concessions as a prelude to Swiss membership, was nearly rejected in the League referendum. Thereafter the government continually cited the latent but strong grass-roots opposition to the League's activities as a factor preventing a more active Swiss policy of international cooperation. The continued, fundamental divergence of popular Swiss attitudes toward collective security was vividly demonstrated during the January 1936 debates over the Italian crisis, when even the government's policy of grudging and limited cooperation with the League was heavily criticized from various quarters (and by parliament as a whole) for its alleged willingness to compromise Swiss interests.

The problem of determining the strength of domestic opposition was greater in the Rhodesian case, partly because no formal parliamentary debate over the crisis was ever held. In addition, the peculiar structure of the Swiss Federal Council, composed (since 1959) of representatives of all the major parties in rough proportion to their electoral strength, has rendered the traditional distinction between "government" and "opposition" less meaningful in the modern Swiss political system. Even so, the role of opposition was amply filled by the grass-roots antiforeignization movements of the late 1960s, which capitalized on their early successes in limiting the number of foreigners in Switzerland by opposing Switzerland's gradual opening to world affairs. Their successes were best seen in the surprising 1976 referendum defeat of the government's regular IDA contribution (Lambelet 1980), and particularly in the following year (1977), when popular control over Swiss foreign policy was tightened through the constitutional extension of the earlier optional referendum on foreign treaties, and the creation of a new, mandatory referendum on certain important treaties (those relating to membership in multinational communities and collective security organizations). Clearly the government's maneuverability in foreign affairs, particularly in accommodating international sanctions obligations, continues to be sharply restricted by the opposition of important constituencies within the country; and this opposition was amply demonstrated in the 16 March 1986 Swiss referendum on UN membership, in which the government's proposal to accede to the Charter was forcefully rejected, by 75.7 percent of the voting public (*The Times*, 17 March 1986, 1; Ross 1988).

FACTORS ACCOUNTING FOR THE VARIATION IN POLICY

This section will set forth a number of specific factors which have accounted for the differences between Swedish and Swiss sanctions policy. My broader objective in this undertaking, however, is to identify regularities from which empirical generalizations (in this case, of third or source states) could be drawn. Therefore this accounting can help generate a set of generally operative factors, which can be used as potential determinants of how neutral (and other) states might react in other cases of international sanctions—always keeping in mind that it is more difficult to identify factors which are causal and general than those which are parsimonious and specific (Przeworski and Teune 1970, 86). This aim also accords with a number of other analysts of the sanctions problem, who have suggested that more attention should be given, in determining the overall success of sanctions operations, to analyzing the problems for the sanctioning states themselves (Hufbauer and Schott 1985, 86–88; Doxey 1987, chapter 7). One obvious reference point for this section is the ongoing issue of whether international enthusiasm for UN sanctions against South Africa is sufficient to warrant a mandatory enforcement operation against Pretoria.

Geographical Proximity

One hypothesis by which we could seek to explain differences in neutral states' responses to sanctions might be that a state's readiness to impose them is positively related to its geographical distance from the target of sanctions. It is plausible to expect that a state close to the target state in terms of distance (particularly a neighboring state) would be less likely to impose sanctions than one far removed, because of the likelihood that sanctions would disrupt everyday working arrangements essential to both states, such as customs and border control, security arrangements such as extradition treaties, and other types of interaction such as bilateral trade between the two states, which would normally be considerable due to the relative ease in transporting goods over short distances. Due to the prospect of severe disruption of these and other essential services, one would expect that a state would be disinclined to support sanctions against a neighbor, notwithstanding the possibility of recouping some of its losses through provisions for mutual support.

The Italian case supports this hypothesis, insofar as Switzerland's proximity to Italy, and Sweden's distance from it, helped determine the extent to which each state cooperated with the League's operation. Sweden was, of course, separated from Italy by all of central Europe, which facilitated its support for sanctions. Switzerland, however, shared a long border with Italy, and in the south and east it was easily accessible by road and rail to northern Italian cities. Switzerland's hesitancy in the embargo resulted from its considerable stake in the continuation of relations with Italy.

However, the Rhodesian situation showed that this factor may be less relevant in reverse, in that considerable distance from the target may not necessarily increase a state's willingness to apply sanctions. For Switzerland, its lengthy distance from Rhodesia did not soften its refusal to apply the embargo, and in some respects it was even less disposed to support the operation than in 1935–36. For Sweden, on the other hand, its long distance from the target certainly did nothing to dampen its enthusiasm for the embargo; indeed it was possibly the single most vehement non-African supporter of sanctions. Thus in the latter crisis, other factors clearly played a more important role than geographical proximity alone, although it would appear that the importance of this factor increases in direct correlation with the strength of the target state. Thus while in the Italian case it was a crucial consideration for Italy's immediate neighbors (Albania, Hungary, Rumania, as well as Switzerland and even France), it was not nearly so important for Rhodesia's neighbors (Zambia, Tanzania, Botswana, and later Mozambique).

Cultural Affinity

A second hypothesis could be that a state's willingness to impose sanctions is inversely related to the degree of its cultural affinity with the target state. This seems a reasonable assumption due to the frequent coincidence of close political relations and cultural ties between nation-states. As discussed in chapter 2, the term "nationhood" has traditionally been defined in cultural (e.g., linguistic, ethnic, or racial) terms; and in a situation where national characteristics cut across state boundaries, we could expect some degree of political affinity, thereby reducing the probability of participation. The reverse situation would, in turn, suggest that lack of cultural affinity would increase the probability of participation.

The Italian crisis demonstrated the validity of this hypothesis. Sweden's Scandinavian ethnicity had little in common with Italian culture, which meant that the Swedes had no cultural hindrance to imposing the embargo. However, close cultural ties linked Italy and Italian-speaking regions of southern Switzerland, and the two countries shared an official language and a network of economic interlinkages fostered by these linguistic and ethnic ties. Significantly, these cultural links were reflected directly in the attitude of the Swiss foreign minister (Giuseppe Motta), whose sympathy for Italy's predicament reflected his Italo-Swiss origins and Roman Catholicism.

The importance of the cultural factor is rather more difficult to gauge in the Rhodesian case. Notwithstanding the ruling white minority's European origins, there appeared to be little cultural affinity between Rhodesians and either the Swiss or Swedish populations. This factor, however, seemed to be significant for Sweden almost in reverse, whereby the very differences between Sweden's white racial unity and the black African majority arguably contributed to Swedish expressions of a common bond and feeling of solidarity with the native African population—an attitude also expressed, if less forcibly, in 1935–36. This general attitude of solidarity was related both to Sweden's domestic social welfare policies (including its considerable efforts to assimilate foreign workers and political refugees into the Swedish system), and also to its increasing level of Third World development aid by the late 1960s.

Strategic Vulnerability

A third, and closely related, hypothesis could be that a state's willingness to impose sanctions is inversely related to its degree of strategic vulnerability to the target state. This seems plausible mainly because of the expected tendency of the target state to threaten, or actually respond with, some form of retaliation against participating states or their nationals. Such action might be prompted by anger or resentment over being singled out for punishment, particularly if the target state's actions were not unprecedented, or might be considered more acceptable (in geopolitical or strategic terms) in other times or situations. A state which is relatively vulnerable to such retaliation could be expected to be less favorable to active participation than a state which is less exposed to retaliation.

The Italian crisis seems clearly to bear out this hypothesis, insofar as Sweden's support for the embargo was partly a function of its strategic protection from Italian countermeasures, particularly as compared with Switzerland. It is true that Italy's aerial bombardment of Sweden's Red Cross facilities in Abyssinia proved that no state is absolutely safe strategically, even though those attacks did not endanger (nor were they even directed against) the security apparatus of the Swedish state. On the other hand, Switzerland's potential vulnerability to Italian retaliation was highlighted by their long common border and by the presence of thousands of Swiss nationals working in Italy, who were often subjected to restrictions and harassment by the Italian authorities. The League's presence in Geneva was another very important factor, which caused some Swiss to fear an Italian preemptive strike against the League's Palais des Nations complex in Geneva, in order to head off a possible escalation of the economic embargo to military action.

However, Rhodesia's remoteness from both states, and particularly its limited military and economic resources, meant that neither neutral state was in any way strategically vulnerable to Rhodesian retaliation. Thus in the latter crisis this was a negligible factor in the neutrals' responses. From the foregoing it would appear that this factor, as with point (1) above concerning geographical proximity, works in direct correlation to the relative strength of the target state. Again we can usefully contrast the reluctance of Italy's immediate neighbors to impose sanctions in 1935, with the vigorous support for further sanctions by Rhodesia's African-ruled neighbors.

There may be some use in speculating at this point on what might have happened in two other cases of (League) sanctions, in which the results might have supported the present hypothesis. Perhaps a fairer test of these states' respective sanctions policies would have resulted from an embargo against Germany—advocated by some (e.g., Lord Robert Cecil) in response to Germany's remilitarization of the Rhineland in March 1936, and occasionally mentioned as a potentially effective League action in the years following Italy's conquest of Abyssinia—given that both states appeared similarly exposed to German retaliation. Another intriguing hypothetical scenario would involve their respective responses to an embargo against Soviet Russia, as was in fact contemplated within League circles in 1939 after the Soviet attack against Finland. In this latter scenario, it was even conceivable that their respective attitudes of 1935 would have been reversed, given Switzerland's traditional hostility toward socialist ideology, in contrast to Sweden's close proximity and apparent strategic vulnerability to the USSR.

Initial Political Attitudes

Another hypothesis could be that willingness to impose sanctions is also partly determined by political attitudes toward the target country at the outset of the dispute. It is plausible to expect a correlation between close political relations and a hesitancy to apply sanctions, if only because of the natural tendency for states to support their allies and oppose their enemies in international actions. Taken alone, this factor might seem at variance with the traditional neutral requisites of impartiality and refusal to consider any state an enemy. Even so, there seems little reason to suppose that neutral states would be immune from the political and emotive pressures inherent in any coercive sanctions operation; and both Sweden and Switzerland acknowledged the force of world political and moral opinion during the two crises, and its influence on their own actions.

The contrast between the initial Swedish and Swiss political views toward Italy was striking enough. Sweden's favorable attitude toward sanctions was largely attributable to the widespread perception, within government and party circles, of a fundamental antipathy between Swedish social democracy and Italian fascism. Other political factors, including Sweden's distrust of French intentions (causing it to support Britain's role as the principal sanctioning state), and increasingly close ties with Abyssinia by the mid-1930s, also shaped its policy. And in 1965, the ruling white Rhodesian minority found precious few sympathizers in Sweden, even within the opposition Conservative Party. Many Swedes, particularly Social Democrats and Liberals, strongly denounced the Rhodesian régime for being, like fascist Italy, reactionary, antidemocratic, and (however vaguely) "right-wing."

Similarities can also be detected in Switzerland's initial political attitude in the two crises. In 1935–36, its economic, cultural, and historical ties with neighboring Italy predisposed the Swiss against supporting sanctions. These factors also caused the Swiss to discount any problems arising from their differing political ideologies, as emphasized by the sympathetic Swiss ministers in Rome, Wagnière and (later) Ruegger. Revealing incidents during and after the crisis, notably the Alemannic- (and even Romande-) Swiss insistence on absolute neutrality, and the curious post-invasion decision in Lausanne to honor Mussolini for his foreign policy "successes," demonstrated a widespread Swiss reluctance to cooperate with an embargo against Italy. The force of these pro-Italian sympathies tended to overwhelm the equally vehement, but much less influential, political arguments by the Swiss Socialists in favor of greater cooperation with the League's operation. The Federal Council's tendency to dwell on the legal minutiae of neutrality during the operation also appeared designed to divert attention from these strong political motivations. Even so, Switzerland was not simply an Italian ally, and its attitude toward Italy was clearly much less sympathetic than that of several of Italy's other neighbors, particularly Albania, Yugoslavia, and Austria.

From the outset of the Rhodesian crisis, Switzerland also refused full participation. This refusal was not because of any commitment to close relations with Rhodesia, but rather because of its commitment to neutrality and (later) to its independence from the UN as a nonmember. Nonetheless, Switzerland's continuing economic and financial (and for some years, also consular) relations with Rhodesia; its controversial role in aiding Rhodesia's defiance of the embargo; its close economic connections with Rhodesia's benefactor, South Africa; and its offer of asylum to the deposed Portuguese president after the April 1974 Lisbon coup, all variously indicated a lenient attitude toward the triumvirate of related (white minority) régimes in Africa. The government's curiously indifferent attitude toward the principles of majority rule and national self-determination in southern Africa also suggested an attitude of political sympathy for the Smith régime's predicament.

Attitudes Toward International Organizations

A fifth hypothesis by which a state's sanctions policy might be determined is that the degree of its acceptance of sanctions would be in positive correlation with its overall attitude toward political cooperation within the context of international organizations. The degree of international cooperation has also been suggested as a variable in a recent analysis of economic sanctions (Hufbauer and Schott 1985, 34–36). The linkage here would appear to be obvious, given that sanctions are one of the basic elements of global international organizations. Nonetheless the connection is not always watertight. For example, Sweden's gradual acceptance of sanctions by 1935–36 followed, rather than coincided with, its overall bearing toward the League's general aims, which had been clearly positive from the outset. For Switzerland, rather, its seeming support for the principle of international cooperation, indicated by its decision to host the League organization itself, was definitely not translated into support for sanctions when the crisis arose. The basis for this dichotomy was in fact established by the League itself by its exemption of Switzerland from military sanctions, which, as discussed in chapter 5, sowed the seeds for Switzerland's dilemma in case sanctions were actually implemented.

In the Rhodesian case, Sweden's active cooperation with UN activities by the 1950s and 1960s devolved easily and naturally into full support for sanctions. Yet for Switzerland, its cooperation and participation in most of the broad range of the nonpolitical activities of the UN system did not translate into support for sanctions. Almost the opposite was true: Swiss policy, particularly its determination to maintain its token amounts of trade with Rhodesia, was laden with symbolism, as a means of demonstrating Swiss resolve not to bow to Security Council directives so long as it remained a nonmember of the UNO itself. Thus in these cases, Sweden's attitude toward sanctions generally reflected its overall attitude toward international cooperation; Switzerland's did to a much lesser degree.

Density and Volume of Trade

Still another hypothesis by which we might seek to explain how a state could be expected to respond to the imposition of sanctions is that its willingness to impose them is inversely related to the density and volume of its trade with the target state. This variable is also suggested by Hufbauer and Schott (1985, 39), who hold that the outcome of sanctions can be affected by the size of trade links between the source and target states. More specifically, it seems reasonable to expect that a state which maintains a high level of trade with the target states (in terms both of its overall amount and its percentage of the neutral's trade, and also the nature of that trade and its significance for the neutral state's economy) would be less likely to apply sanctions than a state whose trade with the target state was minimal or insignificant. This correlation could be expected because of the mutually beneficial nature of bilateral commerce, which implies that disruptive measures undertaken by one state against an important trade partner would damage its own economy as much, or even more, than it would the target state itself. Moreover, it seems reasonable to suppose that the importance of this factor would be related to the degree of sensitivity of the participating state's economy to external economic developments. In the case of both Sweden and Switzerland, their traditionally open economies, highly exposed to shifting patterns of world trade, make this a particularly crucial variable.

Here the difference between the two countries in 1935-36 is instructive. As discussed in chapter 5, Switzerland was the fourth leading buyer of Italian exports (and second among League member states), and Italy was the third most important supplier of goods to Switzerland. Annual Italo-Swiss trade was not far short of SwFr 200m, which accounted for 7–8 percent of all Switzerland's imports and around 9 percent of its exports. The significance of these figures was perhaps slightly mitigated by the contraction in Italo-Swiss trade in the early and mid-1930s (a result of the worldwide depression), but this factor did not materially reduce the importance of the Italian market to the Swiss economy. Indeed in some ways the erosion of Switzerland's economic health increased its determination to avoid all measures which would damage these traditionally strong trade ties further. Switzerland's acceptance of Italy's right to expand economically into Abyssinia would seem to support this interpretation, since such expansion would indirectly serve Switzerland's own interests.

In sharp contrast, Italy was only Sweden's eleventh most important trade partner (and ninth within the League), in terms of both import and export trade. Italy accounted for around 1½ percent of all Sweden's imports and somewhat over 2 percent of all its exports; substantial figures, but hardly crucial for Sweden's economic security. Another factor was the nonessential nature of Sweden's imports from Italy, which consisted mainly of fruits and vegetables, wine and yarn, which meant that even its full acceptance of Proposal III did not create acute difficulties for the Swedish economy. On the other hand, the figures show that Italy had become, during the previous decades, a much more significant trade partner for Sweden; whereas in 1913 it took just 0.5 percent of Sweden's total exports, by 1934 this level had risen to 2.4 percent (*SKM* 1936, vol. 23, 18:646). These increases, which attested to and coincided with Sweden's development as a European industrial power, highlighted the subsequent, major reductions which the Swedish government brought about during the crisis itself. Thus the gap in the relative importance of Italy for the Swedish and Swiss economies was being somewhat narrowed by 1935. Nonetheless it remains clear that the prospect of losing much of the Italian market, particularly in time of economic depression, was a much more vital factor for Switzerland than for Sweden; and these dangers were reiterated time and again by Switzerland's delegates to the League's working subcommittees and the Committee of Eighteen from the earliest stages of the crisis.

Here it is also tempting to speculate on how Sweden would have reacted to a complete embargo of exports to Italy, given that the nature of those exports (paper pulp, iron and steel, and machinery) were very important in terms of its overall economy. As it stood, Sweden's full compliance with the partial export embargo (Proposal IV) was not problematic, mainly because it was a relatively minor supplier of iron ore to Italy in spite of its overall position as one of the world's leading iron ore producers. In 1935 Sweden exported to Italy only SEK 0.3m worth of iron ore and iron alloys, which (along with Swedish-produced pig iron) could be cut off without great difficulty, whereas the USSR, Algeria (then under French rule), and Spain were all significantly more important sources of iron ore for Italy. Nonetheless, it would seem unfair to suggest that Sweden would not have complied with a complete export embargo. And again using the hypothetical scenario of an embargo against Germany, it could be supposed that these two states' responses may have shown greater similarity (and both more disposed against applying sanctions), considering the fact that Germany accounted for well over 20 percent of each country's trade totals; it was by far Switzerland's primary trade partner, as well as Sweden's most important supplier of goods (accounting for 23 percent of its imports in 1935), and its second most important export market after the UK (*SKM* 1936, vol. 23 [15–16]:576–79).

In the Rhodesian case, overall trade levels for both Sweden and Switzerland were low by any standard, at or less than 1 percent of each state's total trade volume, in both directions. However, in this crisis, other related issues increased the importance of the embargo for both states. For example, Sweden's traditionally close trade links with Great Britain disposed the Swedes to accept an embargo led mainly by Britain itself. This factor had also affected Sweden's attitude in 1935, in light of Britain's leading League role in the Italian embargo.

For Switzerland, meanwhile, its low level of trade with Rhodesia was an insufficient indicator of its importance, which was increased by two other factors. One was the existence (and disreputable expansion) of indirect trade connections, utilizing dummy corporations registered in Switzerland which facilitated illicit trade to and from Rhodesia via legitimate channels through South Africa and the Portuguese colonies, thus aiding Rhodesia's defiance of the embargo. The second additional factor was the maintenance of private bank accounts in Switzerland by many individual Rhodesians, despite the Swiss government's decision to freeze the Rhodesian Reserve Bank's assets held there. This factor, coupled with the government's refusal to prevent the entry of Rhodesian citizens into its territory, effectively gave Rhodesian officials and businessmen free access to foreign currency accounts and vital business contacts in Switzerland. As we saw earlier, close banking relations were also an important consideration in the Italian crisis, in light of Italy's substantial gold stocks held in Swiss banks, and the controversial Italo-Swiss clearing agreement of December 1935. Thus in assessing the effect of trade on states' willingness to impose sanctions, one must also account for other, indirect but related trade and financial connections.

For Sweden, a rather different and instructive situation arose in connection with the issue of sanctioning South Africa alongside, and in conjunction with, the Rhodesian embargo. The validity of this connection between the strength of trade ties and the willingness to impose sanctions could well be tested regarding the neutrals and South Africa. There were in fact signs that Sweden's enthusiasm for sanctions against Pretoria, at least in the early stages, was tempered by the substantial and increasing trade and industrial contacts between these two states in the postwar period, which continued despite the growing opposition to the policy of apartheid expressed by most of the Swedish political community.

Although by 1968 Sweden's UN delegate Sverker Åström began voicing support for Security Council deliberations leading to mandatory international sanctions, as late as 1975–76 the Swedish government refused to assent to coordinated Scandinavian measures against South Africa without further Security Council action. This continuing hesitancy was particularly noteworthy in light of (and despite) the increasingly strident tone of Prime Minister Olof Palme's foreign policy statements during the two years leading up to the Social Democrats' defeat in the 1976 general election. The government decided to ban all new Swedish investments in South Africa only in 1979, two years after SC Resolution 418 designated the South African situation a threat to the peace and suggested that member states apply an economic embargo; and these measures were tightened in 1985. Thus it seems reasonable to conclude that strong Swedish–South African trade links acted as a partial deterrent to Sweden's early call for sanctions against Pretoria. It should also be noted, however, that Sweden's restrictions on, for example, new investments in South Africa and Namibia, pre-dated most other international restrictions placed against Pretoria.

The case of Switzerland and South Africa is also highly relevant in this context. From the foregoing it would be expected that Switzerland's close financial and trade connections with South Africa would have caused the Swiss to oppose any UN embargo. By the mid-1980s Switzerland had become South Africa's third major trading partner, taking 6.6 percent of South Africa's exports (only the United States at 8.39 percent, and Japan at 7.7, were higher). An equally important factor is the central role of large Swiss banks in providing substantial loans to maintain the liquidity of the South African economy. It was no surprise, then, that the intermediary chosen to head off a potential South African default on its loans during 1984–85 was Dr. Fritz Leutwiler, former head of the Swiss National Bank. The Federal Council itself had already indicated its opposition to an international embargo against South Africa.

This distinction between the Rhodesian and South African cases also broaches the more general question of whether a sanctions operation can ever succeed if important trade partners of the target state are opposed to an international embargo. There is firm evidence that the lack of cooperation by some important trading states limited the success of both embargoes: first, by hindering attempts to agree on which products to prohibit, and second, by enabling active circumvention of the sanctions once they were in place. In the Italian crisis, the oil embargo was initially delayed, and later shelved, because the League's member states knew that some major oil traders would not be obliged to join (principally the United States); the same was true with iron and steel products, which, unlike iron ore, were exempted since the League membership did not control even a majority of the world's iron and steel trade.

And in the Rhodesian case, South Africa's refusal to apply sanctions—and worse still, from the UN's viewpoint, its systematic circumvention of the embargo—enabled a small, landlocked colony to survive a quasi-universal embargo for fourteen years, far beyond all expectations at the outset. Thus an embargo, which is never guaranteed success even under the most favorable circumstances, is unlikely to succeed if important trade partners of the target state are not in favor of it. More pointedly, if this hypothesis is true (and the evidence suggests its validity), it is likely that important trade partners will refuse to participate, in which case a sanctions operation would be likely to fail, if indeed it were tried at all.

Balance of Trade

One final hypothesis could be that a state's receptivity to sanctions is related to its balance of trade with the target state. More specifically, it seems plausible that a neutral state's attitude would be more favorable in a situation in which it carried a balance of trade surplus with the target state, and less favorable if it ran a trade deficit with it. This point, however, must remain more speculative than the others, insofar as deductive or a priori reasoning might indicate otherwise—that a trade deficit might actually increase a state's willingness to apply an embargo, since this would enable it to improve its overall balance of payments by eliminating a source of debt.

The relevance of this factor would seem to be related directly to the density and volume of trade. The issue can be subdivided into two elements: elimination of the deficit, and elimination of trade altogether. Taking the latter point first, sanctions operations often aim to eliminate all trade with the target state. The implementation of such a stoppage would be difficult for any state, particularly in a case where major trade linkages existed. The difficulties would be still greater in a case where a significant trade deficit existed, as an embargo could conceivably damage the economy of the state applying it more than the target state itself. As discussed in chapter 5, this argument figured prominently in the debate over League sanctions against Italy (though confined mainly to discussion of Swiss policy); and it was deemed valid by at least one authoritative independent source (RIIA 1938, 192).

That said, however, the second option—namely, steps to bring about an even trade balance while maintaining overall levels of trade—would be a more feasible and likely alternative for the source state. The reason is that such a move would be in the state's own self-interest (as a way to eliminate a source of deficit) as well as in the interests of the international organization. The two goals of eliminating the trade balance while continuing trade can be mutually compatible since a state can rectify a bilateral trade imbalance in one of two ways: either by increasing its exports to the target state or by decreasing its imports from it. Thus without much difficulty it could eliminate the deficit without materially reducing its overall level of trade. Such a step would, equally, advance the aims of the organization, insofar as an existing trade deficit translates into a trade surplus, and hence a foreign exchange windfall, for the target state itself. By eliminating this source of revenue for the target state, the neutral could justifiably argue that it had thereby done its duty in promoting international solidarity. Again, such partial action would be likely since it would serve the interests of both the state applying the measure and, at least to a limited degree, the organization calling for sanctions—depending on the significance of the trade links and the relative size of the trade deficit.

Bearing in mind the speculative nature of this hypothesis, all four cases are revealing. Prior to the Italian embargo, Sweden's trade with Italy was heavily in surplus, by over SEK 12m for 1934, although this declined to 7m for 1935. Given that Sweden's imports from Italy (in 1934) were some 40 percent less than its exports to it, the application of sanctions would, all things being equal, damage the Swedish economy less than Italy's. This would be the case in the event of a comprehensive trade embargo, equally applicable to export and import trade; and Sweden's situation in this particular case was helped by the one-sided nature of the embargo, by which the total ban on imports (Proposal III) was not accompanied by a similarly complete ban on exports to Italy.

Another factor concerns the relative importance of the goods traded between the two countries. As mentioned in this chapter and in chapter 4, the main Swedish imports from Italy (fruits and vegetables, wines, yarn) were much less vital for the Swedish economy than was the export to Italy of some of Sweden's most important products, mainly paper pulp and iron and steel, neither of which were subject to the embargo. Given this discrepancy, the import embargo would have been less important to Sweden than a (hypothetically) total export embargo, even if an even trade balance had existed; and the actual surplus in favor of Sweden eased its problems further. As a result of its restrictions, Sweden's trade surplus with Italy rose in 1936 (though the increase, from SEK 7m to 10m, was hardly massive). A better indication is given through the comparison of import and export figures during the embargo itself (December 1935–June 1936), from table 4-2, which shows import figures of SEK 1,981,000, against an export total to Italy of SEK 14,085,000; thus Sweden's exports to Italy outweighed its imports from it by a factor of more than seven during the crisis itself.

In vivid contrast, Switzerland's difficulties in the embargo were exacerbated by its very large, though declining, trade deficit with Italy during the period leading up to sanctions. Table 5-1 shows this striking discrepancy: Swiss-Italian trade left the Swiss with a huge, SwFr 53m deficit in 1933, although this figure had been reduced substantially, to around 18m in 1935, due primarily to a large drop in Swiss imports from Italy in both 1934 and 1935. This factor, combined with (and in contrast to) Italy's overall situation as a chronic debtor nation, provided the basis for the well-founded Swiss claim that a full imposition of Proposal III would hurt Switzerland more than Italy itself. Switzerland's trade deficit with Italy also caused the government to defy Proposal IIA of the embargo, by concluding a special clearing agreement with Italian banking authorities, aiming at balancing its trade and eliminating the necessity of cash payments for goods. Even so, this agreement was not in Italy's best interests, since it prevented Italy from deriving foreign exchange out of a surplus situation; and the Swiss could (and did) thereafter argue that they had taken an important step to hinder Italy's war-making capacity, which few other states had to even consider taking.

This correlation between trade balance and willingness to apply sanctions was also demonstrated in the Rhodesia case, although here its significance was less evident. Again, Sweden's trade with the target was heavily in surplus (SEK by 7.6m, out of an export total of 17.7m in 1965); but Swiss imports from Rhodesia in 1965 (worth over SwFr 24.5m) were higher than its exports to Rhodesia (slightly over SwFr 7m) by a factor of nearly 3½. Even so, this (1965) figure was not fully indicative of Swiss-Rhodesian commercial links, in light of the suspicious large-scale export of precious and semiprecious stones from Rhodesia to Switzerland in the year prior to sanctions, which was reported by the UN Sanctions Committee (see table 8-2, col. 6). The 1964 figures were closer to an even balance, standing at SwFr 10.5m and 6.5m for imports and exports respectively, though Switzerland remained in deficit. Thus while this trend fits in neatly with the hypothesis, it was less revealing in the

Rhodesian case: partly because the embargo was (eventually) total and not merely selective, but primarily since the overall trade amounts involved were much less significant for the two countries than in 1935–36. Nonetheless, this does demonstrate the continuation of an interesting pattern, which thereby contributes to its theoretical value and practical plausibility.

IMPLICATIONS FOR THE NEUTRALITY-SANCTIONS PROBLEM

This section will discuss the extent to which the analysis of Sweden's and Switzerland's policies enables us to draw conclusions regarding neutrality in general, particularly on the question of the extent to which neutrality is compatible with collective security arrangements. One of my principal aims at the outset was to determine what the similarities, or differences, between these two states' attitudes tell us about neutrality policy; to determine how far it is possible to generalize about neutrality policy from a comparative study of two states which practice it. Here it bears mentioning that the guidelines for modern neutrality, as specified by the Hague Conventions of 1907, have become increasingly obsolete due to intervening developments in the technology and scope of modern warfare, particularly in the nuclear age. It follows that modern neutrality is characterized by a lack of rigorous and universally applicable guidelines, and is increasingly being determined on an ad hoc basis, shaped by the actual policies (peacetime as well as wartime) of individual neutral states themselves.[2] This development, in turn, suggests that much can be learned from an analysis of two individual neutral states' policies; in this case, as a basis for reassessing the traditionally accepted notion that neutrality is, in principle, incompatible with sanctions.

The four cases examined here have indicated that neutrality has varied considerably in importance as a factor hindering participation by neutral states in sanctions operations. In Sweden's case, the government considered neutrality to be a relatively unimportant factor in its decision to participate in either embargo. In the Italian crisis, Sweden did not specifically cite neutrality as a hindrance to full participation, although the issue was raised in connection with parliamentary discussions over the imposition of sanctions legislation in April 1936. Moreover, the specter of a collapse in the League's authority after the failure of the Italian operation caused the Swedes, along with most other small European states, to revert to the neutral theme. During the Rhodesian dispute, neutrality was widely considered in Sweden, even by the political opposition, as an inappropriate response and indeed as superfluous to the crisis. The decision to implement permanent sanctions legislation, which was designed to solidify Sweden's economic sanctions obligations under the UN Charter, was based on the general belief that neutrality was no hindrance to full, and even outspoken, participation in an economic embargo of another state, if requested by the UN Security Council. We can thus conclude that Swedish policy since 1920 has been marked by a growing acceptance of economic sanctions obligations. In itself, this development gives reason for asserting that participation in a limited sanctions operation is, in practical terms, compatible with a credible policy of neutrality.

Switzerland, however, reiterated the long-standing belief that its neutrality hinders its cooperation with even a limited sanctions operation at the outset of both operations. In the Italian crisis, this attitude cost the Swiss some international credibility, since they also accepted the view that nonmilitary sanctions obligations were not, in principle, incompatible with neutrality in the strict sense of the term. In the Rhodesian affair, many of the government's arguments on this point were subsequently modified. For example, the Federal Council gradually changed its stated arguments for its nonparticipation in the operation (though without admitting as much), from emphasizing its neutrality to stressing its nonmembership in the UN. This distinct shift indicated that neutrality decreased in importance as a factor in Switzerland's attitude during this particular operation. It is also true that Switzerland's refusal to cooperate with the UN embargo was modified by the 1970s, and that the government launched a public campaign to achieve Swiss membership in the UN at the very time of the Rhodesian affair. This campaign was indeed based largely on the government's changing attitude toward sanctions. The new argument, developed through its series of reports on the UN during 1969–77 and in its 1981 message, was that limited UN sanctions no longer represented an inherent danger to its neutrality; and conversely, that neutrality was no longer an absolute barrier to Swiss participation in sanctions operations.[3] Nonetheless, there is little evidence that the Rhodesian operation itself induced the Federal Council to accept sanctions in principle; and the Swiss public's overwhelming rejection of UN membership in early 1986 clearly indicates that the Swiss government will in the future have every incentive to remain aloof from UN coercive sanctions operations.

These results indicate more dissimilarity than convergence in their attitudes regarding the sanctions problem, indeed more than was expected at the outset of the study. Nevertheless two points stand out. One is that neutrality policy has demonstrated considerable unity in diversity; the very differences in their sanctions policies indicate clearly that neutrality in the postwar period has lost much of its earlier, static legal connotations, and has become an increasingly flexible policy, and determined more on an ad hoc basis, relative to interpretation by neutral states themselves.

Second, in terms of Swedish and Swiss policy, neither state has proven itself willing to modify its neutrality to the extent required for participation in full-fledged collective security operations. It bears repeating that economic sanctions are only part of the full range of collective security actions (theoretically) at the disposal of international organizations. Here Sweden's attitude is instructive, given its close identification with UN operations. Swedish policy was generally supportive of the League's and the UN's aims, but in neither crisis was its neutrality or other essential interests actually threatened. In addition, the underlying neutrality-sanctions dilemma for Swedish policy never really materialized in practice, and its policy of cooperation was thereby relatively convenient and safe.

It might even be argued that Swedish policy in the two crises betrayed an element of opportunism, and it would be useful to examine briefly this (possible) charge. For example, Sweden scored potentially valuable political points and bolstered its activist profile without high costs; its advocacy of sanctions enhanced its reputation for international solidarity while its losses were small. Haskel (1976) would no doubt argue (correctly) that Sweden cooperated with both operations because the opportunities in so doing far outweighed the costs for Swedish policymakers. In the earlier case, Sweden solidified its reputation as a defender of the interests of the smaller League states and the international legal order; and in the latter case, it bolstered its reputation as a friend and benefactor of the developing world by punishing the white settler régime. Palme's "small state" doctrine, espoused with increasing vigor after his important Gävle speech of 1965 (Kleberg 1977), also represented an interesting reemergence of Sweden's earlier League policy of defending the interests of the smaller member states. In the Rhodesian case Sweden indeed proved adept at pursuing a middle course, professing support for the general aims of the developing world while distancing itself from Assembly resolutions which were not strictly in line with the UN Charter (i.e., those calling specifically for sanctions, and those advocating the use of British and/or UN force; see Huldt 1974).

Despite Sweden's relative lack of difficulty or danger in the two operations, it nonetheless would be presumptuous and even unfair to conclude that Sweden would not have accepted greater risks through sanctions, if called upon to do so. On the contrary, in both cases Sweden clearly was willing to shoulder a considerable, even if not disproportionate, burden, to suffer some loss of trade and political influence through loyal application of the embargoes. During the Italian crisis Sweden lost some SEK 12m worth of imports from Italy, and its total imports from Italy were only one-sixth the total of the previous year; Sweden also sharply reduced its exports of electrical machinery and pig iron to Italy, even though neither product was subject to the trade embargo recommended by the Coordination Committee. Another indication of Sweden's willingness to assume some loss was the autonomous agreement within the Swedish private banking consortium to sever all credits to Italy, without governmental pressure to do so, thus unilaterally depriving themselves of a source of credit (although a less charitable interpretation of this action, as noted in chapter 4, is that it helped prevent possible defaults by Italian debtors).

In the latter crisis, Sweden severed its trade with Rhodesia rapidly and completely, thus eliminating an entire market. This market was of course insignificant in terms of the overall Swedish economy; but then again this was also the case for nearly all the other UN member states. Another indication of Sweden's willingness to deprive itself, in certain cases perceived as involving matters of principle, was the government's 1979 decision to ban new Swedish investments in South Africa and Namibia, a year before this became common Nordic policy; and the extension of these restrictions in February 1985 was carried out in spite of vigorous opposition from the Swedish business community (*Financial Times*, 21 February 1985, 2:1). In sum, Sweden was willing to assume some losses in the cause of international solidarity; but its actual losses were not great in either event.

Some similar conclusions can be drawn with regard to Swiss policy. Switzerland has managed to retain much of its general reputation for international solidarity (in related areas such as hosting international conferences and the UN's European offices), in spite of the government's rather tortuous and spotty record on the sanctions question. The Swiss have in fact demonstrated a remarkable ability to induce special recognition of their neutrality on the basis of its tradition and presumed benefits for the general "cause of peace"— substantiating Christopher Hughes's view that the Swiss attitude sometimes verges on the assertion "whatever *we* do, is neutral" (1975, 149). A prime case in point would be Switzerland's position regarding League sanctions at the outset and at the close of the League era. Switzerland's accession to the Covenant in 1919–20, and its agreement to apply economic sanctions against an aggressor, was expressly based on the principle that such a policy would be conducive to international peace and security; yet its headlong and unilateral retreat into full neutrality in April 1938 was based on the nearly identical assertion that, in doing so, Switzerland "is rendering an undeniable service to the cause of peace" (*OJ*, May–June 1938, 312). Its success in obtaining official League approval of these views on both occasions also indicated the continually ambiguous nature of Switzerland's "differential neutrality" within League membership, particularly since the League gave no such dispensation to any other neutral, including Sweden. Switzerland's tendency to draw parallels between its policies and the pursuit of peace is not, of course, unique among states. Even so, the shifts in Swiss sanctions policy during this period were major and indeed striking, and yet they received the sanctity of League approval, or at least acquiescence, on both occasions.

Switzerland's performance in the two operations themselves shows clearly that it resisted all measures potentially threatening its neutrality and other essential interests. Switzerland rejected full participation in the Italian embargo because of two strong arguments: first, that its military neutrality would be threatened by an international embargo against a powerful immediate neighbor, and second, that applying sanctions would damage its own economy more than Italy's. The Federal Council was clearly intent on limiting the damage to Switzerland, while also making limited gestures to League solidarity.

In the Rhodesian case, the Federal Council argued similarly that its participation would endanger its essential interests. In this case, however, those interests were very different: the government intended to demonstrate its absence of obligations to the UN operation. Here Switzerland's independence from the UN operation, both legal and political, was being tested; and the government's painstaking emphasis on its autonomous position clearly demonstrated the importance with which the Federal Council viewed this matter. The government later began to cooperate more openly with the UN, prompted in part by the embarrassing publicity which accompanied Swiss circumvention of the embargo. But at no stage did the government consider this (grudging) cooperation to be fundamentally inimical to its own economic and political interests.

When directly comparing the two states' policies, it is difficult to avoid the conclusion that they cooperated with the operations only insofar as their basic interests were not endangered, but no further. Both have repeatedly cited their humanitarian traditions and dwelled on higher, abstract principles (notably the themes of international peace and justice); and yet a strong case can be made that national self-interest largely conditioned their responses. This, however, is not to suggest that they did not make some effort to accommodate the League and the UN, and both countries, particularly Sweden, willingly suffered some losses in terms of trade, credit, and political influence. Nonetheless the obvious and subtle differences between the two states stand out more than their similarities—primarily insofar as Sweden has generally accepted economic sanctions obligations of its own accord, whereas Swiss cooperation (insofar as it has been tendered) has been more reactive and forced by circumstances. In terms of neutrality, Switzerland tended to give an automatic, reflex defense, based on its symbolic value as a focus of national unity, whereas Sweden did not dwell on the neutral theme, given the more flexible interpretation of neutrality within its overall foreign policy schema, and in light of its realistic view that its neutrality was not threatened in either instance.

The problem of reconciling neutrality with collective security obligations thus has lessened, due as much to the demonstrated limitations of collective security in the modern era as to the increasing flexibility of neutral policies. The inability for international organizations to escalate economic to military sanctions has demonstrated that the increasing scale of rigor for sanctions systems remains more theoretically appealing than practically viable. While it is true that limited nonmilitary sanctions can, and often do, lead to more comprehensive nonmilitary sanctions (or to similar measures against other states), the threshold of international military operations has generally proven "beyond the pale" and too weighty an option for member states to accept. Even the scope of concerted economic sanctions remains very limited, particularly in an era in which key member states renege on their financial assessments to UN operations, and when the UN membership itself finds precious few issues on which to agree.

While prediction remains a hazardous occupation, it seems reasonable to assume that sanctions will remain a much-discussed but rarely utilized form of action by international organizations—a paradox, perhaps, in contrast with their increasing popularity as unilateral punitive measures. So long as the UN Charter's enforcement provisions remain unaltered (such as, for example, through the institution of a majority-type voting system in the Security Council, or greater powers for the General Assembly under a revamped Uniting for Peace plan), neutrals will be unlikely to face acute problems in UN action. The sanctions dilemma for neutral states has declined from a potential and even an actual one during the League era, to a merely symbolic one in the UN period; Bernard Dutoit thus argues reasonably that "the actual evolution of the international organization has succeeded in mitigating the incompatibility between neutrality and collective security" (1962, 43). Sweden's policy, in itself, has shown that a neutral state can participate fully in an economic sanctions operation with limited risk and without threatening the essence of its neutrality. Swiss policy, on the other hand, has shown that sanctions can still pose at least a symbolic dilemma for neutrals, and that limits to full neutral cooperation with sanctions remain. Such limits are, however, determined largely by idiosyncratic problems for the individual neutral state itself, rather than by any established neutral formulae.

NOTES

1. See on the first point Renwick, 1981, p. 80; Daoudi and Dajani, 1983, p. 65; and S. R. Chowdhury, who even claims that the League "released Switzerland from the duties of economic sanctions obligations" (1966, p. 201). Even the authoritative Chatham House report on the crisis included Switzerland in its table of "Italy's Trade with Non-Sanctioning Countries" (RIIA 1938, p. 93, table 1).

On the second point, see Boczek, 1969, p. 98; and Robert, 1950, p. 24, who states that "the Federal Council applied the economic and financial sanctions . . . only as much as permitted by the Hague Conventions," which is wrong since the Hague rules were inapplicable to a case of limited economic sanctions, as she herself states elsewhere (p. 79), and as Motta held at the outset of the crisis.

2. From the legal side, see Fenwick, 1969, pp. 100–2; Guggenheim, 1945, pp. 27, 45–46; Kelsen, 1950, pp. 110, 162–63; and especially Norton, 1976. On the increasing relevance of neutrality and other similar quasi-legal designations in peacetime, see Sims, 1966, p. 8; Rothstein, 1968, p. 245; Hakovirta, 1983; Rudolph in Grahl-Madsen and Tonen, 1984, pp. 162–63; Ferencz, 1973, pp. 4–5.

3. See on this trend the Federal Council's series of UN reports: 1969, p. 118; 1971, p. 52; 1977, pp. 132, 134, 144; and 1981, pp. 50–51. The government nonetheless continued to assert its independence in both sanctions and peacekeeping operations even as a potential UN member (e.g., *BS, CN,* 1982, vol. I, p. 1462).

Bibliography

PRIMARY SOURCES

League of Nations Documents

"Documents Concerning the Accession of Switzerland to the League of Nations," and Annexes. *International Conciliation* 152 (July 1920):315–47.
League of Nations Official Journal. For 1919, 1920, 1921, 1935, 1936, 1937, 1938.
League of Nations Official Journal, Special Supplements. Nos. 6, 14, 130, 133, 138, 145, 146, 147, 150, 151, 154, 180, 183.
Monetary Review. 1935–36. Geneva: League of Nations Economic Intelligence Service, 1936.
World Economic Survey. 5th year, 1935–36. Geneva: League of Nations Economic Intelligence Service, 1936.

United Nations Documents

Documents of the United Nations Conference on International Organization [UN-CIO]. Vols. 3, 4, and 6. San Francisco: 1945.
United Nations General Assembly, Official Records and Supplements. United Nations, New York: Department of Public Information, yearly.
United Nations Security Council, Official Records. Reports of the Special Sanctions Committee on Rhodesia:
First Report: UN Doc. S/8954, *SCOR*, 23rd year, Suppl. for October–December 1968.
Second Report: UN Doc. S/9252 and Add. 1, *SCOR*, 24th year, Suppl. for April–June 1969.
Third Report: UN Doc. S/9844/Rev. 1, *SCOR*, 25th year, Suppl. for July–September 1970.
Fourth Report: UN Doc. S/10229 and Add. 1 and 2. *SCOR*, 26th year, 1971, SS no. 2.

Fifth Report: UN Doc. S/10852/Rev. 1, and Add. 1 and 2. *SCOR*, 28th year, 1973, SS no. 2.

Sixth Report: UN Doc. S/11178/Rev. 1, *SCOR*, 29th year, 1974, SS no. 2 and 2a.

Seventh Report: UN Doc. S/11594/Rev. 1, *SCOR*, 30th year, 1975, SS no. 2, Vols. I and II.

First Special Report: UN Doc. S/11597, *SCOR*, 30th year, 1975, SS no. 3.

Eighth Report: UN Doc. S/11927/Rev. 1, *SCOR*, 31st year, 1976, SS no. 2, Vols. I and II.

Ninth Report: UN Doc. S/12265, *SCOR*, 32nd year, 1977, SS no. 2, Vols. I–III.

Tenth Report: UN Doc. S/12529/Rev. 1, *SCOR*, 33rd year, 1978, SS no. 2, Vols. I and II.

Eleventh Report: UN Doc. S/13000, *SCOR*, 34th year, 1979, SS no. 2, Vols. I–III.

Twelfth Report: UN Doc. S/13750, *SCOR*, 35th year, 1980, SS no. 2, Vols. I and II.

United Nations Security Council, Official Records and Quarterly Supplements. United Nations, New York: Department of Public Information, yearly.

Yearbook of the International Law Commission. Vols. 1 and 2, 1964, 1966. United Nations, New York: Department of Public Information, 1965, 1967.

Yearbook of the United Nations. United Nations, New York: Department of Public Information, yearly.

Swedish Government Documents

Aktstycken Rörande Den Svenska Röda Kors-Ambulansen i Abessinien 1935–36. Stockholm: P.A. Norstedt & Söner, 1937.

"Bistånd 1982–83." *Svensk u-arbete*. Stockholm: SIDAs informationsbyrå, 1982.

Documents on Swedish Foreign Policy. New series. Stockholm: Ministry for Foreign Affairs, 1950–51 to present.

Förenta Nationernas Generalförsamlings Första Ordinarie Mötes Andra Del. New York, 1946. Aktstycken Utgivna av Kungl. Utrikesdepartementet. Stockholm: P. A. Norstedt & Söner, 1947.

"Kungl. Maj:ts Proposition till Riksdagen Angående Medgivande att Vidtaga de Åntgärder, som erfordras för Sveriges anslutning till Förenta Nationerna: given Stockholms slott den 8 mars 1946." BRP, 1 saml. no. 96, 1946, pp. 1–191.

"Kungl. Maj:ts Proposition till Riksdagen Angående Sveriges Anslutning till Nationernas Förbund; Given Stockholms slott den 14 februari 1920." BRP, no. 90, 1920, pp. 1–244.

Nationernas Förbunds Församlings Andra Ordinarie Möte i Genève 1922. Aktstycken Utgivna av Kungl. Utrikesdepartementet. Stockholm: 1923.

Nationernas Förbunds Församlings Nittonde Ordinarie Möte i Genève 1938. Aktstycken Utgivna av Kungl. Utrikesdepartementet. Stockholm: P. A. Norstedt & Söner, 1939.

Nationernas Förbunds Församlings Sextonde Ordinarie Möte i Genève 1935. Aktstycken Utgivna av Kungl. Utrikesdepartementet no. 24. Stockholm: P. A. Norstedt & Söner, 1925.

Nationernas Förbunds Församlings Sjuttonde Ordinarie Möte i Genève 1936. Aktstycken Utgivna av Kungl. Utrikesdepartementet no. 26. Stockholm: P. A. Norstedt & Söner, 1937.

Nordiska Rådet. 17:e Sessionen, 1969. Stockholm: Kungl. Boktryckeriet, P. A. Norstedt & Söner, 1969.

"Rapport du Comité d'Experts chargé par le Gouvernement Suédois de l'Examen du Protocole dit le Genève, relatif au Règlement Pacifique des Differends Internationaux." Documents Publies par le Ministère des Affairs Etrangères. Stockholm: 1925.

Riksdagens Protokoll. Första och Andra Kammaren, and Bihang till Riksdagens Protokoll. [Note: after 1971 both chambers were merged into a single, unicameral Riksdag]

"Speech by Karin Söder, Sweden's Foreign Minister, to the United Nations General Assembly, 29 September 1977." Stockholm: mimeographed by the Swedish Foreign Ministry, 1978.

Svensk FN–Lag: Sanktioner och Deras Genomförande. SOU. 1970: 19.

Svensk Författningssamling. Stockholm: Kungl. Boktryckeriet, P. A. Norstedt & Söner, yearly.

Sverige i Förenta Nationernas [FNs] Säkerhetsråd 1975–76. Aktstycken utgivna av Kungl. Utrikesdepartementet, Ny serie 3:32, 1978.

Sveriges Budgetredovisning för budgetåret 1978–79. Stockholm: Liberförlag, 1980.

Sveriges Kommersiella Meddelanden. utgivna av Kungl. Kommerskollegium. Stockholm: Isaac Marcus Boktryckeri-Aktiebolag, yearly.

Sveriges Officiella Statistik. Utrikeshandel. Stockholm: Statistiska Centralbyrån, Kungl. Boktryckeri, P. A. Norstedt & Söner, yearly.

"Zimbabwe." *Svensk u-samarbete.* Stockholm: SIDAs informationsbyrå, 1982.

Swiss Government Documents

Bulletin sténographique officiel de l'Assemblée fédérale/Amtliches stenographisches Bulletin der schweizerischen Bundesversammlung, yearly.

"Beziehungen zum Ausland." Jurisprudence des autorités administratifs de la Confédération. Berne: Département politique fédérale, 26 November 1954, pp. 9–13.

"Commission Consultative Suisse pour l'éxamen de la Charte des Nations Unies. Compte rendu des séances tenues les 14 et 15 novembre 1945 sous la presidence de M. le Conseiller fédéral Max Petitpierre" (2 vols). Berne: Département politique fédérale, 1945.

Feuille fédérale de la Confédération Suisse/Schweizerisches Bundesblatt, yearly.

"Message du Conseil fédéral à l'Assemblée fédérale sur le CICR, du 27 mai 1981." *FF* 1981, 2:981–97.

"Message du Conseil fédéral a l'Assemblée fédérale concernant l'adhésion de la Suisse à Cour Internationale de la Justice à la Haye, du 8 juillet 1947." *FF* 1947, Vol. 2.

"Message du Conseil fédéral à l'Assemblée fédérale concernant l'adhésion de la Suisse à l'Organisation des Nations Unies (ONU), du 21 décembre 1981." *FF* 1982, 1:505–702. [Referred to as 1981 UN Message]

"Message du Conseil fédéral à l'Assemblée fédérale concernant la participation de la Suisse à l'accord rélatif à un programme internationale de l'énergie, du 5 février 1975." *FF* 1975, 1:757–99.

Message from the Federal Council of Switzerland to the Federal Assembly concerning the Question of Accession of Switzerland to the League of Nations, 4 August 1919, and Annexes. Cambridge: Cambridge University Press, 1919. (Original text in *FF* 1919, 4:567–713). [Referred to as 1919 League Message]

"Rapport de la Commission consultative pour les relations de la Suisse avec l'ONU au Conseil fédéral," du 20 août 1975. Berne: Département politique fédérale, 1975.

Rapport du Conseil fédéral a l'Assemblée fédérale sur la gestion. En: 1921, 1935, 1936, 1937, 1938, 1946, 1967, 1969, 1970, 1973, 1974, 1975, 1976, 1977, 1978.

Rapport du Conseil fédéral a l'Assemblée fédérale sur les grandes lignes de la politique gouvernementale pendant la legislature. [Published every four years, at the outset of each parliamentary session]

"Rapport du Conseil fédéral à l'Assemblée fédérale sur la politique de securité de la Suisse [Conception de la défense générale] du 27 juin 1973." FF 1973, 2:112 ff.

"Rapport du Conseil fédéral à l'Assemblée fédérale sur les relations de la Suisse avec l'Organisation des Nations Unies et ses institutions specialisées de 1969 à 1971 du 17 novembre 1971." FF 1972, 1:1–68. [Referred to as 1971 UN Report]

"Rapport du Conseil fédéral à l'Assemblée fédérale sur les relations de la Suisse avec l'Organisation des Nations Unies et ses institutions specialisées de 1972 à 1976, du 29 juin 1977." FF 1977, 2:781-948. [Referred to as 1977 UN Report]

"Rapport du Conseil fédéral à l'Assemblée fédérale sur la seconde initiative populaire contre l'emprise étrangère, du 22 septembre 1969." FF 1969, 2:1050–73.

Recueil officiel des lois et arrêtés fédéraux de la Confédération Suisse/Amtliche Sammlung der Bundesgesetze und Verordnungen der schweizerischen Eidgenossenschaft, yearly.

"Report of the Federal Council to the Federal Assembly Concerning Switzerland's Relations with the United Nations, of 16 July 1969." Berne: Eidgenossisches Politisches Departement, Abteilung für internationale Organisationen, 1969. (Original text in FF 1969, 2:1457–1617). [Referred to as 1969 UN Report]

Statistique du Commerce Suisse, Rapport Annuel. 1935, IIe partie. Berne: Publie par la direction générale des douanes fédérales, 1936.

Statistique Mensuelle du Commerce extérieur de la Suisse. Berne: publie sous la direction générale des douanes fédérales, monthly.

Statistisches Jahrbuch der Schweiz/Annuaire Statistique de la Suisse. Berne: publie par le bureau fédéral de la statistique, yearly.

Miscellaneous Documents and Collections of Documents

Brodin, Katarina, Kjell Goldmann, and Christian Lange. "The Policy of Neutrality: Official Doctrines of Finland and Sweden." *C & C* 3, no. 1 (1968)18–51.

Documents on International Affairs for 1935. Vols. I and II. Ed. John W. Wheeler-Bennett and Stephen Heald. London: Oxford University Press, issued under the auspices of the Royal Institute of International Affairs, 1937.

"The Effect of the United Nations Charter on the Development of International Law with Special Reference to the Status of Neutrality and The Hague and Geneva Conventions." Report of the Forty-First Conference of the International Law Association. Cambridge (1946):39–63.

Grahl-Madsen, Atle and Jiri Toman. *The Spirit of Uppsala, Proceedings of the Joint UNITAR–Uppsala University Seminar on International Law and Organization for a New World Order (9–18 June 1981).* Berlin: Walter de Gruyter, 1984.

International Legal Materials. Vol. 5, no. 2 (March 1966). Washington D.C.: The American Society of International Law, 1966.

Miller, David Hunter. *The Drafting of the Covenant.* Vols. 1 and 2. New York: C. P. Putnam and Sons, 1928.

Official Documents Bearing on the Armed Neutrality of 1780 and 1800. Washington, D.C.: Carnegie Endowment for International Peace, 1917.

Roberts, Edward Adam, and Richard Guelff, eds. *Documents on the Laws of War.* Oxford: Clarendon Press, 1982.

Survey of International Affairs for 1935, Vol. 2: Abyssinia and Italy. Ed. Arnold J. Toynbee. London: Oxford University Press, Issued under the Auspices of the Royal Institute of International Affairs, 1936.

Treaties and Alliances of the World: An International Survey Covering Treaties in Force and Communities of States. New York: Charles Scribners and Sons for Keesings Publications Ltd., 1974.

Windrich, Elaine. *The Rhodesian Problem: A Documentary Record, 1923–73.* London: Routledge and Kegan Paul, 1975.

SECONDARY SOURCES

General Books

Abrahamsen, Samuel. *Sweden's Foreign Policy.* Washington, D.C.: Public Affairs Press, 1957.

Almond, Gabriel, and Sidney Verba. *The Civic Culture.* Princeton: Princeton University Press, 1963.

Anderson, Perry. *Lineages of the Absolutist State.* London: NLB, 1974a.

———. *Passages from Antiquity to Feudalism.* London: NLB, 1974b.

Andersson, Ingevar. *A History of Sweden.* London: Weidenfeld and Nicholson, 1956.

Andrén, Nils. *Power-Balance and Non-Alignment.* Stockholm: Almquist & Wiksell, 1967.

Archer, Clive. *International Organisations.* London: George Allen and Unwin, 1983.

Baer, George W. *Test Case: Italy, Ethiopia and the League of Nations.* Stanford, Calif.: Stanford University Press, 1976.

Baldwin, David A. *Economic Statecraft.* Princeton: Princeton University Press, 1985.

Belin, Jacqueline. *La Suisse et Les Nations Unies.* New York: Manhattan Publishing Company, 1956.

Bellquist, Eric. *Some Aspects of the Recent Foreign Policy of Sweden.* Berkeley: University of California Press, 1929.

Black, Cyril E., Richard A. Falk, Klaus Knorr, and Oran R. Young. *Neutralization and World Politics.* Princeton: Princeton University Press, 1968.

Blix, Hans. *Sovereignty, Aggression, Neutrality.* Stockholm: Almquist & Wiksell, 1970.

Board, Joseph B. *The Government and Politics of Sweden.* Boston: Houghton Mifflin Co., 1970.

Bonjour, Edgar. *Swiss Neutrality: Its History and Meaning.* London: George Allen and Unwin, 1946.

————. *Geschichte der Schweizerischen Neutralität.* Bande I–VI. Basle: Helbing and Lichtenbahn, 1970.

————. *La Neutralité Suisse: Synthèse de son Histoire.* Neuchâtel: A La Baconnière, 1978.

Bonjour, Edgar, H. S. Offler, and G. R. Potter. *A Short History of Switzerland.* Oxford: Oxford University Press, 1952.

Bowles, Thomas Gibson. *The Declaration of Paris of 1856.* London: Sampson, Low, Marston and Co., Ltd., 1900.

Bozeman, Adda Bruenner. *Regional Conflicts Around Geneva.* Stanford: Stanford University Press, 1949.

Brooks, Robert Clarkson. *Civic Training in Switzerland.* Chicago: University of Chicago Press, 1930.

Brown, Neville. *European Security 1972–1980.* London: Royal United Services Institute for Defence Studies, 1972.

Brown-John, C. Lloyd. *Multilateral Sanctions in International Law: A Comparative Analysis.* New York: Praeger, 1975.

Burgenemeier, Beat. *Théorie et pratique des investissements suisse a l'étranger.* Genève: Librairie Droz, 1981.

Burton, John, ed. *Nonalignment.* London: André Deutsch Ltd., 1966.

Carlgren, W. M. *Swedish Foreign Policy During the Second World War.* London: Ernest Benn Ltd., 1977.

Carlsson, Sten, and Jerker Rosen. *Svensk Historia.* Vol. 2, *Tiden Efter 1918.* Stockholm: Esselte Studium, 1961.

Carr, Edward Hallett. *The Twenty Years' Crisis.* London: Macmillan, 1939.

Castrén, Erik. *The Present Laws of War and Neutrality.* Helsinki: Academia Scientiarium Fennica Annales, Ser. B. Tom. 85, 1954.

Chowdhury, Subrata Roy. *Military Alliances and Neutrality in War and Peace.* Bombay: Orient Longmans, 1966.

Claude, Inis L., Jr. *Power and International Relations.* New York: Random House, 1962.

————. *Swords into Plowshares: The Problems and Progress of International Organization.* New York: Random House, 1964.

Codding, George. *The Federal Government of Switzerland.* London: George Allen and Unwin, 1961.

Cohn, Georg. *Neo-Neutrality.* New York: Columbia University Press, 1939.

Crabb, Cecil V., Jr. *The Elephants and the Grass: A Study of Nonalignment.* New York: Praeger, 1965.

————. *Nations in a Multipolar World.* New York: Harper and Row, Inc., 1968.

Daoudi, M. S. and M. S. Dajani. *Economic Sanctions: Ideals and Experience.* London: Routledge and Kegan Paul, 1983.

Deutsch, Karl. *Nationalism and Social Communication.* Cambridge, Mass.: M.I.T. Press, 1966.

Deutsch, Karl, and William J. Foltz. *Nation-Building.* New York: Atherton Press, 1966.

Dorfer, Ingemar. *System 37 Viggen.* Oslo: Universitetsförlaget, 1973.

Doxey, Margaret P. *Economic Sanctions and International Enforcement.* London: Macmillan for the Royal Institute of International Affairs, 2d ed., 1980.

————. *International Sanctions in Contemporary Perspective*. London: Macmillan, 1987.

Dutoit, Bernard. *La Neutralité Suisse a l'Heure Européenne*. Paris: R. Pichon et R. Durand-Auzias, 1962.

Eek, Hilding. *Sveriges utrikespolitik och FN som internationell organisation*. Stockholm: Skrifter utgivna av Utrikespolitiska Institutet, no. 9, 1955.

————. *Folkrätten. Staternas och de Mellanstatliga Organisationernas Rättsordning*. Stockholm: P. A. Norstedt & Söner, 1968a.

Ehni, Reinhart. *Die Schweiz und die Vereinten Nationen von 1944–1947*. Tübingen: Studien zur Geschichte und Politik no. 21, 1967.

Falk, Richard A. *The Status of Law in International Society*. Princeton: Princeton University Press, 1970.

Ferencz, Benjamin B. *Defining International Aggression: The Search for World Peace*. Vol. 1. New York: Oceana Publications, Inc., 1973.

Forsythe, David P. *Humanitarian Politics: The International Committee of the Red Cross*. Baltimore: Johns Hopkins University Press, 1977.

Fox, Annette Baker. *The Power of Small States: Diplomacy in World War II*. Chicago: University of Chicago Press, 1959.

Frei, Daniel. *Dimensionen neutraler Politik: Ein beitrag zür Theorie der Internationalen Beziehungen*. Genève: Etudes et Travaux de l'Institut Universitaire de Haute Etudes Internationales, no. 8, 1969.

Gihl, Törsten. *Nationernas förbund och sanktionerna*. Stockholm: Utgiven av svensk förening för nationernas förbund, 1936.

Goodrich, Leland M., Edward Hambro, and Anne Patricia Simons. *Charter of the United Nations*. 3d ed. New York: Columbia University Press, 1969.

Grotius, Hugo. *The Law of War and Peace*. Trans. by Frances W. Kelsey. Oxford: Clarendon Press, 1925.

Guggenheim, Paul. *Traité de Droit international public*. Tome I. Genève: Librairie de l'Université, Georg et Cie S.A., 1967.

Gustafsson, Lars. *The Public Dialogue in Sweden*. Stockholm: P. A. Norstedt & Söner, 1964.

Hadenius, Stig, Hans Wislander, and Bjorn Molin. *Sverige Efter 1900: En modern politisk historia*. Stockholm: Aldus/Bonniers, 1967.

Haegler, Rolf P. *Schweizer Universalismus, UNO-Partikularismus*. Berne: Peter Lang, 1983.

Halldin Norberg, Viveca. *Swedes in Haile Selassie's Ethiopia, 1924–52: A Study in Early Development Co-operation*. Uppsala: Offsetcenter ab, 1977.

Hancock, M. Donald. *Sweden: The Politics of Post-industrial Change*. New York: Praeger, 1972.

Handel, Michael. *Weak States in the International System*. London: Frank Cass, 1981.

Hart, Thomas G. *The Cognitive World of Swedish Security Elites*. Stockholm: the Institute of International Affairs, 1976.

Haskel, Barbara, *Scandinavian Option*. Oslo: Universitetsförlaget, 1976.

Håstad, Elis. *Regeringssättet i den schweiziska demokratin*. Uppsala: Skrifter utgivna av Statsvetenskapliga Föreningen, VI, 1936.

————. *The Parliament of Sweden*. London: The Hansard Society for Parliamentary Government, 1957.

Hermele, Kenneth, and Karl-Anders Larsson. *Solidaritet Eller Imperialism: Om Sverige, Världsordningen och Tredje Världen*. Stockholm: Liberförlag, 1977.

Higgins, Rosalyn. *The Development of International Law Through the Political Organs of the United Nations.* London: Oxford University Press, 1963.

Holmström, Barry. *Koreakriget i svensk debatt.* Uppsala: Statsvetenskapliga Föreningen, Skrifter 61, 1972.

Howe, Russell Warren. *Weapons, the International Game of Arms, Money and Diplomacy.* Garden City, N.Y.: Doubleday, 1980.

Hufbauer, Gary Clyde, and Jeffrey J. Schott. *Economic Sanctions Reconsidered: History and Current Policy.* Washington, D.C.: Institute for International Economics, 1985.

Hughes, Christopher J. *The Federal Constitution of Switzerland.* Oxford: Oxford University Press, 1954.

————. *The Parliament of Switzerland.* London: Cassell and Company, Ltd., 1962.

————. *Switzerland.* London & Tonbridge: Ernest Benn Ltd., 1975.

Huldt, Bo. *Sweden, the United Nations, and Decolonization.* Lund: Esselte Studium, 1974.

International Sanctions: A Report by a Group of Members of the Royal Institute of International Affairs. London: Oxford University Press, 1938. [Referred to as RIIA]

James, Alan. *The Politics of Peace-Keeping.* London: Chatto & Windus for the International Institute for Strategic Studies, 1969.

Jessup, Philip C. *Neutrality: Its History, Economics, and Law.* Vol. 1: *The Origins;* Vol. 4: *Today and Tomorrow.* New York: Columbia University Press, 1935–36.

Johnson, Peter. *Neutrality: a Policy for Britain.* London: Maurice Temple Smith, 1985.

Joll, James. *Europe Since 1870: An International History.* Middlesex: Penguin Books, 1976.

Jones, S. Shepard. *The Scandinavian States and the League of Nations.* Princeton: Princeton University Press, 1939.

Kapungu, Leonard T. *The United Nations and Economic Sanctions.* Lexington, Mass.: Lexington Books, 1973.

Katzenstein, Peter J. *Small States in World Markets: Industrial Policy in Europe.* Ithaca, N.Y.: Cornell University Press, 1985.

Kay, David A. *The New Nations in the United Nations, 1960–1967.* New York: Columbia University Press, 1970.

Kelsen, Hans J. *The Law of the United Nations—A Critical Analysis of its Fundamental Problems.* London: Stevens & Sons, Ltd., 1950.

————. *Collective Security Under International Law.* Washington, D.C.: U.S. Government Printing Office, 1957.

Koblik, Steven. *Sweden: The Neutral Victor.* Stockholm: Läromedelsförlagen, 1972.

Kohn, Hans. *Nationalism and Liberty: The Swiss Example.* London: George Allen & Unwin, 1956.

————. *The Idea of Nationalism.* New York: Macmillan, 1958.

Lasserre, Victor. *Une Suisse Insoupçonnee: Lettre Ouverte à Jean Ziegler.* Paris: Editions Buchet/Chastel, 1977.

Leebaert, Derek, ed. *European Security: Prospects for the 1980s.* Lexington: Lexington Books, 1979.

Lipset, Seymour M., and Stein Rokkan, eds. *Party Systems and Voter Alignments: Cross-National Perspectives.* New York: Free Press, 1967.

Lönnröth, Eric. *Den Svenska Utrikespolitikens Historia.* Vol. 5, 1919–1939. Stockholm: P. A. Norstedt & Söner, 1959.

Lyon, Peter. *Neutralism.* Leicester: Leicester University Press, 1963.

Macridis, Roy, ed. *Foreign Policy in World Politics.* Englewood Cliffs, N.J.: Prentice-Hall, Inc., 1958.

Maldéveloppement Suisse-Monde. Commission des Organisations suisses de cooperation au développement. Genève: CETIM, 1975.

Marks, Sally. *The Illusion of Peace: International Relations in Europe, 1918–1933.* London: Macmillan, 1976.

Mårold, Bert. *Den Svenska Freds—och Neutralitets—Rörelsens Uppkomst.* Göteborg: Akademiförlaget, 1974.

Martin, Lawrence W., ed. *Neutralism and Nonalignment.* New York: Praeger, 1962.

Masnata, François. *Le Parti Socialiste et la Tradition Démocratique en Suisse.* Neuchâtel: à la Baconnière, 1963.

Mayer, Lawrence C., and John H. Burnett. *Politics in Industrialized Societies: a Comparative Perspective.* New York: John Wiley & Sons, 1977.

The Military Balance 1981–82. London: International Institute for Strategic Studies, 1981.

Morgenthau, Hans. *Politics Among Nations: The Struggle for Power and Peace.* 3d ed. New York: Alfred Knopf, 1960.

Moseley, Leonard. *Haile Selassie: The Conquering Lion.* London: Weidenfeld and Nicholson, 1964.

Northedge, F. S. *The International Political System.* London: Faber & Faber, 1976.

Northedge, F. S., *The League of Nations: Its Life and Times [1920-1946].* Leicester: Holmes and Meier, 1986.

Oakley, Stewart. *The Story of Sweden.* London: Faber & Faber, 1966.

Ogley, Roderick. *The Theory and Practice of Neutrality in the Twentieth Century.* London: Routledge and Kegan Paul, 1970.

Oppenheim, Lassa Francis Laurence. *International Law: A Treatise.* Vol. 2, *Disputes, War, and Neutrality,* ed. H. Lauterpacht. 7th ed. New York: Longmans, Green and Co., 1952.

Ørvik, Nils. *The Decline of Neutrality, 1914–1941.* London: Frank Cass & Co., Ltd., 1971.

Peace and Security After the Second World War. A Swedish Contribution. Stockholm: Utrikespolitiska Institutet, Skrifter 5: 1945.

Petitpierre, Max. *Seize Ans de Neutralité Active.* Neuchâtel: Editions de la Baconnière, 1980.

Pointet, Pierre Jean. *La neutralité de la Suisse et la liberté de la Presse.* Zürich: Editions polygraphiques, 1945.

Politis, Nicholas. *Neutrality and Peace.* Trans. from the French by F. C. Macken. Washington, D.C.: Carnegie Endowment for International Peace, 1935.

Przeworski, Adam, and Henry Teune. *The Logic of Comparative Social Enquiry.* New York: John Wiley and Sons, 1970.

Rajan, M. S. *United Nations and Domestic Jurisdiction.* Bombay: Orient Longmans, 1958.

Rappard, William E. *The Government of Switzerland.* New York: Van Nostrand Co., Inc., 1936.

———. *Collective Security in the Swiss Experience, 1291–1948.* London: George Allen and Unwin, 1948.

Renwick, Robin. *Economic Sanctions*. Harvard Studies in International Affairs, no. 45. Cambridge, Mass.: Center for International Affairs, 1981.

Rigonalli, Marzio. *Le Tessin dans les relations entre la Suisse et l'Italie, 1922–1940*. Locarno: Tipografia Pedrazzini, 1983.

RIIA, see International Sanctions, General Books, p. 222.

Robert, Denise. *Etude sur la neutralité suisse*. Zürich: Zürcher Studien zum Internationalen Recht, no. 16, 1950.

Roberts, Edward Adam. *Nations in Arms: The Theory and Practice of Territorial Defence*. London: Chatto & Windus for the International Institute for Strategic Studies, 1972.

Rosenau, James N. *The Study of Political Adaptation*. London: Francis Pinter Ltd., 1981.

Rothstein, Robert L. *Alliances and Small Powers*. New York: Columbia University Press, 1968.

de Rougemont, Denis. *La Confédération helvétique*. Monaco: Rocher, 1953.

Rowan-Robinson, H. *Sanctions Begone! A Plea and a Plan for the Reform of the League*. London: Clowes, 1936.

La Ruche, Francis. *La Neutralité de la Suède*. Paris: Nouvelles Editions Latines, 1953.

Sampson, Anthony. *The Arms Bazaar*. London: Hodder and Stoughton, Ltd., 1977.

Schwarz, Urs. *The Eye of the Hurricane: Switzerland in World War Two*. Colorado: Westview Press, 1980.

Scott, Franklin D. *Sweden: The Nation's History*. Minneapolis: The University of Minnesota Press, 1977.

Scott, James Brown. *The Armed Neutralities of 1780 and 1800*. New York: Oxford University Press, 1918.

Senn, Alfred Erich. *The Russian Revolution in Switzerland, 1914–1917.* Madison: University of Wisconsin Press, 1971.

Seton-Watson, Hugh. *Nations and States*. London: Methuen & Co., Ltd., 1977.

Siegfried, André. *Switzerland: A Democratic Way of Life*. Trans. from the French by Edward Fitzgerald. London: Jonathan Cape, 1950.

Sims, Nicholas A. *Neutralism and International Conflict*. London: Colleges & Universities Campaign for Nuclear Disarmament, 1966.

Smith, David, and Colin Simpson. *Mugabe*. London: Sphere Books, 1981.

Stanley, Timothy W., and Darnell M. Whitt. *Détente Diplomacy: United States and European Security in the 1970s*. New York: Dunellan Co. Inc., 1970.

Steinberg, Jonathan. *Why Switzerland?* Cambridge: Cambridge University Press, 1976.

Steiner, Jürg. *Amicable Agreement Versus Majority Rule*. Chapel Hill: University of North Carolina Press, 1974.

Stettler, Bernhard. *Die Stellung der Schweiz zum Sanktions-system des Volkerbundes von 1919 bis zür Anwendung gegen Italien 1935–36*. Berne: Peter Lang, 1977.

Stone, Julius. *Aggression and World Order: A Critique of United Nations Theories of Aggression*. London: Stevens and Sons Ltd., 1958.

Stranner, Henri. *Neutralité suisse et solidarité européenne*. Lausanne: 1959.

Svänström, Ragnar, and Carl Fredrik Palmstierna. *A Short History of Sweden*. Oxford: Oxford University Press, 1934.

Sweden in World Society: Thoughts about the Future. Swedish Secretariat for Futures Studies. Oxford: Pergamon Press, 1980.

Taylor, A. J. P. *The Origins of the Second World War*. Middlesex: Penguin Books, 1961.
———. *English History 1914–1945*. Oxford: Oxford University Press, 1965.
Tilly, Charles, ed. *The Formation of National States in Western Europe*. Princeton: Princeton University Press, 1975.
Tingsten, Herbert. *Svensk Utrikesdebatt Mellan Världskrigen*. Stockholm: Aldus/ Bonniers, 1944. [NB: the English translation by Joan Bulman is entitled *The Debate on the Foreign Policy of Sweden, 1918–1939*. London: Oxford University Press, 1949.]
———. *The Swedish Social Democrats*. Trans. from the Swedish by Greta Frankel and Patricia Howard-Rosen. New Jersey: Bedminster Press, 1973.
Toynbee, Arnold J. *A Study in History*. Vol. 9. London: Oxford University Press, 1954.
U-debatt: Om mål och metoder i biståndsarbetet. Stockholm: Raben & Sjögren, 1971.
Undén, Bo Östen. *Neutralitet och Folkrätt*. Stockholm: Albert Bonniers Boktryckeri, 1939.
———. *Tankar om Utrikespolitik*. Stockholm: Raben & Sjögren, 1963.
de Vattel, Emerich. *Le Droit de Gens*. Book 3. Washington: Carnegie Institution, 1916.
Verdross, Alfred. *The Permanent Neutrality of the Republic of Austria*. Wien: Österreichischer Bundesverlag, 1967.
Vergotti, Jacques M. *La Neutralité de la Suisse*. Lausanne: Imprimerie la Concorde, 1954.
Vincent, John Martin. *Switzerland at the Beginning of the Sixteenth Century*. Baltimore: Johns Hopkins, 1904.
Wallace, William. *Foreign Policy and the Political Process*. London: Macmillan, 1971.
Wallace, William, and W. E. Paterson, eds. *Foreign Policy-Making in Western Europe*. London: Saxon House, 1978.
Wallensteen, Peter, and Miroslav Nincic, eds. *Dilemmas of Economic Coercion: Sanctions in World Politics*. New York: Praeger, 1983.
Walters, F. P. *A History of the League of Nations*. Vols. 1 and 2. London: Oxford University Press, 1952.
Webster, C. K. *The Congress of Vienna*. London: G. Bell & Sons Ltd., 1934.
Wicker, Cyrus French. *Neutralization*. London: Oxford University Press, 1911.
Wilson, Hugh Robert. *Switzerland—Neutrality as a Foreign Policy*. Philadelphia: Dorrance and Company, 1974.
Wiskemann, Elizabeth. *Undeclared War*. New York: St. Martins Press, 1967.
Wright, P. Quincy, ed. *Neutrality and Collective Security*. Chicago: University of Chicago Press, 1936a.
Zacklin, Ralph. *The United Nations and Rhodesia, a Study in International Law*. New York: Praeger, 1974.
Ziegler, Jean. *Switzerland Exposed*. Translated from the French by Rosemary Sheed Middleton. London: Allison & Busby, 1978.
Zimmern, Sir Alfred E. *The League of Nations and the Rule of Law, 1918–1935*. London: Macmillan, 1936a.

General Articles

Anton, Thomas. "Policy-Making and Political Culture in Sweden." *Scandinavian Political Studies* 4 (1969):88–102.

Arnold, Guy, and Alan Baldwin. "Rhodesia: Token Sanctions or Total Economic Warfare." In *The Rhodesian Problem: A Documentary Record, 1923–1973,* edited by Elaine Windrich. 269–274. London: Routledge and Kegan Paul, 1975.

Baer, George W. "Sanctions and Security: The League of Nations and the Italo-Ethiopian War." *International Organization* 27, no. 2 (1973): 165–80.

Barnes, Ian Ronald. "Swedish Foreign Policy. A Response to Geo-Political Factors." *C & C* 9, no. 4 (1974):243–61.

———. "The Changing Nature of the Swedish Aid Relationship During the Social Democratic Period of Government." *C & C* 15, no. 4 (1980):141–50.

Beckman, Björn. "Aid and Foreign Investments: The Swedish Case." *C & C* 14, nos. 2–3 (1979):133–148.

Bergquist, Mats. "Trade and Security in the Nordic Area." *C & C* 4, no. 4 (1969):237–246.

Bindschedler, Rudolf L. "La délimitation des Compétences des Nations Unies." Academie de Droit International. *Recueil des Cours* 1 (1963):305–423.

———. "Das Problem der Beteiligung der Schweiz an Sanktionen der Vereinigten Nationen, besonders im Falle Rhodesiens." In *Zeitschrift für Ausländisches Öffentliches Recht und Völkerrecht* 28, no. 1 (März 1968):1–15.

Bindschedler-Robert, Denise. "Les bons Offices dans la Politique étrangère de la Suisse." In *Handbuch der Schweizerischen Aussenpolitik,* edited by Alois Riklin. Berne: Paul Haupt, 1975. 679–91.

Birnbaum, Karl E. "The Formation of Swedish Foreign Policy." *C & C* 1, no. 1 (1965):6–31.

Bjork, Kaj. "Varför reagerar inte socialdemokratin i Schweiz." *Tiden* 5 (1953):276–80.

Boczek, Boleslaw A. "Permanent Neutrality and Collective Security: The Case of Switzerland and the United Nations Sanctions Against Southern Rhodesia." *Case Western Reserve Journal of International Law* 1, no. 2 (1969):73–104.

Bohn, David. "Neutrality—Switzerland's Policy Dilemma: Options in the New Europe." *Orbis* 21, no. 2 (Summer 1977):335–52.

Borchard, Edwin. "Sanctions v. Neutrality." *AJIL* 30, no. 1 (January 1936):91–94.

———. "War, Neutrality, and Non-Belligerency." *AJIL* 35, no. 4 (October 1941):618–25.

Brierly, J. L. "Some Implications of the Pact of Paris." *BYBIL* 10 (1929):208–10.

Brown, Philip Marshall. "Malevolent Neutrality." *AJIL* 30, no. 1 (January 1936):88–90.

Brownlie, L. "Volunteers and the Law of Neutrality." *International and Comparative Law Quarterly* 5 (October 1956):570–80.

Carlgren, Wilhelm. "Sweden: The Ministry for Foreign Affairs." In *The Times Survey of Foreign Ministries of the World,* edited by Zara Steiner. 455–70. London: Times Books, 1982.

Cefkin, J. Leo. "The Rhodesian Question at the United Nations." *International Organization* 22, no. 3 (Summer 1968):649–69.

Chaumont, Charles. "Nations Unies et Neutralité." *Recueil des Cours* 1 (1956):1–56.

Daalder, Hans. "Building Consociational Nations." In *Building States and Nations,* edited by S.N. Eisenstadt and Stein Rokkan, Vol. 2. 14–31. Beverly Hills: Sage Publications. 1973.

Dahlberg, Brita. "Neutralitet Mot Ny Bakgrund." *Tiden* 9 (1968):517–22.

"Declaration by Norway, Sweden and Denmark Relative to the Establishment of Uniform Rules of Neutrality (December 21, 1912)." *AJIL* Supplement 7 (1913):187–91.

Dehn, C. G. "The Problem of Neutrality." Grotius Society. *Transactions* 33 (1945):139–49.

Deutsch, Karl W., and Hermann Weilenmann. "The Swiss City Canton: a Political Invention." *Comparative Studies in Society and History.* 7, no. 4 (July 1965):393–408.

Dolman, Antony J. "The Like-Minded Countries and the New International Order: Past, Present and Future Prospects." *C & C* 14, nos. 2–3 (1979):57–86.

Edberg, Rolf. "Tema med Variationer." *Tiden* 4 (1951):193–98.

Eek, Hilding. "Sverige i FN:s Säkerhetsråd 1957–58." *Världpolitikens dagsfrågor* 3 (1959).

———. " 'Neutralitet,' Politiska Flyktingar." *Svensk Tidskrift* 55, no. 3 (1968b):152–56.

Elder, Neil. "Parliament and Foreign Policy in Sweden." *Political Studies* 1, no. 3 (October 1953):193–206.

Emerson, Rupert. "The New Higher Law of Anti-Colonialism." In *The Relevance of International Law*, edited by Karl W. Deutsch and Stanley Hoffman, 153–74. Cambridge, Mass: Schenkman Publishing Co., 1968.

Faurby, Ib. "Premises, Promises, and Problems of Comparative Foreign Policy." *C & C* 11, no. 3 (1976):139–62.

Fenwick, C. G. "The 'Failure' of the League of Nations." *AJIL* 30 (1936):506–9.

———. "When is There a Threat to the Peace?" *AJIL* 61, no. 3 (July 1967):753–55.

———. "Is Neutrality Still a Term of Present Law?" *AJIL* 63, no. 1 (January 1969):100–2.

Forsman, L. "Neutralitet i en Föränderlig Värld." *Tiden* 61, no. 2 (1969).

Frei, Daniel. "Neutrality and Nonalignment: Convergencies and Contrasts." Paper (unpublished) presented to the 11th World Congress of the International Political cal Science Association, Moscow, 12–18 August 1979, 1–14.

Freymond, Bernard. "Switzerland: The Federal Department of External Affairs." In *The Times Survey of Foreign Ministries of the World*, edited by Zara Steiner. 471–92.London: Times Books, 1982.

Freymond, Jacques. "Supervising Agreements: The Korean Experience." *Foreign Affairs* (April 1959):496–503.

———. "The Foreign Policy of Switzerland." In *Foreign Policies in a World of Change*, edited by Joseph E. Black and Kenneth W. Thompson, 149–170. New York: Harper and Row, 1963.

———. "The Foreign Policy of Switzerland." In *The Other Powers*, edited by R.P. Barston, 92–120. London: George Allen and Unwin, 1973.

———. "La Suisse devant l'ONU." In *La Suisse et la diplomatie multilatérale*, edited by Franz A. Blankart, 283–300. Genève: 1976.

Friedman, Julian R. "Alliances in International Politics." In *Alliances in International Politics*, edited by Julian R. Friedman, 1–28. Boston: Allyn and Bacon, Inc., 1970.

Galtung, Johan. "On the Effects of Economic Sanctions." *World Politics* 19, no. 3 (April 1967):378–416.

Gaudard, Gaston. "La Suisse Face à la Nouvelle Structure de l'économie mondiale." Conférence prononcée le 15 novembre 1976 lors du Dies Academicus de l'Université de Fribourg, Editions Universitaires Fribourg, Suisse (1976):5–24.

Gihl, Törsten. "Neutralitetsproblem." *Internationell Politik* 1, Skrifter utgivna av Kommitten för utrikespolitisk upplysning. Stockholm: Kooperativa förbundets bokförlag (1938).

Grieve, Muriel J. "Economic Sanctions: Theory and Practice." *International Relations* 3, no. 6 (October 1968):431–43.

Grieve, W. P. "The Present Position of 'Neutral' States." Grotius Society. *Transactions* 33 (1948):99–118.

Guggenheim, Paul. "La sécurité collective et la problème de la neutralité." *Schweizerisches Jahrbuch für internationales Recht/Annuaire Suisse de droit international* 2 (1945):9–47.

Gunter, Michael M. "Switzerland and the United Nations." *International Organization* 30 (1976):129–52.

Haekkerup, Per. "Scandinavia's Peace-Keeping Forces for U.N." *Foreign Affairs* 42, no. 4 (July 1964):675–81.

Hägglöf, M. Gunnar. "A Test of Neutrality: Sweden in the Second World War." *International Affairs* 36, no. 2 (April 1960):153–67.

Hakovirta, Harto. "Neutral States and Bloc–Based Integration." *C & C* 13, no. 2 (1978):109–32.

———. "The International System and Neutrality in Europe 1946–1980–1990." *Yearbook on Finnish Foreign Policy, 1980.* Helsinki: Institute of International Affairs (1980):39–48.

———. "Effects of Non-Alignment on Neutrality in Europe: An Analysis and Appraisal." *C & C* 18, no. 2 (1983):57–75.

Halderman, John W. "Some Legal Aspects of Sanctions in the Rhodesian Case." *International and Comparative Law Quarterly* 17, no. 3 (July 1968):672–705.

Halperin, Jean. "The Transformation of Switzerland." In *The Opening of an Era: 1848,* edited by François Fejto, 50–66. New York: Fertig, 1966.

Hansen, Peter. "Adaptive Behavior of Small States—the Case of Denmark and the European Community." In *Sage International Yearbook of Foreign Policy Studies,* edited by P. McGowan, Vol. 2, 143–74. Beverly Hills: Sage Publications, 1974.

Håstad, Elis. "Sweden's Attitude Toward the United Nations." In *Sweden and the United Nations,* 9–163. New York: Manhattan Publishing Company, 1956.

Haug, Hans. "Switzerland and the United Nations." In *Modern Switzerland,* edited by Murray J. Luck, 457–72. Palo Alto, Calif.: The Society for the Promotion of Science and Scholarship, Inc., 1978.

Higgins, Rosalyn. "International Law, Rhodesia, and the U.N." *The World Today* 23 (March 1967):94–106.

Hoffman, Stanley. "International Law and the Control of Force." In *The Relevance of International Law,* edited by Karl W. Deutsch and Stanley Hoffman, 21–46. Cambridge, Mass.: Schenkman Publishing Co., 1968.

Hoffmann, Fredrik. "The Functions of Economic Sanctions: A Comparative Analysis." *Journal of Peace Research* 4, no. 2 (1967):140–59.

Houghton, N. D. "The Present Status of the League of Nations." *International Conciliation* 317 (February 1936):67–108.

Howell, John M. "A Matter of International Concern." *AJIL* 63, no. 4 (October 1969):771–82.

Hudson, Manley D. "Switzerland and the International Court of Justice." *AJIL* 41, no. 4 (October 1947):866–71.

"The International Law of the Future." *AJIL* Supplement 38 (1944):41–140.

"International Law and Military Operations Against Insurgents in Neutral Territory." Note from *Columbia Law Review,* In *The Vietnam War and International Law,* edited by Richard A. Falk, 572–96. Princeton: Princeton University Press, 1969.

"Issues Before the 23rd General Assembly." *International Conciliation,* no. 569 (September 1968): 71–80.

Jessup, Philip C. "The Birth, Death, and Reincarnation of Neutrality." *AJIL* 26 (1932):789–94.

Katzenstein, Peter J. "Capitalism in one Country? Switzerland in the International Economy." *International Organization* 34, no. 4 (Autumn 1980):507–40.

Keller, Rene. "La Participation de la Suisse aux organisations internationales: problèmes politiques." In *La Suisse et la diplomatie multilatérale,* edited by Franz A. Blankart, 29–48. Genève: 1976.

Kleberg, Olof. "De stora och de små—Olof Palmes syn pa supermakter och småstater." In *Är svensk neutralitet möjlig?,* 67–87. Stockholm: Liberförlag, 1977.

Korovin, Eugene A. "The Second World War and International Law." *AJIL* 40, no. 4 (October 1946):742–55.

Kunz, Josef L. "The Geneva Conventions of August 12, 1949." In *Law and Politics in the World Community,* edited by George A. Lipsky, 280–89. Berkeley: University of California Press, 1953.

Lalive, J. F. "International Organization and Neutrality." *BYBIL* 75 (1947):72–89.

Lambelet, Jean Christian. "Analyse Statistique du Référendum Fédéral du 13 juin 1976 sur le prêt en faveur de l'Association Internationale de développement (IDA)." *Annuaire Suisse de Science Politique/Schweizerisches Jahrbuch für Politische Wissenschaft,* Vol. 20, 239–48. Berne: Paul Haupt, 1980.

Languetin, Pierre. "La Politique extérieure de la Suisse: les négociations multilatérales du GATT." In *La Suisse et la diplomatie multilatérale,* edited by Franz A. Blankart, 177–94. Genève: 1976.

Lauterpacht, Hersch. "Rules of Warfare in an Unlawful War." In *Law and Politics in the World Community,* edited by George A. Lipsky, 89–113. Berkeley: University of California Press, 1953.

Lenway, Stephanie Ann. "Economic Sanctions and Statecraft." *International Organization* 42, no. 2 (Spring 1988):397–426.

Light, Margot. "Neutralism and Non-Alignment: The Dialectics of Soviet Theory." *Millenium* 14, no. 1 (Spring 1985):79–92.

Lijphart, Arend. "Consociational Democracy." *World Politics* 21 (January 1969):207–25.

———. "Comparative Politics and the Comparative Method." *The American Political Science Review* 65 (September 1971):682–93.

———. "The Comparable-Cases Strategy in Comparative Research." *Comparative Political Studies* 8, no. 2 (July 1975):158–77.

Malinverni, Georges. "Democracy and Foreign Policy: The Referendum on Treaties in Switzerland." *BYBIL* 49 (1978):207–19.

Markenstein, Klaus. "Swedish Foreign Assistance." *C & C* 5, no. 2 1970):95–101.

McDougall, Myres S., and W. Michael Reisman. "Rhodesia and the United Nations: The Lawfulness of International Concern." *AJIL* 62, no. 1 (January 1968):1–19.

Morgenthau, Hans J. "The End of Switzerland's 'Differential' Neutrality." *AJIL* 32, no. 3 (July 1938):558–62.

———. "The Resurrection of Neutrality in Europe." *The American Political Science Review* 33, no. 3 (June 1939):473–86.

Mowat, R. B. "The Position of Switzerland in the League of Nations." *BYBIL* 4 (1923–24):90–95.

Munch, Peter. "Les Etats Neutres et le Pacte de la Société des Nations." In *Les Origines et l'oeuvre de la Société des Nations,* publie sous la direction de P. Munch. Tome 1, 161–88. Copenhague: Rask Ørstedfonden, 1923.

Muret, Charlotte. "The Swiss Pattern for a Federated Europe." *International Political Communities: An Anthology,* 149–73. Garden City, N.Y.: Doubleday & Company, Inc., 1966.

Myrdal, Alva. "Neutralitetspolitik som princip och praktik." *Tiden* 3 (1969):146–53.

"Neutralization." *Encyclopedia of the Social Sciences.* Vol. 2, 365–66. New York: Macmillan, 1933.

"Neutrality." *Encyclopedia of the Social Sciences.* Vol. 2, 361–64. New York: Macmillan, 1933.

Nilsson, Törsten. "Utrikespolitik och Handelspolitik." *Tiden* 3 (1969):139–45.

Norton, Patrick M. "Between the Ideology and the Reality: The Shadow of the Law of Neutrality." *Harvard International Law Journal* 17 (Spring 1976):249–311.

Ogley, Roderick C. "Towards a General Theory of International Organisation." *International Relations* 3, no. 8 (November 1969):599–619.

Petersen, Nikolaj. "Adaptation as a Framework for the Analysis of Foreign Policy Behavior." *C & C* 12, no. 4 (1977):221–50.

Petitpierre, Max. "Is Swiss Neutrality Still Justified?" In *Switzerland, Present and Future.* Zürich: New Helvetic Society, 1963. Extracted in Roderick Ogley, *The Theory and Practice of Neutrality in the Twentieth Century,* 173–81. London: Routledge & Kegan Paul, 1970.

Pictet, François Charles. "Les Institutions des Nations Unies établies en Suisse." In *Handbuch der schweizerischen Aussenpolitik,* edited by Alois Riklin, 575–82. Berne: Paul Haupte, 1975a.

———. "La Participation de la Suisse aux Organes et aux Institutions specialisées des Nations Unies." In *Handbuch der schweizerischen Aussenpolitik,* edited by Alois Riklin, 543–48. Berne: Paul Haupte, 1975b.

Pictet, Jean. "La Suisse et les Conventions de Genève de 1949 pour la Protection des Victimes de la Guerre." In *Handbuch der schweizerischen Aussenpolitik,* edited by Alois Riklin, 329–41. Berne: Paul Haupte, 1975.

Podelford, Norman J. "The New Scandinavian Neutrality Rules." *AJIL* 32 (1938):789–93.

"Political and Economic Effects of Sanctions on Rhodesia." *The World Today* 23 (January 1967):1–5.

Potter, Pitman B. "The Wal-Wal Arbitration." *AJIL* 30 (1936):27–44.

Qurasi, B. "L'évolution de l'attitude officielle de la Suisse à l'égard d'une adhésion éventuelle à l'ONU de 1944 à 1978." *Diplomatische Akademie, Jahrbuch.* Vol. 14, 97–9. Wien: 1978–79.

Rabinowitz, Charles. "U.N. Application of Selective Mandatory Sanctions Against Rhodesia: A Brief Legal and Political Analysis." *Virginia Journal of International Law* 7, no. 2 (1967):147–62.

Rappard, William E. "La Suisse et la Société des Nations." In *Les Origines et l'oeuvre de la Société des Nations*, publie sous la direction de P. Munch. Tome 1, 361–427. Copenhague: Rask-Ørstedfonden, 1923.

————. "La Suisse et la Charte de San Francisco." *Annuaire "La Suisse."* Vol. 4, 1–19. Berne: Publie par la Nouvelle Société Helvétique, 1946a.

————. "The United Nations from a European Point of View." *Yale Law Journal* 55 (1946b):1036–48.

————. "The Refutation of Articles 10 and 16." In *From Collective Security to Preventive Diplomacy*, edited by Joel Larus, 33–56. New York: John Wiley & Sons, Inc., 1965.

Rist, Gilbert. "La Suisse, Monde du Silence." Dans *Les cahiers protestants*. No. 4, 7–24. Lausanne: 1968.

Rokkan, Stein. "Center-Formation, Nation-Building, and Cultural Diversity: Report on a UNESCO Program." In *Building States and Nations*. edited by S. N. Eisenstadt and Stein Rokkan, 13–40. Beverly Hills: Sage Publications, 1973a.

————. "Cities, States, and Nations: A Dimensional Model for the Study of Contrasts in Development." In *Building States and Nations*, edited by S.N. Eisenstadt and Stein Rokkan, 73–97. Beverly Hills: Sage Publications, 1973b.

Rosenau, James N. "Pre-Theories and Theories of Foreign Policy." In *Approaches to Comparative and International Politics*, edited by R. Barry Farrel, 27–92. Evanston: Northwestern University Press, 1966.

————. "Adaptive Polities in an Interdependent World." *Orbis* 16, no. 1 (Spring 1972):153–73.

Ross, J. F. L. "Conference of Neutral and Non-Aligned States in Stockholm 1982." *The Non-Aligned World* 1, no. 1 (January–March 1983):123–27.

————. "Government versus the People: The Foreign Policy Debate in Switzerland, 1965–86." Paper presented to the Northeast Political Science Association, Providence, Rhode Island, November 1988, 1–34.

Rothstein, Robert L. "Alignment, Nonalignment, and Small Powers: 1945–1965." *International Organization* 20, no. 3 (Summer 1966):397–418.

Rowe, Edward T. "The Emerging Anti-Colonial Concensus in the United Nations." *Journal of Conflict Resolution* 3 (1964):209–30.

Särlvik, Bo. "Recent Electoral Trends in Sweden." In *Scandinavia at the Polls: Recent Political Trends in Denmark, Norway, and Sweden*. edited by Karl H. Cerny, 73–129. Washington, D.C.: American Enterprise Institute for Public Policy Research, 1977.

"Southern Rhodesia." *International Conciliation* 569 (September 1968):70–77.

Stadler, Karl P. "The Kreisky Phenomenon." *West European Politics* 4, no. 1 (January 1981):5–18.

Stavropoulos, Constantin A. "The Practice of Voluntary Abstentions by Permanent Members of the Security Council under Article 27, para. 3 of the Charter of the United Nations." *AJIL* 61, no. 3 (July 1967):737–52.

Stourzh, Gerald. "Some Reflections on Permanent Neutrality." In *Small States in International Relations*, edited by August Schou and Arne Olav Brundtland, 93–99. Stockholm: Almquist and Wiksell, 1971.

Sundberg, H. G. F. "Är Sverige 'Neutralt'?" *Svensk Tidskrift* 55, no. 7 (1968):336–39.

Sundelius, Bengt. "Interdependence, Integration and Foreign Policy Decentralization in Sweden." *C & C* 19, no. 2 (1984):93–120.

Tarschys, Daniel. "Neutrality and the Common Market: the Soviet View." *C & C* 6, no. 2 (1971):65–75.

———. "The Changing Basis of Radical Socialism in Scandinavia." In *Scandinavia at the Polls: Recent Political Trends in Denmark, Norway, and Sweden*, edited by Karl H. Cerny, 133–53. Washington, D.C.: American Enterprise Institute for Public Policy Research, 1977.

Taubenfeld, Howard J. "International Actions and Neutrality." *AJIL* 47, no. 3 (July 1953):377–96.

Tham, Wilhelm. "Tiden Efter 1920." In *Sveriges Historia Genom Tiderna*. Stockholm: Saxon & Lindströms Förlag, 1948.

Trygger, Ernst. "L'entrée de la Suède dans la Société des Nations." In *Les Origines et l'oeuvre de la Société des Nations*, publie sous la direction de P. Munch. Tome 1, 428–40. Copenhague: Rask Ørstedfonden, 1923.

Verdross, Alfred. "Austria's Permanent Neutrality and the United Nations Organization." *AJIL* 50, no. 1 (January 1956):61–68.

———. "Neutrality within the Framework of the U.N. Organization." *Symbolae Verzije*, 410–18. La Haye: Martinus Nijhoff, 1958.

Wahlbäck, Krister. "Från medlare till kritiker," *Internationella Studier* 3 (1973).

Wallensteen, Peter. "Characteristics of Economic Sanctions." *Journal of Peace Research* 5, no. 3 (1968):248–67.

———. "Aktiv utrikespolitik—Finns det ett borgerligt alternativ?" *Är svensk neutralitet möjlig?*, 88–103. Stockholm: Liberförlag, 1977.

Weber, Max. "The De Facto Integration of Switzerland in Europe." In *Switzerland: Present and Future*, 130–36. Zürich: New Helvetic Society, 1963.

Weilenmann, Herman. "The Interlocking of Nation and Personality Structure." In *Nation-Building*, edited by Karl W. Deutsch and William J. Foltz, 33–55. New York: Atherton Press, 1963.

Wengler, Wilhelm. "The Meaning of Neutrality in Peacetime." *McGill Law Journal* 10, no. 4 (1964):369–79.

Wickman, Krister. "Svensk Utrikesdebatt." *Tiden* 43, no. 4 (April 1951):199–208.

Wildhaber, Luzius. "Switzerland, Neutrality and the United Nations." *Malaya Law Review* 12, no. 1 (July 1970):140–59.

Wilkinson, Anthony R. "From Rhodesia to Zimbabwe." In *Southern Africa: the New Politics of Revolution*, edited by Basil Davidson, Joe Slovo and Anthony R. Wilkinson, 215–352. Middlesex: Penguin Books, 1976.

Woolsey, L. H. "The Fallacies of Neutrality." *AJIL* 30 (1936):256–62.

Wright, P. Quincy. "The Future of Neutrality." *International Conciliation* 242 (September 1928):353–442.

———. "The Meaning of the Pact of Paris." *AJIL* 27 (1933):39–61.

———. "The Test of Aggression in the Italo-Ethiopian War." *AJIL* 30 (1936b): 45–56.

Würtemberg, Marks von. "L'oeuvre commune des Pays scandinaves relative à la Société des Nations." In *Les Origines et l'oeuvre de la Société des Nations,* publie sous la direction de P. Munch. Tome 1, 210–13. Copenhague: Rask Ørstedfonden, 1923.

Zahler, Walter R. "Switzerland and the League of Nations, a Chapter in Diplomatic History." *The American Political Science Review* 30, no. 4 (August 1936):753–57.

Zartman, I. William. "Neutralism and Neutrality in Scandinavia." *Western Political Quarterly* 7, no. 2 (June 1954):125–60.

Zemanek, Karl. "Neutral Austria in the United Nations." *International Organization* 15 (Summer 1961):408–23.

———. "Das Problem der Beteiligung das immerwährend neutralen Österreich an Sanktionen der Vereinten Nationen, besonders im Falle Rhodesiens." *Zeitschrift für Ausländisches Öffentliches Recht und Völkerrecht* 28, no. 1 (März 1968):16–32.

Zimmern, Alfred. "The Problem of Collective Security." In *Neutrality and Collective Security*, edited by P. Quincy Wright. Chicago: University of Chicago Press, 1936b.

Ph.D. Dissertations

Dohlman, Ebba. "Sweden's Foreign Trade Policy and National Security." Ph.D. diss., University of London, 1985.

Highley, Albert H. *"The Actions of States Members of the League of Nations in Application of Sanctions Against Italy, 1935–36."* Université de Genève, thèse no. 36. Genève: Imprimerie du "Journal de Genève." 1938.

Holt, Peter. "Some Problems of Permanent Neutrality in Europe: Austria and Switzerland." Ph.D. diss., University of Sussex, 1978.

Ralston, Jerry W. "The Defence of Small States in the Nuclear Age: Sweden and Switzerland." Université de Genève, thèse no. 194, 1969.

Rist, George. "Image du Tiers Monde et conceptions du développement." Université de Genève, thèse no. 294. Saint Saphorin: Editions Georgi, 1978.

Newspapers

Dagens Nyheter
The Financial Times
International Herald Tribune
Journal de Genève
Neue Zürcher Zeitung
New York Times
Svenska Dagbladet
The Times
Tribune de Genève

Index

About the Author

JOHN F. L. ROSS is currently Assistant Professor of Political Science at Northeastern University in Boston, Massachusetts, where he teaches International Relations, West European Politics, and International Organization. He is also Faculty Associate at Harvard University's Center for International Affairs. He received his M.Sc. in Government and his Ph.D. in International Relations from the London School of Economics and Political Science. He took his B.A. in Political Science from the University of North Carolina at Chapel Hill, where he graduated with Highest Honors.

His many academic honors include the Montague Burton Award in International Relations from the London School of Economics, a national CVCP award for overseas scholars in the United Kingdom, the Gilbert Murray Trust Fund Award, the Terry Sanford Award for Excellence in Political Science Honors from the University of North Carolina, and Phi Beta Kappa.

Dr. Ross has lived and researched in Europe during the past ten years. In addition to Great Britain, he has spent considerable time in Scandinavia, the Alpine countries, and southern Europe, studying political culture and foreign policy. He has written and spoken extensively on European and international affairs, and has published articles in several countries, including Sweden and India.